T0272025

Cambridge IGCSE®

Accounting

STUDENT'S BOOK

Also for Cambridge O Level

David Horner, Leanna Oliver

William Collins' dream of knowledge for all began with the publication of his first book in 1819.

A self-educated mill worker, he not only enriched millions of lives, but also founded a flourishing publishing house. Today, staying true to this spirit, Collins books are packed with inspiration, innovation and practical expertise. They place you at the centre of a world of possibility and give you exactly what you need to explore it.

Collins. Freedom to teach.

Published by Collins

An imprint of HarperCollins*Publishers*
The News Building
1 London Bridge Street
London
SE1 9GF

HarperCollins*Publishers*
Macken House, 39/40 Mayor Street Upper
Dublin 1, D01 C9W8, Ireland

Browse the complete Collins catalogue at
www.collins.co.uk

© HarperCollins*Publishers* Limited 2018

10

ISBN 978-0-00-825411-7

British Library Cataloguing in Publication Data

A catalogue record for this publication is available from the British Library.

Author: David Horner, Leanna Oliver
Development editor: Penny Nicholson
Commissioning editor: Lucy Cooper
Project manager: Amanda Harman
In-house editors: Alexander Rutherford, Letitia Luff
Copyeditor: Patricia Hewson
Proofreader: Piers Maddox
Illustrator: Jouve India
Cover illustrator: Maria Herbert-Liew
Cover designers: Kevin Robbins and Gordon MacGilp Internal designer / Typesetter: Jouve India
Production controller: Tina Paul
Printed and Bound in the UK by Ashford Colour Ltd
All exam-style questions and sample answers in this title were written by the authors. In examinations, the way marks are awarded may be different.

® IGCSE is a registered trademark.

The publishers gratefully acknowledge the permission granted to reproduce the copyright material in this book. Every effort has been made to trace copyright holders and to obtain their permission for the use of copyright material. The publishers will gladly receive any information enabling them to rectify any error or omission at the first opportunity.

p 1 Billion Photos/ Shutterstock, p 14 Makistock/ Shutterstock, p 17 pixfly/ Shutterstock, p 33 wrangler/ Shutterstock, p 70 Syda Productions/ Shutterstock, p 120 MAGNIFIER/ Shutterstock, p 171 Pressmaster/ Shutterstock, p 181 Alexander Raths/ Shutterstock, p 195 David Papazian/ Shutterstock, p 237 InnaFelker/ Shutterstock, p 280 nd3000/ Shutterstock, p 282 abdrahimmahfar/ Shutterstock, p 286 Syda Productions/ Shutterstock, p 290 LDProd/ Shutterstock, p 294 Adam Gregor/ Shutterstock, p 298 Dusan Petkovic/ Shutterstock, p 302 Caftor/ Shutterstock, p 307 nd3000/ Shutterstock, p 312 D K Grove/ Shutterstock, p 318 wavebreakmedia/ Shutterstock, p 321 S_Photo/ Shutterstock, p 327 chrisdorney/ Shutterstock, p 330 Syda Productions/ Shutterstock, p 336 Patryk Kosmider/ Shutterstock, p 344 Monkey Business Images/ Shutterstock, p 357 Indypendenz/ Shutterstock

MIX
Paper | Supporting responsible forestry
FSC™ C007454

This book contains FSC™ certified paper and other controlled sources to ensure responsible forest management.

For more information visit: www.harpercollins.co.uk/green

Contents

Introduction

Welcome to *Collins Cambridge IGCSE Accounting*, which has been carefully designed and written to help you develop the knowledge and skills you will need to succeed in the Cambridge IGCSE Accounting and Cambridge O Level Accounting courses.

Accounting is the study of financial record keeping. It involves the classification, recording and analysis of financial records for all types of businesses, ranging from small one-person organisations right up to large multinational businesses operating in the global market. Your Cambridge Accounting course will help you to develop the following set of skills used within finance and accounting:

- How to record transactions using double entry book-keeping
- How to update the accounts of a business
- How to check the accuracy of the accounts, and correct them if necessary
- How to calculate the profit or loss for different types of businesses
- How to produce financial statements for different types of businesses
- How to analyse and evaluate the financial performance of a business using financial ratios.

The course covers aspects of financial accounting. Chapters 1 to 4 cover the classification and recording of financial transactions. These chapters are concerned with double entry book-keeping and other methods of recording transactions. Additionally, these chapters examine the methods used for checking the accuracy of accounts and making corrections to any errors found. Chapters 5 to 7 cover the production of the financial statements, specifically the income statement and balance sheet, for different types of business. They also look at the advantages and disadvantages of operating as different types of business and how to assess the performance of a business using information from the financial statements.

By the end of this course, you should have the knowledge and the skills you need to not only succeed in your Cambridge Accounting course but to better understand the world of business. Good luck with your study of accounting!

How to use this book

This Student's Book covers all the content for the Cambridge IGCSE and O Level Accounting syllabuses. It is divided into seven chapters – one for each of the areas of the syllabus. Each chapter is divided into units which cover the essential knowledge and skills you need as specified by each unit of the syllabus. Each of the units is organised in the same way and has the following features:

- **Learning objectives** list the key knowledge and skills you need to acquire.
- **Starting point** questions allow you to check your understanding of previous topics and help you understand the links between topics.
- **Exploring** questions ask you to think about the topic you are about to study in a broader sense. They encourage you to identify issues and come up with solutions that will be developed in the unit.
- The **Developing** section presents the knowledge and skills required by the corresponding unit of the syllabus. This section has some special features to help you achieve the learning objectives for the unit.
  - **Key terms** and **key knowledge** boxes provide definitions of accounting terms and highlight important information for at-a-glance reference and to support your understanding.

- **Worked examples** show how the facts, terms, principles, policies, procedures and techniques you learn are applied to produce accounts and financial statements and in other accounting situations. The accompanying commentary in the margin provides further explanation.

- Throughout the text there are many examples of **accounts** and **financial statements** to show the internationally agreed conventions for the presentation of these documents.

- **Questions** within the text allow you to check your understanding of key concepts or encourage you to come up with an answer before it is explained in the text.

- **Case studies** show real-life examples of some of the ideas which you have encountered in the text.

- The **Applying** section provides an opportunity to bring together your learning through discussion with your peers. This might be through discussion questions or a task.

- **Knowledge check** questions at the end of each unit allow you to check your knowledge and understanding of the material in the unit.

- **Check your progress** helps you to evaluate how you are doing.

The Student's Book also includes two other sections to support your knowledge and understanding of the syllabus content:

- **Chapter reviews** allow you to practise what you have learned in the chapter with exam-style questions designed to help you prepare for the examination.

- A **glossary** provides definitions of all the key terms highlighted in the text. Words in coloured bold throughout the book can be found in the glossary.

There is also an accompanying Workbook available, which offers further exercises for support, practice, stretch and revision.

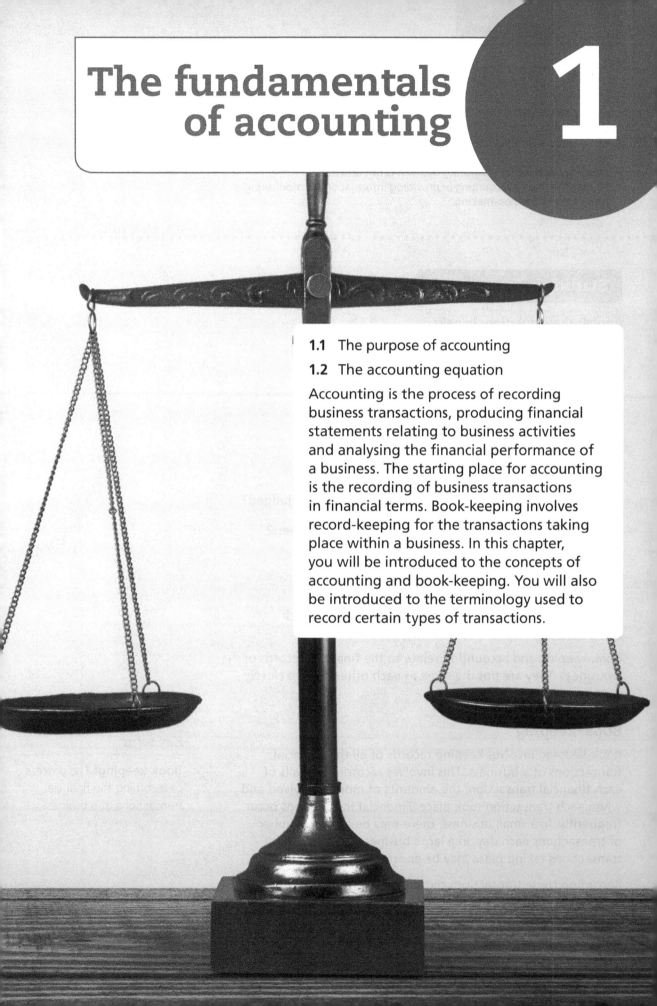

The fundamentals of accounting

1

1.1 The purpose of accounting

1.2 The accounting equation

Accounting is the process of recording business transactions, producing financial statements relating to business activities and analysing the financial performance of a business. The starting place for accounting is the recording of business transactions in financial terms. Book-keeping involves record-keeping for the transactions taking place within a business. In this chapter, you will be introduced to the concepts of accounting and book-keeping. You will also be introduced to the terminology used to record certain types of transactions.

The purpose of accounting

Learning objectives

By the end of this unit, you should be able to:

- understand and explain the difference between book-keeping and accounting
- state the purposes of measuring business profit and loss
- explain the role of accounting in providing information for monitoring progress and decision-making.

Starting point

Answer these questions in pairs.

1 Why do we need to record business transactions?

2 What skills do you think an accountant needs?

Exploring

Discuss these questions in pairs.

1 How do you think business performance can be judged?

2 What do you think are the main goals of a business?

Developing

The differences between book-keeping and accounting

Book-keeping and accounting relate to the financial records of a business. They are not the same as each other but are closely connected.

Book-keeping

Book-keeping involves keeping records of all the financial transactions of a business. This involves recording details of each financial transaction, the amounts of money involved and when each transaction took place. Financial transactions occur frequently. In a small business, there may be a small number of transactions each day. In a large business, the number of transactions taking place may be enormous.

Recording these transactions requires care and attention to detail. Transactions should be recorded soon after they occur

Key term

Book-keeping: The process of recording the financial transactions of a business.

and accurately. Inaccurate records result in a risk of incorrect decision-making which can have serious consequences. For example, if expenses are not recorded then a manager may buy more materials than can be afforded out of the business bank account.

Book-keeping involves recording transactions in the 'books' of the business. These books are divided up by type of transaction. Transactions are recorded in two separate places:

- All similar transactions are recorded in specific books according to the type of transaction. These are known as **books of prime entry** (explored in Unit 2.3).

- Transactions are also recorded in the **ledger accounts** of the business. The ledgers (explored in Unit 2.1) contain the accounts of the business.

Accounting

Book-keeping involves the recording of financial transactions within a business. The activity of **accounting** includes book-keeping but also involves other activities.

Accountants use the financial records produced by those completing book-keeping. The records are used to construct the **financial statements** of the business. These statements tell users of accounting data important information about the state of the business.

Two important financial statements are:

1. The **income statement**, which shows the profit earned or loss made by the business

2. The **statement of financial position**, which shows business resources and how those resources are financed.

Another function of accounting is to analyse the financial performance of the business. This involves using financial data from the financial statements to assess how well the business is performing.

The purpose of measuring business profit and loss

Business objectives are the aims and goals of a business. Most businesses have profit-related objectives. **Profit maximisation** is a common business objective. This is where the business aims to make as high a level of profit as is possible. Other business objectives include:

- Growth – measured by sales value or by sales volume (the quantities of goods sold)

- Market share (how much of the market the businesses' sales account for)

Key terms

Accounting: The process of recording financial transactions, producing financial statements and analysing financial performance of a business.

Financial statements: Statements produced for an accounting period summarising business performance. They include an income statement and a statement of financial position

Key term

Profit maximisation: Aiming to earn as high a level of profit as is possible.

- Survival
- Break-even (often a financial objective of not-for-profit organisations, such as charities)
- Social objectives
- Environmental objectives.

Business objectives can change over time for the same business. For example, a business experiencing difficult economic conditions may aim for survival rather than profit maximisation.

 Explain how and why the objectives of businesses may change over time.

Profit is measured as the difference between the income earned and the expenses paid by a business for an accounting period. If income is greater than expenses, a profit is made. However, if expenses are greater than income, the business makes a loss for that period.

Profit is not the same thing as money. For example, a business can spend money buying items to be sold for profit. This means money is leaving the business but the money received from the sale of the items may not happen until a much later time period after profit has already been recorded.

Key knowledge

Income greater than expenses → Profit

Expenses greater than income → Loss

An **accounting period** is the period used to calculate the profit or loss made by the business. For most businesses, the accounting period is one year. The accounting year may not start on 1 January. Many businesses have accounting periods starting on 1 April. Some businesses start their accounting periods at other times. All accounting periods are likely to start at the beginning of a month.

Key knowledge

Profit is stated in the **income statement** of a business.

The income statement is a financial statement produced for an accounting period showing the total income earned and the total expenses paid by the business. The income statement will show the profit or loss made by the business for that period.

2 Why do many businesses have 1 April as the start of the annual accounting period?

It is important to measure how much profit is made in order to make decisions about how it can be used:

- Business owners may take money out of the business for their personal use. It is important that they do not take out so much that it affects the running of the business.

Key terms

Profit: Total income less total expenses for a period of time.

Accounting period: The time period for which financial statements are prepared.

Income statement: A financial statement showing a business's income and expenses for an accounting period and the resulting profit or loss.

- Profit can be reinvested within the business to enable the business to expand.

- Profit can be used to pay any debts the business has.

As well as decisions about spending, there are other reasons why knowing how much profit has been made is important for a business:

- Paying tax – Many businesses pay tax as a percentage of their profit so calculating how much profit has been made is necessary in order to calculate the amount of tax to be paid.

- Obtaining credit – Lenders will often only lend a business money if they have proof that the business is likely to survive and be able to repay the money lent. Profit is a good indicator of the long-term success of a business.

- Keeping shareholders happy – Limited companies are businesses owned by shareholders. Limited companies regularly give profits to shareholders as dividend payments and making these payments is very important in keeping shareholders happy and attracting new shareholders if necessary.

- Attracting investors – Companies may need to attract new investors and profit is a sign of a good investment.

- Encouraging entrepreneurship – Profit provides a motive for people to take calculated risks in running a business, such as the decision to expand or to launch new products.

The role of accounting in providing information for monitoring progress and decision-making

Accounting involves producing the financial statements of the business. These provide useful information about the business.

Monitoring progress

Financial statements are analysed to monitor the progress of the business. Which areas of the financial statement are monitored will depend partly on who is looking at the information contained on the statements. Financial statements are explored in Chapters 5 and 6.

- Business owners are interested in the profit earned as it is the main objective of most businesses. They will look at the size of the profit compared with previous years' profits and the profits earned by similar businesses.

- The size of the debts of the business will be monitored closely. If debts rise, there is a risk that the business will not be able to meet the repayments or that the interest on the debts may rise to a level similar to or even greater than the profits earned by the business.

- Suppliers want to be sure that they will receive payment before allowing a business to buy goods on credit. The financial statements provide information on the stability of a business.

3 Why would a bank be interested in the progress of a business?

Decision-making

The information contained within the financial statements can help in business decision-making:

- Knowing the size of the profit allows the owners to decide whether they can afford to buy more assets.

- Knowing the cash balance of the business allows decisions to be made on whether to arrange another source of finance.

- Knowing the sales revenue allows decisions to be made about expansion of operations and recruitment of staff.

Management accounting is another aspect of accounting. It involves the use of financial and accounting data by managers to make decisions. Managers compare the actual performance of the business, for example in terms of sales revenue or profits earned, with budgeted levels of performance. They also plan by setting targets for future performance.

Key term

Management accounting: Using financial information to make business decisions concerning costs, revenues and output.

> **Applying**

Discuss these questions in pairs.

1 Explain why the workers in a business would be interested in the profits earned by the business

2 Explain why rising profits may not be seen as satisfactory progress by business owners.

Knowledge check

1 Which of the following is not a likely business objective?

   A Profit maximisation   **C** Survival

   B Growth   **D** Income statement

2 A business sells 1100 units at $8 each. Total expenses are $5400. Calculate the profit for this period.

   A $8800   **C** $3400

   B $5400   **D** $14 200

3 Which of the following is not a reason for buying shares in a limited company?

   A To receive dividends   **C** To control the business

   B To profit from rising share prices   **D** To obtain credit

4 State three reasons why it is important to measure profit (or loss) for an accounting period.

5 Explain the difference between book-keeping and accounting.

6 Explain how accounting can provide information for

    A monitoring progress   **B** making decisions.

Check your progress

Read the unit objectives below and reflect on your progress in each.

- Understand and explain the difference between book-keeping and accounting

- State the purposes of measuring business profit and loss

- Explain the role of accounting in providing information for monitoring progress and decision-making.

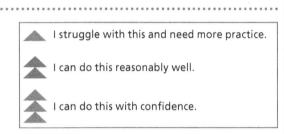

I struggle with this and need more practice.

I can do this reasonably well.

I can do this with confidence.

The accounting equation

Learning objectives

By the end of this unit, you should be able to:
- explain the meaning of assets, liabilities and owner's equity
- explain and apply the accounting equation.

Starting point

Answer these questions in pairs.

1 What sources of finance are used by owners setting up a business?

2 Why do businesses borrow money?

3 Why is it difficult for new businesses to borrow money?

Exploring

Discuss these questions in pairs.

1 Why is it important to keep full accounting records?

2 How do you think assets used by a business are valued?

Developing

Assets, liabilities and owner's equity

Key knowledge

Every transaction has two effects on the financial records of the business. This is the **duality principle** of business transactions.

Many business transactions involve assets, liabilities and the owner's equity. These financial terms describe items that are recorded in the accounts of the business.

- **Assets** are items used by people to run and manage a business. Examples of assets include business premises, machinery, inventory (stocks of materials or finished goods) and money held as cash or in the business bank account.

- **Liabilities** are amounts owed by the business to other businesses or people. These include short-term debts, such as a temporary delay between buying and paying for goods for

Key terms

Duality principle: This principle states that a business transaction always has two effects on the business and requires two entries, one debit and one credit, to be made in the accounts; also known as 'double entry'.

Assets: Resources used within the business for its activities.

Liabilities: Amounts borrowed to fund business activity.

Owner's equity: Business resources supplied by the owner of the business.

resale. Liabilities also includes long-term debts, such as bank loans. Liabilities will be repaid in the future.

- **Owner's equity** refers to resources used by the business that have been supplied by the business owner (or owners). These resources may be the owner's personal savings, or other resources, such as a car or a computer. Owner's equity may also be referred to as the capital of the business.

The accounting equation

Key knowledge

The accounting equation: Assets = Owner's equity + Liabilities

A basic principle found within most accounting records is that of **duality**. Duality means that each business transaction is viewed from two different perspectives. The **accounting equation** uses the principle of duality as it can be thought of as looking at the business in two different ways.

The accounting equation underpins the work you will complete when learning how to record accounting transactions. The accounting equation is based on these two elements:

- The resources the business has – the assets of the business
- How these resources were financed – by the owner's equity and the liabilities of the business.

The accounting equation states that these two elements, the two 'sides' of the equation, must always be equal. This is sometimes described as the equation 'balancing'.

Key knowledge

The accounting equation will always be true. It cannot be false at any time.

Resources used within the business *must* have either come from the owner or have been borrowed. Even if the business owner receives a gift or donations from someone else, this still counts as the owner's resources. Any profit made by a business is added to the owner's equity. Profit can be used to buy more assets.

Worked example 1

A business purchases a car on credit for $5000. How does this effect the accounting equation?

Assets increase by $5000.

Liabilities increase by $5000.

As a result, both sides of the accounting equation increase by the same amount.

Buying a car means that the business has the use of the car as an asset.

The car was purchased on credit. This means the business has a new liability which is the amount owing on the car purchased.

The accounting equation always 'balances'. For example, if the car purchased in Worked example 1 was financed from the business bank account instead of being purchased on credit, the accounting equation would still hold true; the value of the car is added to the total assets but the value of another asset (the bank account of the business) falls by the same amount. These two changes lead to no overall change in total value of assets – meaning the accounting equation still balances.

Rearranging the equation

 How do you calculate the value of liabilities for a business if this information is not available?

You can rearrange the accounting equation to calculate a missing value.

> Assets = Liabilities + Owner's equity

can be rearranged as

> Owner's equity = Assets – Liabilities

and can also be rearranged as

> Liabilities = Assets – Owner's equity

Worked example 2

The owner of a business has assets valued at $16 500. She knows she has borrowed $3250. What is the value of the owner's equity?

Owner's equity = Assets – Liabilities

= $16 500 – $3250

= $13 250

The accounting equation and the statement of financial position

Keeping up-to-date records of business transactions is very important. Each transaction can be recorded using the **statement of financial position**. This statement shows the assets and liabilities of a business and the owner's equity in the business.

The statement shows the effects on the assets, liabilities and owner's equity of all business transactions. It is useful as it shows how much the business owes.

You will study the statement of financial position in more detail in Chapter 5. A simplified statement of financial position will consist of two sides.

To calculate owner's equity, you use the accounting equation in the form Owner's equity = Assets – Liabilities.

Key terms

Statement of financial position: A financial statement showing the assets of the business and the financing for these assets, either from owner's equity or liabilities.

Liquidity: A measure of how easy it is to convert an asset into cash without it losing its value.

Inventory: Goods held by a business for resale. They may be in the form of finished goods, partly finished goods or raw materials.

- One side shows the resources used within the business (the assets)
- The other side shows how the assets were financed, either with borrowed money (liabilities) or from the business owner (owner's equity).

The statement of financial position appears as follows:

Business name	
Statement of financial position as at date	
Resources used within the business:	How the assets were financed:
Assets ($)	Owner's equity and Liabilities ($)

The statement shown has assets on the left-hand side and owner's equity and liabilities on the right-hand side. This is known as the **horizontal format**. The **vertical format** is an alternative layout for presenting this statement and this will be used in Chapter 5.

The following examples look at the start-up of a very simple business organisation. The statement of financial position is updated after each transaction.

Worked example 3

Transaction 1: Introducing owner's equity

Ramondo is setting up a business. On 1 August, he deposited $8000 into a business bank account and used $3500 to purchase a van for business use. Prepare the statement of financial position after these transactions.

Notice that the title of the statement states that this is a statement of financial position, as well as the appropriate time period for the statement; 'as at' means for the date shown only.

Ramondo			
Statement of financial position as at 1 August			
Assets	$	Owner's equity and Liabilities	$
Van	3500	Owner's equity	8000
Bank	4500		
	8000		8000

In a statement of financial position the assets appear in order of **liquidity**. Liquidity is a measure of how easy it is to convert an asset into cash. The least liquid assets appear at the top of the column. Liabilities appear in order of their likely repayment date – with those furthest away from repayment appearing at the top of the column.

Key terms

Trade payable: The amount that a business owes to a supplier for goods or services sold on credit. The supplier may also be known as a trade payable or a creditor.

Trade payables: The sum of the amounts that a business owes to its suppliers for goods or services sold on credit. All the suppliers of a business may also be referred to collectively as trade payables.

Trade receivable: The amount that a business is owed by a customer for goods or services supplied on credit. The customer may also be known as a trade receivable or a debtor.

Trade receivables: The sum of the amounts that a business is owed by its customers for goods or services sold on credit. All the credit customers of a business may also be referred to collectively as trade receivables.

The totals of the two sides of the statement of financial position are the same. This should be expected as the statement of financial position is a representation of the accounting equation, which is always true.

The totals of each side of the statement should be presented on the same row as each other.

Worked example 4

Transaction 2: Buying inventory on credit

On 4 August, Ramondo bought **inventory** (goods ready for resale) from Iqbal, who is a trader. The inventory was valued at $800 and was purchased on credit.

Prepare a statement of financial position for the business after this transaction.

When goods are bought on credit, the goods are paid for after they have been supplied

Ramondo			
Statement of financial position as at 4 August			
Assets	$	Owner's equity and Liabilities	$
Van	3500	Owner's equity	8000
Inventory	800	Trade payables (Iqbal)	800
Bank	4500		
	8800		8800

It also creates a new liability, known as a **trade payable**. This is the amount that the business owes to Iqbal for the purchase of the inventory on credit.

Buying inventory on credit creates a new asset, inventory.

The statement of financial position still balances but the totals have changed. Both assets and liabilities have increased by $800, the cost of the inventory.

On the statement of financial position, the amounts that a business owes to its suppliers for goods or services bought on credit are usually grouped together as one total under the heading **trade payables**.

Worked example 5

Transaction 3: Buying an asset

On 8 August, Ramondo bought equipment for the business. The cost of $2400 was paid from the business bank account. Prepare a statement of financial position after this transaction.

Ramondo			
Statement of financial position as at 8 August			
Assets	$	Owner's equity and Liabilities	$
Van	3500	Owner's equity	8000
Equipment	2400	Trade payables (Iqbal)	800
Inventory	800		
Bank	2100		
	8800		8800

There is no overall change to the total value of the assets. One asset has increased (equipment) and one asset has fallen in value (bank).

Worked example 6

Transaction 4: Selling inventory on credit

On 12 August, Ramondo sold $400 of the inventory for the same price on credit to Narinder. Prepare a statement of financial position after this transaction.

Ramondo				
Statement of financial position as at 12 August				
Assets	$	Owner's equity and Liabilities	$
Van	3500	Owner's equity	8000
Equipment	2400	Trade payables (Iqbal)	800
Inventory	400		
Trade receivables (Narinder)	400		
Bank	2100		
	8800		8800

One asset decreases in value (inventory).

However, a new asset is created, known as a **trade receivable**. This is the amount that Narinder owes the business for the goods he purchased on credit.

On the statement of financial position, the amounts that a business is owed by its customers for goods and services bought on credit are usually grouped together as one total under the heading trade receivables.

 How would the statement of financial position be affected by a sale of inventory for a profit?

Worked example 7

Transaction 5: Borrowing money

On 15 August, Ramondo obtained a loan for the business of $3000 from Quick Finance Co. This money was paid directly into the business bank account. Prepare a statement of financial position for the business.

Ramondo				
Statement of financial position as at 15 August				
Assets	$	Owner's equity and Liabilities	$
Van	3500	Owner's equity	8000
Equipment	2400	Loan (Quick Finance Co)	3000
Inventory	400	Trade payables (Iqbal)	800
Trade receivables (Narinder)	400		
Bank	5100		
	11800		11800

Liabilities have increased (the loan from Quick Finance Co).

Assets have also increased (increased bank balance as the loan was paid into the bank).

3 Following on from Worked example 7, on 17 August Ramondo paid the amount owing to Iqbal from the bank. Prepare a statement of financial position to show this transaction.

This approach to recording business transactions is technically correct. However, preparing a new statement of financial position for every transaction is very time-consuming. A more efficient method of recording business transactions is to use the system of **double entry book-keeping.** This is explored in Unit 2.1.

Applying

Discuss these questions in pairs.

1 Explain why the statement of financial position always balances (the totals are always the same).

2 How would a loss made on the sale of an asset affect the accounting equation?

Complete this task in pairs.

Task

Jason is setting up a new business. The following transactions occurred in the first week of business activity. From these transactions prepare a statement of financial position as at 10 May 2018.

1 May Jason places $25 000 into the business bank account.

1 May He withdraws $560 from the bank and holds it as cash.

3 May He buys inventory worth $1190 on credit from Sabkha.

4 May A bank loan of $10 000 is paid directly into business bank account.

6 May He buys a laptop for $1000 and pays by cheque.

7 May He buys office equipment for $240 and pays in cash.

Knowledge check

1 Which of the following is an asset?

   A A bank loan   **C** Mortgage

   B Amount owing to suppliers   **D** Inventory bought on credit

2 Use the following data to calculate the value of the owner's equity:

   Machinery $54 000, Equipment $8200, Bank balance $1150, Bank loan $15 900

   A $47 450   **C** $62 450

   B $78 450   **D** $63 350

3 Classify the following into assets or liabilities:

   A Money owed by customers

   B Amounts owing to the bank

   C Machinery used by the business

   D Goods bought with the intention of being sold for a profit

   E Mortgage used by the business to buy premises

4 Use the following information to prepare a statement of financial position for 31 October.

	$
Property	230 000
Vehicles	38 750
Inventory	11 900
Bank	4 535
Trade payables	8 927
Bank loan	85 000
Owner's equity	?

Check your progress

Read the unit objectives below and reflect on your progress in each.

- Explain the meaning of assets, liabilities and owner's equity
- Explain and apply the accounting equation.

 I struggle with this and need more practice.

 I can do this reasonably well.

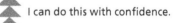 I can do this with confidence.

Chapter review

1   Which of the following is NOT a likely reason why profit is important to the owner of a business?

    A To inform competitors

    B To keep shareholders happy

    C To calculate the right amount of tax to be paid

    D So that borrowing is possible

2   A business sells 600 units at $4 each. Total expenses are $2200. Calculate the profit earned.

    A $2400   **C** $800

    B $200   **D** $2200

3   Which of the following is the best description of the term profit maximisation?

    A Earning more profit than all other businesses

    B Earning more profit than in all previous years

    C Earning as much profit as is possible

    D Maximising spending by the business

4   Which of the following is not a liability?

    A Trade credit given by suppliers   **C** Bank loan

    B Trade credit given to customers   **D** Mortgage on property

5   Which of the following is correct?

	Assets ($)	Liabilities ($)	Owner's equity ($)
A	80910	24151	57759
B	4414	1312	4102
C	27909	12311	15598
D	41411	31747	8664

6   Which of the following is not true?

    A Assets = Liabilities + Owner's equity   **C** Liabilities – Owner's equity = Assets

    B Owner's equity = Assets – Liabilities   **D** Assets – Owner's equity = Liabilities

7   Which of the following is not correct?

	Assets ($)	Liabilities ($)	Owner's equity ($)
A	12414	6464	5950
B	3141	990	2151
C	8010	6352	1658
D	19813	11311	8062

Sources and recording of data

2

This chapter looks at how accounting records are processed and maintained. The records begin with a business transaction which generates a business document. The next stage of the process is to transfer the details from the business document into the appropriate book of prime entry. Once the information has been transferred, the details of the transaction can then be posted to the double entry accounts in the various ledgers of the business. To prepare the financial statements of the business, the accountant balances these accounts and transfers the balances to the financial statements.

The double entry system of book-keeping

Learning objectives

By the end of this unit, you should be able to:

- outline the double entry system of book-keeping
- process accounting data using the double entry system
- prepare ledger accounts
- post transactions to the ledger accounts
- balance ledger accounts as required and make transfers to financial statements
- interpret ledger accounts and their balances
- recognise the division of the ledger into the sales ledger, the purchases ledger and the nominal (general) ledger.

Starting point

Answer these questions in pairs.

1 What kinds of resources will an owner need to begin operating a small business? Which of these resources do you think are essential for a small business?

2 Does the owner have to provide their own money for the business to get started? Where can people get money from to start a business?

3 What will the business need to do before it is likely to be allowed to borrow money?

Exploring

Discuss these questions in pairs.

1 What do you think the term 'double entry' means in relation to the recording of accounting transactions?

2 How is record keeping within a business more difficult when there is more than one owner of the business?

Developing

Double entry book-keeping

The system of double entry book-keeping looks at every business transaction from two perspectives. This maintains the principle of duality and is a further extension of the accounting equation (which you met in Unit 1.2). Each transaction requires two entries to be made in the financial records (the books) of the business. The books of the business refer to the documents used to record financial information. Book-keeping involves the maintenance and updating of these financial records. The different types of book are explored in Unit 2.3.

Double entry book-keeping has been used to record business transactions for hundreds of years. The creation of the system of double entry book-keeping is widely attributed to the work of Luca Pacioli in 1494.

Double entry accounts

Business transactions are recorded as part of double entry book-keeping and are entered into accounts. Double entry accounts are sometimes referred to as ledger accounts as a ledger is a book that contains the accounts of the business.

Accounts appear as:

Account name					
Debit side (abbreviated as Dr)			Credit side (abbreviated as Cr)		
Year		$	Year		$
Date	Account details	Amount	Date	Account details	Amount
	(name of other account in which double entry appears)			(name of other account in which double entry appears)	

Key knowledge

Features of each double entry account include:

The name of the account

This refers to the type of transaction taking place. For example, when the business buys a new piece of machinery, it is recorded in an account named 'Machinery'. There are separate accounts for each type of asset, each type of liability and many other accounting items.

Each account is split into two halves:

- The left-hand side of the account is known as the Debit side (abbreviated as Dr)
- The right-hand side of the account is known as the Credit side (abbreviated as Cr).

When making entries into the account, the following information is recorded on the correct side of the account.

- The date of the transaction
- The details of the transaction, namely the account containing the other half of the double entry
- The amount of money involved.

Rules of double entry book-keeping

Precision matters greatly when recording accounting transactions. For book-keeping to be done correctly the rules of double entry book-keeping must always be followed.

The first rules you need to learn apply to the accounts of assets, liabilities and owner's equity.

Asset accounts	
Debit	Credit
Increases entered on this side	Decreases entered on this side

Liabilities accounts	
Debit	Credit
Decreases entered on this side	Increases entered on this side

Owner's equity account	
Debit	Credit
Decreases entered on this side	Increases entered on this side

Worked example 1

Melissa is setting up a small business. On 1 June 2018, she places $10 000 into a business bank account. Enter this transaction in the correct double entry accounts:

Bank					
		$			$
1 June	Owner's equity	10 000			

Owner's equity					
		$			$
			1 June	Bank	10 000

The business bank balance has increased. Bank is an asset. Using the rule for asset accounts you debit that account with $10 000.

Owner's equity in the business has increased. The rule tells you to credit the owner's equity account with $10 000.

In both cases, the details of each entry give the name of the account that contains the other half of the double entry transaction.

Worked example 2

On 3 June 2018, the business buys equipment costing $2500 and pays using money in the bank account. Enter this transaction in the correct double entry accounts:

Equipment		$			$
3 June	Bank	2500			

Bank		$			$
2018					
1 June	Owner's equity	10000	3 June	Equipment	2500

The business is gaining a new asset (equipment) so an account is opened for this asset and a debit entry is made in this account for the correct amount ($2500).

Notice that the entry in the bank account from 1 June appears here in lighter text.

The payment for the equipment was made from the bank so this means that there will be a reduction in this asset. Therefore, a credit entry is made in this account for $2500.

Worked example 3

On 5 June 2018, the business buys a computer. The computer was purchased on credit from Mehdi and cost $1000. Enter this transaction in the correct double entry accounts:

Computer		$			$
5 June	Mehdi	1000			

Mehdi		$			$
			5 June	Computer	1000

The business gains a new asset (computer) so an account is opened for this and a debit entry is made for the $1000.

The business does not immediately pay for the computer. The business gains a liability which is named after the person (Mehdi) allowing the amount to be borrowed. This liability increases so you credit this account.

Worked example 4

On 12 June 2018, the business pays Mehdi the full amount owing from the business bank account. Enter this transaction in the appropriate double entry accounts.

Bank		$			$
1 June	Owner's equity	10000	3 June	Equipment	2500
			12 June	Mehdi	1000

A payment is made from the bank account. This represents a reduction in this asset. Therefore, you credit the bank account with the amount needed to pay for the computer ($1000).

Mehdi						
		$				$
12 June	Bank	1000	5 June	Computer		1000

The entries from earlier transactions remain in the account.

Paying the debt owing to Mehdi means the business reduces a liability. To reduce a liability, you debit Mehdi's account with the amount paid.

Accounting for inventory

How an asset is classified depends on why the asset was purchased. A computer bought to be used within the business appears in an asset account called 'computer'. However, a business that buys and sells computers as its main business operation would include the purchases and sales of computers in the relevant inventory account. An asset bought specifically for resale is classed as inventory.

Many businesses are traders. Traders make a profit by buying goods that they then sell for a higher price than the amount for which they were purchased. Inventory is an asset. Inventory follows the double entry rules for asset accounts. However, accounting for inventory is more complicated than it might initially appear.

Key term

Trader: A business organisation that aims to make profit from the buying and selling of goods. No production takes place.

Worked example 5

Looking at this account. What do you think is the value of the inventory held by the business after 20 June 2018?

Inventory						
		$				$
16 June	Purchases	2000	20 June	Sales		2000

At first glance, it looks like there is no inventory held by the business after the sale on 20 June.

Key knowledge

Only assets bought specifically for resale are classed as inventory.

However, it is highly likely that the inventory was sold for a higher price than the amount paid for it so it is not possible to state the value of inventory held by the business after 20 June.

Worked example 5 shows that it is not possible to keep all the transactions relating to inventory in one account only.

 Why do you think inventory is not likely to be sold for the same amount as was paid for it?

There are four separate accounts used for inventory transactions. Each account represents a different inventory movement:

- **Purchases account** – for purchases of inventory
- **Sales account** – for sales of inventory
- **Purchases returns account** – for the return of inventory by the business to the original supplier
- **Sales returns account** – for inventory returned by a customer to the business.

Inventory may be bought on credit or it may be paid for immediately. Purchases paid for immediately are referred to as cash purchases but payment can be made either in cash or from the bank account.

Similarly, inventory may be sold on credit or it may be paid for immediately. Sales paid for immediately are referred to as cash sales but the business may receive the payment in cash or directly into the bank account.

Recording inventory in the double entry accounts

Increases in inventory	Decreases in inventory
Account to be debited	Account to be credited
Purchases	Sales
or	or
Sales returns	Purchases returns

2 Why do you think the sales returns and purchases returns are not simply entered into the opposite side of the respective sales and purchases accounts?

Key knowledge

Inventory appears in one of four accounts depending on:
- the direction of movement (into the business or out of the business)
- the reason for this movement.

Key terms

Purchases: Inventory bought by the business either for immediate payment or on credit.

Sales: Inventory sold by the business either for immediate payment or on credit.

Purchases returns: Inventory previously bought by the business returned to the original supplier due to some problem with the inventory (also known as returns outwards)

Sales returns: Inventory previously sold by the business returned by the customer due to some problem with the inventory (also known as returns inwards).

Worked example 6

On 4 October 2018, a business purchases $250 of inventory on credit from James. Enter this transaction in the correct double entry accounts.

Purchases					
		$			$
4 Oct	James	250			

James					
		$			$
			4 Oct	Purchases	250

Purchasing inventory increases this asset held by the business. This is recorded as a debit in the purchases account.

The inventory is purchased on credit. Amounts owing for credit purchases are called **trade payables** and are liabilities. This liability is increasing so you credit the account of James.

Worked example 7

On 12 October 2018, the business in Worked example 6 sells $700 of inventory on credit to Hassan. Enter this transaction in the correct double entry accounts.

		Sales				$
		$				$
			12 Oct	Hassan		700

		Hassan				
		$				$
12 Oct	Sales	700				

Inventory is decreasing because of the sale. Inventory is an asset so you credit the sales account.

The inventory is sold on credit. Amounts owing to the business for credit sales are known as **trade receivables** and are assets. This asset is increasing so you debit the account of Hassan.

Worked example 8

On 19 October 2018, inventory valued at $50 previously purchased from James was returned because it was damaged (see Worked example 6). Enter this transaction in the correct double entry accounts.

		Purchases returns				
		$				$
			19 Oct	James		50

		James				
		$				$
19 Oct	Purchases returns	50	4 Oct	Purchases		250

Inventory held is decreasing because it has been returned to the original supplier. This means a reduction in assets held. You therefore credit the purchases returns account.

Returning inventory to James means the business owes less to James. This reduces a liability and means you credit James's account. Note that the entry for the original purchase on 4 October appears on the credit side of James's account.

Worked example 9

On 25 October 2018, Hassan returned $50 of the goods that were sold to him on 12 October as they were faulty. (See Worked example 7.) Enter this transaction in the correct double entry accounts.

		Sales returns				
		$				$
25 Oct	Hassan	50				

		Hassan				
		$				$
12 Oct	Sales	700	25 Oct	Sales returns		50

The asset of inventory is increasing because of goods returned by a customer. You debit the sales returns account with the value of goods returned.

Trade receivables are an asset. The amount owed by Hassan is reduced by the return of goods so you credit Hassan's account. Note that the entry for the original sale on 12 October appears on the debit side of Hassan's account

Accounting for expenses and income

Accounting for expenses

Expenses are incurred in running a business. These are paid from the business bank and cash accounts. Common examples of expenses include:

- Wages and salaries
- Office expenses
- Heating costs
- Rent
- Sundry (General) expenses
- Business rates
- Insurance
- Advertising costs
- Administration costs

Expenses are recorded in the double entry accounts. Any expense involves a payment from either the bank account or the cash account so you credit either the bank account or the cash account. You make the debit entry in the relevant expense account.

Accounting for expenses	
Account to be debited	Account to be credited
Expense account	Bank or cash

A separate account is opened for each individual category of expense. Very small items of expense are sometimes kept in a 'sundry' or 'general' expenses account.

Key knowledge

All expenses and incomes are recorded in their own separate account – unless they are very small and can be grouped together as sundry or general items.

Accounting for income

The main source of income for a business is from selling goods or services. However, there are other types of income for some businesses. These incomes are connected with other business activities, such as renting out property. They may relate to investments made by the business. Common examples of other types of income include:

- Rent received
- Commission received.

Other types of income are recorded in the double entry accounts. Incomes involve receipts into either the bank account or the cash account so you debit either the bank account or the cash account. You make the credit entry in the relevant income account.

Accounting for income	
Account to be debited	Account to be credited
Bank or cash	Income account

Recording expenses and income in the double entry accounts

Worked example 10

On 16 November 2018, a business receives $500 relating to rental income by bank transfer.

On 18 November, the business makes a payment from the bank of $150 for insurance.

Enter both transactions in the correct double entry accounts.

Rent received						
		$				$
			16 Nov	Bank		500

Insurance						
		$				$
18 Nov	Bank	150				

Bank						
		$				$
16 Nov	Rent received	500	18 Nov	Insurance		150

The credit entry for income received is made in the relevant income account – the 'rent received' account, **in which you record the account to be debited.**

The debit entry is made in the relevant expenses account – the 'insurance' account, **in which you record the account to be credited.**

A payment made from the bank account means a decrease in this asset so you credit the bank account.

The business receives money (an asset) so you debit the bank account.

3 Why is it important to have an account for each type of income and expense?

Accounting for drawings

Owner's equity is money or resources invested into the business by the owner. Sometimes the owner will withdraw resources from the business, such as money from the business bank account, for personal use.

Resources taken from the business by the owner are known as **drawings**. It is useful to keep clear records of the amounts entering and leaving the business resulting from the owner's actions, so drawings are kept in a separate account from owner's equity.

The drawings account follows the same rules as the owner's equity account. This means a decrease in owner's equity requires a debit entry in the drawings account.

Drawings take resources out of business use. The owner should not take excessive drawings. This issue is especially important when more than one person owns the business.

Key term

....

Drawings: Assets (money or other resources) that the owner withdraws from the business for personal use.

4 Why should drawings not be excessive?

The rule for recording drawings in the double entry accounts is:

Accounting for drawings	
Account to be debited	Account to be credited
Drawings	Relevant asset account (e.g. cash)

Recording drawings in the double entry accounts

Worked example 11

On 25 August 2018, the business owner takes $50 from the business bank account for her own use. Enter this transaction in the correct double entry accounts.

				Bank		$
			25 Aug	Drawings		50

		Drawings			
		$			
25 Aug	Bank	50			

Money taken from the business bank account leads to a reduction in assets. This requires a credit entry in the bank account.

Entries for drawings follow the same rules as for owner's equity. Drawings are a reduction in the owner's investment in the business. The drawings account is debited.

Key knowledge

Always keep additions to owner's equity and reductions in owner's equity (drawings) in separate accounts.

5 Why do you think additions to owner's equity and reductions (through the drawings account) are kept in separate accounts?

Balancing accounts

At the end of an accounting period the business owner balances the double entry accounts. This enables them to see the **balance** on each individual account. In some accounts, there are likely to be many entries on the debit and credit sides. However, the owner's main concern is not the number of entries in the account but the balance on the account.

To balance an account, you should first total the debit and credit columns of the account. If the totals are the same the account has no balance. If the totals of the columns are different then there is a balance on the account.

Key term

Balance (of an account): The overall difference between the total on the debit side and the total on the credit side of an account at a point in time.

A balance exists on an account when the totals of the debit and credit columns are different.

Accounts where there is no outstanding balance

The following two accounts have no outstanding balance because the totals of the debit and credit columns in each case are the same.

Bank						
		$				$
2 April	Sales	112	9 April	Purchases		120
12 April	Sundry sales	58	14 April	Computer		790
23 April	Owner's equity	740				
		<u>910</u>				<u>910</u>

In the bank account, you add up both columns. You write in the totals of the two columns on the same row. Double underlining each column finishes the account for that period.

Ali						
		$				$
17 April	Sales	<u>140</u>	26 April	Cash		<u>140</u>

The Ali account is a trade receivable account. In this account, there is no need to add up the columns because there is only one entry on each side of the account. You double underline each side and that balances the account for that period.

Accounts where there is an outstanding balance

Follow these steps to balance an account where there is an outstanding balance.

1 Find the total of each column. Use a calculator, unless the numbers are very easy.

2 Calculate the difference between the totals. This will be the balancing figure on the account.

3 Add the balancing figure to the correct columns to make the totals the same.

The balancing figure is entered in the accounts as the 'balance to be carried down'. This is the amount needed to make the totals of the columns equal and is not the balance on the account.

4 The actual balance on the account, known as 'the balance to be brought down' is the balance on the account at the start of the next accounting period – usually the next month or next year.

Worked example 12

Entries on both sides of the account with different totals

The Alex account is a trade receivable account. In the account of Alex, there are a number of entries on both sides of the account. Balance the account for April.

Alex		$			$
6 April	Sales	15	7 April	Sales returns	21
18 April	Sales	67	12 April	Bank	66
24 April	Sales	28			

Balance the account following the steps above.

1 The total of the debit column is $110.

  The total of the credit column is $87.

2 The balancing figure is $110 – $87 = $23.

Alex		$			$
6 April	Sales	15	7 April	Sales returns	21
18 April	Sales	67	12 April	Bank	66
24 April	Sales	28	30 April	Balance to be carried down	23
		110			110
1 May	Balance to be brought down	23			

3 Enter the balancing figure and add up the columns.

4 Enter the balance to be brought down at the start of the next accounting period – 1 May in this case.

Key knowledge

The following abbreviations are used:

Balance to be carried down = Balance c/d (this is the balancing figure needed to equalise the columns)

Balance to be brought down = Balance b/d (this is the balance on the account).

Worked example 13

Where there are entries on only one side of the account

In both the sales account and the account of Luis, there are entries on only one side of the account. Balance the accounts for the month of April.

Sales						
		$				$
			1 April	Dylan		118
			18 April	Samuel		93
			27 April	Youssef		325

Luis						
		$				$
23 April	Purchases	118				

Sales						
		$				$
30 April	Balance c/d	536	1 April	Dylan		118
			18 April	Samuel		93
			27 April	Youssef		325
		536				536
			1 May	Balance b/d		536

You add up the credit column and enter the total figure. The balancing figure is the same as this total as there are no debit entries. This is entered on the debit side and the balance is brought down to the credit side for the start of the next month.

Luis						
		$				$
23 April	Purchases	118	30 Apr	Balance c/d		118
1 May	Balance b/d	118				

There is only one entry in this account (23 Apr) so the balancing figure is entered on the opposite side and then the balance brought down to the debit side for the start of the next month.

Interpreting ledger accounts and their balances

After an account has been balanced it can be interpreted. This means looking at the balance and recognising what the balance means. For example, the balance on the cash account can be interpreted as telling you how much cash the business has at the date the account was balanced.

Worked example 14

A business balances its ledger accounts at the end of each month. Balance this account at the end of the month and interpret what its balance means for the business.

Bank					
2018		$	2018		$
1 Jan	Balance b/d	165	11 Jan	Ester	88
5 Jan	Sundry sales	110	24 Jan	Insurance	120
15 Jan	Commission received	84			
26 Jan	Adrian	90			

Bank					
2018		$	2018		$
1 Jan	Balance b/d	165	11 Jan	Ester	88
5 Jan	Sundry sales	110	24 Jan	Insurance	120
15 Jan	Commission received	84	31 Jan	Balance c/d	241
26 Jan	Adrian	90			
		449			449
1 Feb	Balance b/d	241			

The debit balance on the bank account is $241. This is the exact amount of money in the business bank account when business opens on that date (1 Feb).

Account balances can always be interpreted. For example:

- Cash balance (always a debit balance) = how much cash the business has
- Debit balance on the bank account = amount the business has in its bank account
- Credit balance on the bank account = amount the business owes to the bank
- Credit balance on sales account = sales made for a period
- Debit balance on purchases account = purchases made for a period
- Debit balance on a **personal account** = amount owed to the business from a customer
- Credit balance on a personal account = amount the business owes to a supplier

Key terms

Personal accounts: Accounts of other businesses or people that the business has a financial relationship with.

Making transfers to financial statements

At the end of the accounting period the income statement is prepared. This shows the size of any profit earned or loss made by the business. Profit or loss is calculated by comparing the income received by the business for the period with the expenses incurred during the period. The ledger accounts are closed and any outstanding balances from these accounts are transferred to the income statement.

Worked example 15

A business ends it year on 31 December. The balance on the sales account for the year is $198000. Show how this balance is transferred to the income statement in the ledger account for sales.

Sales					
		$			$
31 Dec	Transfer to income statement	198000	31 Dec	Balance b/d	198000

Rather than carrying the balance down to the next year, you bring the balance on the account down to the end of year date and transfer the full value of sales, the balance on the account, to the income statement. In effect, this transfer empties the account of its contents – in this case, the sales revenue for the year.

Worked example 16

A business ends its year on 31 December. The balance on the wages account for the year is $39 500. Show how this balance is transferred to the income statement in the ledger account for sales.

					$				$
		Wages							
31 Dec	Balance b/d			39 500		31 Dec	Transfer to income statement		39 500

> As with the sales account in Worked example 15, this transfer empties the account of its contents – in this case, the expense of wages incurred in the year.

Although the income statement does not appear as a ledger account, it does work as a double entry account. Looking at Worked examples 15 and 16, you should be able to see that, following the rule of making a debit entry and a credit entry for each transaction, sales will be credited to the income statement, and wages will be debited to the income statement.

Division of the ledger into the sales ledger, the purchases ledger and the nominal ledger

The double entry accounts of a business are contained in a ledger. For bigger businesses, there are likely to be many accounts. This makes it much harder to locate individual accounts. In most businesses, the ledger is subdivided into three separate ledgers:

- Sales ledger
- Purchases ledger
- Nominal ledger (also known as General ledger).

The three ledgers contain the following types of accounts:

Sales ledger	Purchases ledger	Nominal ledger
Personal accounts of all credit customers (i.e. trade receivables)	Personal accounts of all credit suppliers (i.e. trade payables)	All other accounts: for assets, liabilities, and owner's equity, along with all income and expense accounts.

This makes it easier for a business to track personal accounts. It also allows the business to calculate how much it is owed in total from its customers, as well as how much it owes to all its suppliers. The amount owing can be quickly seen by looking at the balance in the sales ledger. The amount owed can be quickly seen by looking at the balance in the purchases ledger.

 6 Look back at the accounts in the worked examples in this unit. Where would you find each of the accounts – in the sales ledger, the purchases ledger or the nominal ledger?

> **Key terms**
>
> **Sales ledger:** Book recording trade receivables. It contains the personal accounts of all the credit customers of the business.
>
> **Purchases ledger:** Book recording trade payables. It contains the personal accounts of all the credit suppliers of the business.
>
> **Nominal ledger:** Book containing all other accounts not found in sales or purchases ledger.

Applying

Complete this task in pairs.

Task

A business made the following transactions:

- 22 Jan   Wages paid from the bank totalling $5,400
- 22 Jan   Inventory purchased on credit from Akpo $590
- 23 Jan   Inventory purchased on credit from Kobi $410
- 25 Jan   Inventory returned to Akpo valued at $150
- 26 Jan   Sales of goods to Iwelumo on credit for $900
- 27 Jan   Amount paid to Kobi out of the bank account $250
- 29 Jan   Insurance paid from the bank totalling $500
- 30 Jan   Sales of goods to Garcia on credit for $330

Prepare the double entry accounts for these transactions and balance them.

Then prepare the list of balances under the headings Debit balances and Credit balances. Find the totals of the balances under these two headings.

Knowledge check

1   A business sells goods on credit that are later returned by the customer because they are unsuitable. Which of the following is the correct double entry to record the goods being accepted back to the business?

	Debit	Credit
A	Sales	Trade receivables
B	Sales returns	Trade payables
C	Sales returns	Trade receivables
D	Sales	Trade payables

2 Adele purchases goods on credit from Wei. Which of the following is the correct record of this transaction in the double entry accounts of Wei?

	Debit	Credit
A	Adele	Sales
B	Wei	Purchases
C	Purchases	Wei
D	Sales	Adele

3 A computer is bought on credit from Poppy to be used in the business's office. The computer is returned as it doesn't work. Which of the following is the correct double entry needed to record the transaction in the business's accounts?

	Debit	Credit
A	Poppy	Purchases returns
B	Poppy	Computer
C	Sales return	Poppy
D	Computer	Poppy

4 For each transaction state which account should be debited and which should be credited:

(a) Computer bought with payment made from the bank account

(b) Delivery van bought on credit from Peng

(c) Owner pays own money into business bank account

(d) Fixtures and fittings sold on credit to Li

(e) Payment received from Li into bank

(f) Equipment sold for cash.

5 For each transaction state which account should be debited and which should be credited:

(a) Inventory purchased and paid for immediately by cheque

(b) Goods returned to the original supplier, Hania, due to them being faulty

(c) Sales of goods on credit to Rachid

(d) Payment to Sunita, a supplier, made from the bank

(e) Goods previously sold to Martin are returned.

6 For each transaction state which account should be debited and which should be credited:

(a) Rent paid from the bank

(b) Wages paid in cash

(c) Commission received and paid into the business bank account

(d) The owner of a business takes computer equipment from the business for personal use

(e) Inventory purchased on credit from Somchi.

7 Prepare the double entry accounts for the month of August for the following transactions:

1 Aug   Keletso starts a business with $400 of cash and $2000 placed into the business bank account

2 Aug   Computer equipment is bought for business use for $900 with payment made from the bank

4 Aug   Computer equipment worth $200 no longer needed for business use is sold on credit to 123 Computers

7 Aug   A loan of $1000 is taken out by the business from Western Bank. The money is placed straight into the bank account of the business

8   Prepare the double entry accounts for the month of May for the following transactions:

1 May   Grace starts a business by depositing $3000 into the business bank account

2 May $500 is transferred from the bank into the cash account

8 May   Equipment is bought on credit from ABC Supplies for $900

12 May   Additional equipment is bought on credit from ABC Supplies for $500

16 May   ABC Supplies is paid the full amount owing for equipment bought, $1400, by bank transfer

20 May   A car is bought for $1000. Payment is made from the bank account

9   Prepare the double entry accounts from the following transactions and balance each account at the end of the month:

1 Sept   Business bank account opened with $6500 of owner's money

4 Sept   Equipment is bought for $1900 payment made from the bank

6 Sept   Insurance of $55 is paid by cheque

7 Sept   Purchases are made on credit of $65 from Santiago and $21 from Janine

10 Sept   A vehicle is bought for $6000 on credit from Oliver

14 Sept   Sales of $380 are made on credit to Maria

16 Sept   Goods worth $34 are returned to Santiago

18 Sept   Maria pays the full amount owing on his account by cheque

21 Sept   Janine is paid $21 out of the bank account

10   A business year ends on 31 December 2018. The following totals exist in the books of a business:

Purchases $48 900   Commission received $289

Prepare the ledger accounts for the transfer of these totals to the financial statements.

11   In which ledger would the following accounts be found?

(a) Sales   (d) Motor repairs

(b) Sales returns   (e) Owner's equity

(c) Venkat – a trade receivable   (f) James – a trade payable

---

Check your progress

Read the unit objectives below and reflect on your progress in each.

▲	I struggle with this and need more practice.
▲▲	I can do this reasonably well.
▲▲▲	I can do this with confidence.

• Outline the double entry system of book-keeping

• Process accounting data using the double entry system

• Prepare ledger accounts

• Post transactions to the ledger accounts

• Balance ledger accounts as required and make transfers to financial statements

• Interpret ledger accounts and their balances

• Recognise the division of the ledger into the sales ledger, the purchases ledger and the nominal (general ledger).

Business documents

Learning objectives

By the end of this unit, you should be able to:

- recognise and understand the following business documents: invoice, debit note, credit note, statement of account, cheque, receipt
- complete pro-forma business documents
- understand the use of business documents as sources of information: invoice, credit note, cheque counterfoil, paying-in slip, receipt, bank statement.

Starting point

Answer these questions in pairs.

1 How does a business keep records of the payments into and out of the business bank account?

2 Other than the double entry accounts, how does a business keep records of each financial transaction of the business?

Exploring

Discuss these questions in pairs.

1 Why do you think businesses allow credit to their customers?

2 What mistakes could occur if a business uses a computer to keep records of accounting transactions?

Developing

Types of business document

Business documents are documents received and issued by businesses. They contain vital information about the transactions made between businesses and are used to make entries in the accounting records of businesses. They are sometimes referred to as **source documents**.

Business documents are used

- as the source of information for making entries in the accounts of the business
- to confirm agreements made between businesses
- as evidence in the event of a dispute.

Key term

Business document:
A document received or issued by a business when a transaction takes place. It contains information relevant to the transaction.

Pro-forma documents refer to the standardised documents used by businesses. Rather than creating a document with all the details required for a business transaction for each transaction, businesses use a pro-forma document which already contains some of the details. Pro-forma documents contain details that relate to all transactions of a certain type. For example, an invoice issued for a credit sale contains the details common to all credit sales – the address of the business making the sale, space for the details for the items being sold, space for the totals, space for any discounts offered, and so on. There are a number of different types of business document.

Invoice

When a credit sale is made, the business making the sale issues a sales invoice. The business buying the products receives this document but calls it a purchases invoice. This is a business document which contains:

- name and address of the business making the sale
- name and address of the customer
- date of sale
- details of sale – items, quantities and prices (for individual items and total for the invoice)
- carriage and delivery costs
- payment conditions – such as trade discounts and discounts for prompt payment.

Businesses want to encourage other businesses to buy from them. They may offer trade discounts to other businesses to encourage them to buy larger quantities. Often a trade discount is only offered to other businesses in the same industry. The trade discount appears on the invoice and is usually expressed as a percentage. The trade discount does not appear in the double entry accounts. Instead the amount after the trade discount has been deducted appears in the accounts.

Cash discounts are different and are explained in Unit 2.3.

Key terms

Invoice: A document issued by a business when making a credit sale.

Trade discount: A discount given by one business to another business. It is calculated as a percentage reduction in the invoice quantity.

Worked example 1

Look at this invoice. Calculate the missing values.

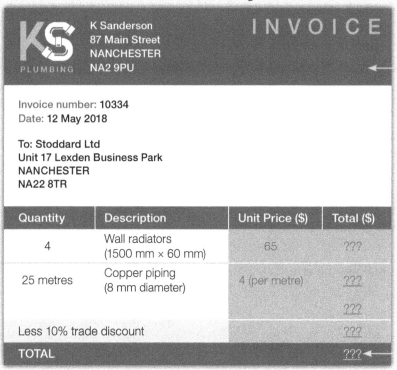

The invoice is issued by K Sanderson for a sale made to Stoddard Ltd. For K Sanderson this is a sales invoice. For Stoddard Ltd this is a purchases invoice.

Quantity	Description	Unit Price ($)	Total ($)
4	Wall radiators (1500 mm × 60 mm)	65	???
25 metres	Copper piping (8 mm diameter)	4 (per metre)	???
			???
Less 10% trade discount			???
TOTAL			???

The total after the deduction of the trade discount is the amount that is debited to the account of Stoddard Ltd and credited to K Sanderson's sales account.

Total for radiators 4 × $65 = $260

Total for the piping 25 × $4 = $100

Total before discount $360

Trade discount = 10% of $360 = $36

Total after trade discount = $360 − $36 = $324

The totals are calculated by multiplying the quantities sold by the selling price of each unit.

1 How can a sales invoice also be a purchases invoice at the same time?

Debit note

After making a purchase, a business may notice that the goods received are not suitable. The goods received may be unsuitable for these reasons:

- wrong quantities received
- faulty products
- incorrect goods
- wrong specification (e.g. wrong colour, wrong size, etc.).

The business will want to return the unsuitable goods to the original supplier. When dealing with unsuitable goods, the business document issued by the customer to the supplier is a **debit note**.

Key term

Debit note: A document issued by a business to the supplier when the goods received are unsuitable.

The information contained on a debit note varies between businesses. However, most debit notes contain the following information:

- name and address of the business (the customer)
- name and address of the supplier
- date
- details of goods that are not suitable and are being returned
- value of unsuitable goods.

The debit note is a request by a customer for a credit note (see below) to be issued by the supplier of the unsuitable goods received by the customer. It does **not** generate a transaction in the double entry accounts. The supplier has to agree to accept the debit note and allow the goods to be returned before any entries can be made in the double entry accounts.

Worked example 2

Look at this debit note. Calculate the total value.

KS PLUMBING

K Sanderson
87 Main Street
NANCHESTER
NA2 9PU

DEBIT NOTE

Debit note number: **34/2018**
Date: **22 May 2018**

To: **Nanchester Plumbing Supplies**
18 High Street
NANCHESTER
NA1 4CV

The following goods are to be returned:

Quantity	Description	Unit Price ($)	Total ($)
2	Wall radiators (2000 mm × 85 mm) – Damaged on arrival	75	150
15 m²	Plasterboard – Wrong specification	7 (per m²)	105
			???

This debit note was issued by K Sanderson as a result of receiving unsatisfactory goods from Nanchester Plumbing Supplies. The goods that are unsuitable are listed on the debit note along with the reason for their return and the value of the goods.

Total of the debit note = $150 + $105 = $255

2 Why do you think no accounting entries are made when a debit note is issued?

Credit note

When accepting returned goods because they are unsuitable, the supplier will issue a **credit note** to the customer. A credit note may also be issued if the customer was originally overcharged on an invoice. Information found on a credit note includes:

- name and address of the business (the business issuing the credit note)
- name and address of the customer (where the credit note is being sent)
- date
- details of the goods being returned by the customer to the business
- the value of the credit note.

Credit notes may be printed in red so that they look different from invoices.

Worked example 3

Look at this credit note. How would Nanchester Plumbing Supplies record this transaction in its double entry accounts?

NANCHESTER
PLUMBING SUPPLIES

CREDIT NOTE

18 High Street
NANCHESTER
NA1 4CV

Credit note number: 2018-7
Date: 29 May 2018

To: K Sanderson
87 Main Street
NANCHESTER
NA2 9PU

Quantity	Description	Unit Price ($)	Total ($)
2	Wall radiators (2000 mm × 85 mm)	75	150
15 m²	Plasterboard	7 (per m²)	105
			255

This credit note is based on the debit note in Worked example 2. The customer (K Sanderson) has returned goods to the supplier (Nanchester Plumbing Supplies). The supplier has sent a credit note for the value of the returned goods. The reason why the goods were originally returned does not have to feature here as the original supplier has accepted that they were unsuitable.

In the accounts of Nanchester Plumbing Supplies the credit note is entered on the debit side of the sales returns account.

The credit entry is in the account of K Sanderson.

The credit entry in K Sanderson's account shows that K Sanderson now owes less to Nanchester Plumbing Supplies.

Statement of account

At the end of each month, a business should send a statement of account to each customer who still owes money to the business. The statement of account is a summary of the transactions between the business and the customer over the month. It indicates the amount still owed by the customer at the end of the month.

A statement of account will normally show:

- name and address of the business
- name and address of the customer
- relevant transactions and dates for the month
- balance owing by the customer at the start and end of the month
- payments received from the customer during the month
- details of invoices (from sales) sent to the customer during the month
- details of any credit notes agreed.

Key term

Statement of account: A document issued to all customers still owing money to the business. It contains details relating to the transactions taking place between the business and the customer.

Worked example 4

This is a statement of account issued by K Sanderson to a credit customer, Levinson Ltd, for May 2018. Calculate how much Levinson Ltd owes the business at the end of the month.

K Sanderson
87 Main Street
NANCHESTER
NA2 9PU

STATEMENT OF ACCOUNT

Account number: 87322
Levinson Ltd
15 Causeway
Nanchester
N1 4RT

Date	Details	Debit ($)	Credit ($)	Balance ($)
1 May	Balance b/d			50
12 May	Invoice Number 10452	450		500
19 May	Credit note Number 39/18		80	420
28 May	Bank		300	???
31 May	Balance owing:			???

The balance owing to the business by Levinson Ltd at 31 May is $120.

The statement of account is a written representation of the double entry account for the credit customer. The amounts in the debit and credit columns match the amounts in the double entry account. This represents how much the customer owes the business at the end of the month. Statements of account are sent out mainly as reminders to the customers of the business of what they still owe.

Subtract the payment of $300 received from the previous balance of $420.

Cheque

Many businesses make payments to other businesses by **credit transfers**, by **standing orders** or by using credit or debit cards. These are automated methods of payment. This means that there is no need for anyone from either business to visit the bank and these can usually be completed online. Another method of making a payment from the business bank account is to use a cheque.

A cheque is a document which authorises payment from a bank account. The bank issues the business with a cheque book which contains a number of pre-printed cheques. These are used by the business for making payments.

Pre-printed cheques contain the following information:

- the name and address of the bank used by the business
- the account details of the business – the sort code (which is a number identifying the branch of the bank with which the business has an account) and the account number (which is unique to the business)
- the name of the business.

To make a payment, the business adds the following details to a cheque before it passes it on to the payee:

- name of payee
- amount to be paid (written in both numbers and words)
- date of payment
- signature of the payer (the business or person making the payment).

The cheque counterfoil is the left-hand portion of the cheque. When the payer writes a cheque, they also complete the cheque counterfoil with the name of the payee, the amount to be paid and the date of the payment. They keep this as a record of the payment. Normally, the cheque can be detached, leaving the counterfoil still attached to the cheque book.

Depending on the business, more than one person may be able to sign a cheque on behalf of the business. The people authorised to sign cheques are called signatories. The bank holds a record of the signature of all the signatories and will only make the payment to the payee if the signature on the cheque matches the signature in their records. This provides security for the payer against fraudulent use of their cheques by people outside of the business.

Some businesses require two signatories on their cheques. This provides security for the business against fraudulent use of their cheques by a signatory of the business.

There are various issues associated with making and receiving payments by cheque, resulting from the fact that a cheque

Worked example 5

Look at the cheque below. What entries would K Sanderson make in his double entry accounts on receiving this cheque?

The payee is K Sanderson.

The payer of the cheque is J B Stroish.

K Sanderson would make the following entries in his double entry accounts:

Bank would be debited by $100

The J B Stroish account would be credited by $100.

In the accounts of J B Stroish, the entries would be similar but on the opposite sides – J B Stroish would debit K Sanderson and credit the Bank.

merely authorises payment from a bank account and must be presented to the bank before the money is transferred between the payer and the payee. These are dealt with in more detail in Chapter 3.

Paying-in slip

Most businesses deposit money regularly into the bank account. A **paying-in slip** is used when paying cheques, notes and coins into the bank account.

Key term

Paying-in slip: A document used to deposit funds (cheques or notes and coins) into a bank account.

Date:	Nanchester Bank High Street Branch		$100 notes		
			$50 notes		
$100 notes			$20 notes		
$50 notes	Date: _____		$10 notes		
$20 notes			$5 notes		
$10 notes	Cashier's stamp	ACCOUNT HOLDER'S NAME	$1 notes		
$5 notes		....	Coins		
$1 notes			Cheques		
Coins		Sort code	Account number		
Cheques	No. of	- - -	TOTAL ($)		
TOTAL ($)	cheques	....			

Banks can issue books of paying-in slips to customers. Like cheque books, these are pre-printed with the business's bank account details. The paying-in slip shown above is a non-personalised one and the business fills in their account details, along with the amount of money to be deposited into the bank account.

There are two ways in which the business records that money has been deposited into the bank account. Either the business receives a stamped copy of the paying-in slip from the bank or they complete the counterfoil attached to the paying-in slip book (the bank stamps the counterfoil and it is kept by the business).

Receipt

A receipt is a written document which is issued by a business when it receives payment from a customer. It provides proof of payment by the customer. A receipt may be printed by machine (as part of a cash till or register) or it may be a handwritten note signed by the business receiving the money.

Receipts normally contain the following information:

- amount received
- date of payment
- what the payment was for (i.e. the goods or services supplied).

Receipts are often not needed in the case of payment by cheque or an automated payment into the bank account. This is because the bank statement will have a record of the amount received. A receipt is issued to the customer and a copy kept by the business as proof of the amount received. A receipt is kept as part of the income records of a business. The information on the receipt appears in the double entry account for cash and whatever the cash being paid or received is in respect of.

> **Worked example 6**
>
> Look at this receipt. What is the correct double entry to record this transaction?
>
>
>
> BUSINESS RECEIPT
>
> NANCHESTER
> PLUMBING SUPPLIES
>
> Amount received in respect of cash sales of plumbing supplies.
> Cash received thanks!
>
> Date: 17 May 2018
>
> M Bloor
>
> Nanchester Plumbing Supplies
>
> Receipt number: 7707
>
> Amount: $118.50
>
> Cash is debited by $118.50.
>
> The sales account is credited by $118.50.

Bank statement

Banks issue bank statements on a regular basis. These contain details of all the money paid into and out of the bank account of the business for a period of time. They are presented from the bank's point of view. This means that if the business has money in the bank account, it appears as a credit balance. (In the business's double entry accounts, money in the bank is shown as a debit balance.)

Bank statements may be posted to the business or the business may receive online statements. They allow the business to check that the details of entries on the statement match the details as they appear in the bank account of the double entry accounts. The statement appears similar to a statement of account – where the balance on the bank account is updated after each entry.

Key term

Bank statement: A document issued by the bank of the business showing all bank transactions for a period of time.

Worked example 7

This bank statement is for May 2018. How much money did K Sanderson have in the bank at the start and the end of this month?

EasternBank

Sort Code 22-11-98
Account No. 01439125

Account name: K Sanderson
31 May 2018   Statement No. 45

Date	Details	Payments ($)	Receipts ($)	Balance ($)
2018				
01 May	Opening balance			??? Cr
04 May	Credit transfer: Bellwood Ltd		240	829 Cr
06 May	Cheque 101450	684		145 Cr
12 May	Direct Debit SE Electricity	86		59 Cr
15 May	Cheque deposited		98	157 Cr
30 May	Cheque 101451	215		58 Dr
31 May	Closing balance			??? Dr

The abbreviated term for credit (Cr) means that the bank owes K Sanderson this amount, i.e. that K Sanderson has money in the account.

K Sanderson has taken out more from the bank than he has in the account. The abbreviation for debit balance (Dr) means that K Sanderson now owes the bank money.

Amount in the bank at the start of the month = $829 – $240 = $589.

At the end of the month the balance is overdrawn by $58.

3 Explain why a bank balance may appear as a credit balance despite there being money in the bank account.

Business documents as sources of information

Business documents provide information used when completing double entry accounts.

Business document	Account to be debited	Account to be credited
(Sales) invoice	Credit customer	Sales
(Purchases) invoice	Purchases	Credit supplier
Cheque counterfoil	Account related to payment	Bank
Cheque received	Bank	Credit customer
Credit note	Sales returns	Credit customer
Receipt	Bank or cash	Account related to receipt
Paying-in slip	Bank	Cash or credit customer*
Bank statement	Bank (if money is received)	Bank (if money is paid out)

* Normally money paid into the bank account will be cheques from customers or cash paid into the bank.

Some of the documents can be used by both the business issuing the document and the business receiving it. A credit note issued by a business will be used for information relating to sales returns. The business receiving the credit note would treat the document as evidence to record purchases returns. The same applies to cheques being issued and received.

Debit note does not appear in the table as it is a request for a business to be allowed to return goods to the supplier. It does not necessarily mean that the supplier will allow the goods to be returned.

Applying

Discuss these questions in pairs.

1. What documents would no longer be needed for a business that does not make credit sales or credit purchases?

2. How do the entries in the double entry account for bank differ from the entries that are on the bank statement?

Knowledge check

1. Which of the following business documents does NOT generate an entry in the double entry accounts of a business?

   A   A paying-in slip

   B   A credit note

   C   A debit note

   D   A sales invoice

2 A business receives an invoice from a supplier. Into which double entry account does the business enter the details?

  A Sales   **C** Credit customer account

  B Purchases   **D** Bank

3 A business issues a receipt for cash sales. Which account does the business credit?

  A Credit customer account   **C** Cash

  B Credit supplier account   **D** Sales

4 Copy and complete this invoice.

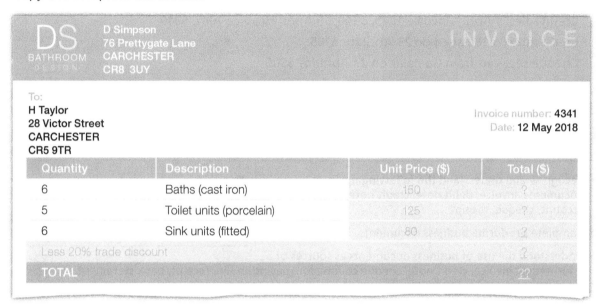

DS BATHROOM DESIGN

D Simpson
76 Prettygate Lane
CARCHESTER
CR8 3UY

INVOICE

To:
H Taylor
28 Victor Street
CARCHESTER
CR5 9TR

Invoice number: **4341**
Date: **12 May 2018**

Quantity	Description	Unit Price ($)	Total ($)
6	Baths (cast iron)	150	?
5	Toilet units (porcelain)	125	?
6	Sink units (fitted)	80	?
	Less 20% trade discount		?
TOTAL			?

5 It is 19 October 2018. You need to pay Molyneux for goods supplied to the value of $356.

Copy and complete this cheque and the counterfoil to make the payment from your bank account.

Date:
___ / ___ / ___

Payee
_____

Amount:
$ _____

000001

Nanchester Bank
High Street Branch

Pay _____

_____

_____

Cheque number
000001

Branch sort code
01-02-13

Account number
01234567

Date:
___ / ___ / ___

$ _____

6 Your business name and address is Partyfood Supplies Ltd, 12 Oakholme Street, Oldtown, OT1 9DR.

On 12 October 2018 Wedding Planners Ltd of 34 Everard Road, Oldtown, OT8 7RD place the following order:

120 cupcakes ($0.80 each), 5 desserts ($8 each), 10 flans ($12 each)

The company receives a trade discount of 5%.

(a) Prepare an invoice for the order.

On 13 October Wedding Planners Ltd return 20 of the cupcakes because they are damaged.

(b) Prepare a credit note.

7   Your business name and address is Dex Systems Solutions, Unit 5, Business Park, Newtown, NT55 1LY.

Prepare the statement of account for April 2018 for this information:

Customer account no: 7280

Customer name and address: Gamalat, 78 Hartope Road, Newtown, NT4 5UN

Credit sales: 5 April – Invoice 1045, $540; 19 April – Invoice 1047, $310

Credit note 05/18 issued on 23 April for $105.

Cheque received from Gamalat on 27 April for $500

Check your progress

Read the unit objectives below and reflect on your progress in each.

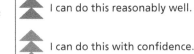

- I struggle with this and need more practice.
- I can do this reasonably well.
- I can do this with confidence.

- Recognise and understand the following business documents: invoice, debit note, credit note, statement of account, cheque, receipt

- Complete pro-forma business documents

- Understand the use of business documents as sources of information: invoice, credit note, cheque counterfoil, paying-in slip, receipt, bank statement.

Books of prime entry

Learning objectives
By the end of this unit, you should be able to:
- explain the advantage of using various books of prime entry
- explain the use of, and process, accounting data in the books of prime entry – cash book, petty cash book, sales journal, purchases journal, sales returns journal, purchases returns journal and the general journal
- post the ledger entries from the books of prime entry
- distinguish between and account for trade discount and cash discounts
- explain the dual function of the cash book as a book of prime entry and as a ledger account for bank and cash
- explain the use of and record payments and receipts made by bank transfers and other electronic means
- explain and apply the imprest system of petty cash.

Starting point

Answer these questions in pairs.

1 Which double entry accounts are used more frequently than others?

2 How can you organise the double entry accounts of the business to make information easier to find?

Exploring

Discuss these questions in pairs.

1 What sort of mistakes can be made when transferring information from business documents to the financial records of the business?

2 In some businesses, more than one person maintains the accounts of the business. How would you divide up their roles and responsibilities?

Developing

Introduction

For small businesses, the double entry accounts can be kept in one book. Individual accounts are easy to find because there are not many separate accounts. Once a business expands, some method of organising the financial records becomes important. Different ledgers are used to store certain types of accounts (covered in Unit 2.1). In addition, businesses can also use a system of **books of prime entry**.

Financial transactions are classified according to type of transaction and then entered in the appropriate book of prime entry. The books of prime entry provide back-up to the double entry system and ensure the double entry accounts are not cluttered with a large number of entries of small value. The books of prime entry provide the link between the business documents (discussed in Unit 2.2) and the ledger accounts (discussed in Unit 2.1). Business documents generate entries into the books of prime entry. The entries in the books of prime entry are then transferred to the ledger accounts by the process of **posting**.

Key terms
....

Book of prime entry: A book, or journal, in which transactions are first recorded before being posted to the double entry accounts.

Posting: The process of transferring information from books of prime entry to the correct double entry account.

Key knowledge
....

Business documents provide information for the books of prime entry. Information from the books of prime entry is then posted as entries in the ledger accounts.

Books of prime entry record details of transactions as they happen. Except for the cash book, they are not accounts. The cash book is both a book of prime entry and an account. There are different books used for different types of transaction, as shown in the table below. Books of prime entry are also known as **journals** or **books of original entry**.

Book of prime entry	Type of transaction recorded in the book
Cash book	All cash and bank transactions
Petty cash book	All small items of cash payment
Sales journal	All credit sales of goods
Purchases journal	All credit purchases of goods bought for resale
Sales returns journal	Sales returns of goods previously sold
Purchases returns journal	Purchases returns of goods previously purchased
General journal	Any transaction not covered by the other journals

Advantages of using books of prime entry

- Totals are posted from the books of prime entry instead of each individual entry. This means the double entry accounts are used less frequently and are easier to read as a result.

- The books of prime entry provide a back-up to information contained in the double entry accounts. This is useful when records are missing.

- Responsibility for maintaining the financial records can be delegated to different workers. Each person maintains a different book of prime entry.

The cash book

The **cash book** is a combination of the cash and bank accounts. It records all cash and bank transactions made by the business. It works in the same way as a double entry account but with two debit columns and two credit columns – one each for cash and for bank.

The cash book is the only book of prime entry which is also a double entry account (two accounts, in reality).

Electronic bank transfers

Cheques can be used to make payments from the bank account of a business to another person or business. However, cheques are used much less than in the past. Electronic transfers of money from one bank account to another are possible. Some of these methods include:

*   Direct debits
*   Standing orders
*   Bank transfers
*   Credit transfers

The different methods of electronic transfer are explored in Unit 3.3.

Key term

Cash book: A combined cash and bank account which records all transactions involving payments and receipts of money.

Worked example 1

For April 2018, these cash and bank transactions are made.

1 April   Balances are as follows: Cash in hand $102, Cash in bank $1190

8 April   Payment of $200 by cheque to Emma

10 April   Cash sales of $89 paid for by cheque

12 April   Cheque received from Kashi for $315

15 April   Cash paid for advertising $95

The cash book appears as:

Cash book							
		Cash	Bank			Cash	Bank
2018		$	$	2018		$	$
1 April	Balances b/d	102	1190	8 April	Emma		200
10 April	Sales		89	15 April	Advertising	95	
12 April	Kashi		315				

Update the cash book by entering the following transactions.

19 April   Cash amount of $45 withdrawn from bank for business use

23 April   Payment of $178 by cheque to Jayden

28 April   Electronic transfer made from business bank of $100 to NW Electricity Ltd

Balance the cash book at the end of the month, stating the closing balances.

The cash book entries are completed by posting into the appropriate columns. This depends on whether the transaction involves money being received – which involves a debit entry (in either the cash or bank column), or money being paid out – which involves a credit entry in the cash or bank columns.

		Cash	Bank			Cash	Bank
Cash book							
2018		$	$	2018		$	$
1 April	Balances b/d	102	1190	8 April	Emma		200
10 April	Sales		89	15 April	Advertising	95	
12 April	Kashi		315	19 April	Cash		45
19 April	Bank	45		23 April	Jayden		178
				28 April	NW Electricity Ltd		100
				30 April	Balances c/d	52	1071
		147	1594			147	1594
1 May	Balances b/d	52	1071				

There might be a debit balance on cash and a credit balance on bank at the same time.

The transaction on 19 April requires a debit entry and a credit entry in the cash book. This is because it is a movement between holding cash in the bank and holding cash in hand.

The cash book balances are both debit balances: $52 for cash and $1071 for bank.

 Why can't the cash account have a credit balance?

Cash discounts

Businesses both buy and sell goods on credit. This means payment is not made until later. To encourage prompt or earlier payment of the debt, a business can offer a **cash discount**. This is where a business deducts a small amount from the total owing if payment is received within a specified time period. Most cash discounts are calculated as a percentage reduction on the outstanding invoice.

Key knowledge

Cash discounts do not require that payment is made in cash. Cash discount is the name used to distinguish it from a trade discount.

There are two types of cash discount that appear in the double entry accounts.

Type of cash discount	Description
Discounts allowed	Offered by the business to its credit customers
Discounts received	Received by the business from its credit suppliers

Key terms

Cash discount: A reduction in the amount owing on a credit transaction to encourage prompt payment.

Discount allowed: A reduction in the invoice total offered by a business to its credit customers to encourage early settlement of invoices.

Discount received: A reduction in the amount a business owes to the credit supplier of the business to encourage early settlement.

Cash discounts differ from **trade discounts**. Trade discounts are reductions in amounts owing offered usually between businesses in the same industry. These do not appear in the double entry accounts. Cash discounts do appear.

Key knowledge

Trade discounts *do* not appear in the double entry accounts.

Cash discounts *do* appear in the double entry accounts.

Worked example 2

A business sells $480 of goods to Jacob and offers a 2.5% discount if payment is received within two weeks. The business has also purchased goods on credit for $800 from Gloria and is offered a discount of 1.25% if payment is made within two weeks.

Both transactions are settled within the two-week period. Calculate the amount received from Jacob and the amount paid to Gloria.

The amount received from Jacob is $480 less 2.5%

2.5% of $480 = $12

Amount received from Jacob = $480 – $12 = $468.

> The business is owed $480 but receives $468 in full settlement. The difference represents the *discount allowed* by the business.

The amount paid to Gloria is $800 less 1.25%

1.25% of $800 = $10

Amount paid to Gloria = $800 – $10 = $790.

> The business owes $800 but pays $790 in full settlement. The difference represents the *discount received* by the business.

Posting discounts in the double entry accounts

Cash discounts are recorded in either the **discounts allowed** or the **discounts received** double entry accounts. Using the information from Worked example 2, the transactions are recorded in the double entry accounts as follows. (The entries in the cash book are not included here.)

Entries needed to record credit sale to Jacob:

Jacob			
	$		$
Sales	480	Bank	468
		Discounts allowed	12

Discounts allowed			
	$		$
Jacob	12		

Entries needed to record credit purchase from Gloria

Gloria			
	$		$
Bank	790	Purchases	800
Discounts received	10		

Discounts received			
	$		$
		Gloria	10

The three-column cash book

A three-column cash book includes an additional column on the debit and credit sides to be used for showing cash discounts. A cash book with no column for discounts is referred to as a **two-column cash book.**

A benefit of using a three-column cash book to record discounts is that the double entry accounts for discounts allowed and received will need fewer entries as a result.

Key knowledge

Most of the time it will not be specified whether a two- or a three-column cash book is being used. However, it is easy to find out. Three-column cash books contain columns for discounts.

Using the information from Worked example 2, the entries into the three-column cash book appear as follows:

Cash book							
	Discounts allowed	Cash	Bank		Discounts received	Cash	Bank
	$	$	$		$	$	$
Jacob	12		468	Gloria	10		790

Worked example 3

For April 2018, the following cash and bank transactions are made.

1 April	Balances brought forward: Cash $175, Bank $290 overdrawn
3 April	Paid Ling by cheque $400 in full settlement of $420 owing
8 April	Paid $50 cash into bank account
15 April	Received cheque from Cheng for $250 in full settlement of sale for $275

The cash book appears as follows:

Cash book									
		Discounts	Cash	Bank			Discounts	Cash	Bank
2018		$	$	$	2018		$	$	$
1 April	Balance b/d		175		1 April	Balance b/d			290
8 April	Cash			50	3 April	Ling	20		400
15 April	Cheng	25		250	8 April	Bank		50	

Update the cash book by entering the following transactions and balancing the account for the end of the month. Complete the discounts allowed and discounts received accounts.

22 April	Received cheque of $90 from Hosna in settlement of sales worth $95
25 April	Cash withdrawn from bank for business use $30
29 April	Paid Kalim by bank transfer $210 in full settlement of sales invoice totalling $225

For the transactions on 22 and 29 April, the discount is entered in the appropriate column.

In this example, the discounts columns are not labelled 'allowed' or 'received'. This is because any payment received from customers is for credit sales and will be linked to discounts allowed to customers. Similarly, the payments made to suppliers for credit purchases will be linked to discounts received from suppliers.

		Discounts	Cash	Bank			Discounts	Cash	Bank
		Cash book							
2018		$	$	$	2018		$	$	$
1 April	Balance b/d		175		1 April	Balance b/d			290
8 April	Cash			50	3 April	Ling	20		400
15 April	Cheng	25		250	8 April	Bank		50	
22 April	Hosna	5		90	25 April	Cash			30
25 April	Cash		30		29 April	Kalim	15		210
30 April	Balance c/d			540	30 April	Balance c/d		155	
		30	205	930			35	205	930
1 May	Balance b/d		155		1 May	Balance b/d			540

Notice how the discounts columns are totalled and not balanced. The totals for the discounts columns are posted to the accounts for discounts allowed and discounts received.

The balances on the cash book at 30 April are: Cash $155 debit; Bank $540 credit.

	Discounts allowed				Discounts received		
	$		$		$		$
Total of April	30					Total of April	35

 2 Why would a business use cheques when it is often easier and quicker to transfer money electronically?

The petty cash book

Some businesses keep a separate **petty cash book** in addition to the cash book. The petty cash book is used for small items of cash payment. Using a petty cash book means the 'main' cash book will not be quickly filled with lots of small payments.

The petty cash book categorises small items of cash expense and totals these every month. The monthly totals are then transferred to the double entry accounts.

The opening balance on the petty cash book is known as the **float**. At the end of each month, the opening balance is restored by a payment made from the main cash book equal to the amount spent on petty cash items during that month.

Key terms

Petty cash book: A book of prime entry used for small items of payment by cash.

Imprest system: A system of maintaining a petty cash book by always ensuring the opening balance of the petty cash book is the same amount for each time period.

Float: The amount of petty cash available at the start of each month.

Maintaining the same float on the petty cash book is known as
the **imprest system**.

Worked example 4

The following are details of petty cash transactions for April 2018.

1 April	The chief cashier debits the petty cash book with $100 to restore the float
4 April	Petrol $12
5 April	Stationery $6
9 April	Tea and coffee $7
11 April	Train tickets $12
18 April	Tea and coffee $4
20 April	Train tickets $15
21 April	Stationery $6
27 April	Folders for office $5

The categories of expenditure used by the business are: Travel costs, Stationery and Sundries. Voucher numbers are used each time a claim is made for petty cash.

The petty cash book appears as follows:

Receipts	Date	Details	Voucher	Total	Travel costs	Stationery	Sundries
$				$	$	$	$
100	1 April	Cash					
	4 April	Petrol	12	12	12		
	5 April	Stationery	13	6		6	
	9 April	Tea and coffee	14	7			7
	11 April	Train tickets	15	12	12		
	18 April	Tea and coffee	16	4			4
	20 April	Train tickets	17	15	15		
	21 April	Stationery	18	6		6	
	27 April	Folders for office	19	<u>5</u>		5	
				?	<u>?</u>	<u>?</u>	<u>?</u>
?	30 April	Cash					
	30 April	Balance c/d		<u>100</u>			
<u>167</u>				<u>167</u>			
100	1 May	Balance b/d					

Total the analysis columns for each category of expenditure and post these to the relevant nominal ledger account. Calculate the amount to be debited to the petty cash book to restore the float.

The totals entered in the petty cash book are:

- Total for travel costs: $39
- Total for stationery: $17
- Total for sundries: $11

Travel costs		
2018		$
30 April	Petty cash book	39

Stationery		
2018		$
30 April	Petty cash book	17

Sundries		
2018		$
30 April	Petty cash book	11

Total to be refunded as part of imprest system: $67.

The total for each category of expenditure is debited to the double entry account for each category of expenditure. The $67 which is debited to the petty cash book to restore the float comes from the credit side of the main cash book.

An employee might spend their own money for the business and then reclaim it as petty cash. In this case, the employee would fill out a petty cash voucher to reclaim the amount spent.

It may help to think of the petty cash book as another double entry account but an account that has credit columns (for payments) split up into categories of expenditure. The columns used are also known as **analysis columns**.

Advantages of maintaining a petty cash book

- It stops the main cash book being quickly filled up with small items of expenditure
- It allows the business to delegate the responsibility for maintaining the petty cash book to a junior member of staff.

Sales journal

The **sales journal** records all credit sales made by the business. This only includes the sales of goods which were purchased by the business specifically for resale. For example, the sale of a motor vehicle on credit which has been used by the business would not appear in the sales journal.

When the business makes a credit sale of goods, it sends an invoice to the customer (see Unit 2.2). The invoice is used to make a record of the sale in the sales journal.

Instead of entering every credit sale made into the sales account, only the total of sales for the month found in the sales journal is transferred to the sales account. However, entries are made for each credit sale in the personal account of the supplier in the sales ledger.

Key term

Sales journal: The book of prime entry used to record credit sales.

Worked example 5

This is an extract from the sales journal of a business for April 2018.

Sales journal			
Date	Details	Invoice no.	Total
2018			$
4 April	Khaled	1011	85
12 April	Farida	1012	160
19 April	Harold	1013	210
25 April	Khaled	1015	56
30 April	Transferred to sales account		???

Post the entries from the sales journal to the correct ledger accounts including the end of month total.

Sales Ledger

Khaled

2018		$	2018		$
4 April	Sales	85			
25 April	Sales	56			

Farida

2018		$	2018		$
12 April	Sales	160			

Harold

2018		$	2018		$
19 April	Sales	210			

Nominal ledger

Sales

2018		$	2018		$
			30 April	Sales journal	511

Each credit sale will be debited to the personal account of the customer of the business.

 3 A business sells a vehicle which had been used by the business on credit. In which journal do you think this would be recorded?

Purchases journal

The **purchases journal** consists of all credit purchases of goods for resale. It only includes purchases of items specifically bought for resale. For example, a business purchasing a computer to be used by the business does not include this within purchases, but a business purchasing a computer specifically for resale does include this within purchases.

Key term

Purchases journal: The book of prime entry used to record credit purchases.

Businesses receive purchases invoices from the suppliers when they make credit purchases. The information found on a purchases invoice is entered in the purchases journal.

Individual purchases are not debited to the purchases account. Instead, the monthly total for the purchases journal is transferred to the purchases account. Individual entries are posted to the personal accounts of the suppliers in the purchases ledger for each purchase made.

Worked example 6

This is an extract from the purchases journal of a business for April 2018.

Purchases journal			
Date	Details	Invoice no.	Total
2018			$
2 April	Samir	564	34
5 April	Omar	565	12
11 April	Omar	566	26
22 April	Nilam	567	55
30 April	Transferred to purchases account		???

Post the entries from the purchases journal to the correct ledger accounts, including the end of month total.

Nominal ledger					
Purchases					
2018		$	2018		$
30 April	Purchases journal	127			

Purchases ledger					
Samir					
2018		$	2018		$
			2 April	Purchases	34

The total of credit purchases for the month is debited to the purchases account in the nominal ledger.

Omar					
2018		$	2018		$
			5 April	Purchases	12
			11 April	Purchases	26

The personal accounts of the suppliers are credited with each credit purchase made. In this case, you credit the account of Omar twice as you made two separate purchases from this supplier.

Nilam					
2018		$	2018		$
			22 April	Purchases	55

Sales returns journal

Sales may be returned to the business by credit customers. A business allowing a customer to return goods issues a **credit note**. Credit notes are recorded in the sales returns journal. The monthly total of sales returns is posted to the sales returns account. Entries are made in the personal account of the customer each time a sales return is authorised.

Key term

Sales returns journal: The book of prime entry used to record sales returns.

Worked example 7

This is an extract from the sales returns journal of the business in Worked example 5 for April 2018.

Sales returns journal			
	Details	Credit note no.	Total
2018			$
19 April	Khaled	1/3	34
26 April	Harold	2/3	12
30 April	Transferred to sales returns account		46

Post the entries from the sales returns journal to the correct ledger accounts, including the end of month total.

Sales Ledger					
Khaled					
2018		$	2018		$
4 April	Sales	85	19 April	Sales returns	34
25 April	Sales	56			

Nominal ledger					
Sales returns					
2018		$	2018		$
30 April	Sales returns journal	46			

Harold					
2018		$	2018		$
19 April	Sales	210	26 April	Sales returns	12

The total of sales returns for the month is debited to the sales returns account in the nominal ledger.

Notice that the original entry for sales appears on the debit side of each account. The sales returns entries are credited to the relevant personal account in the sales ledger. Crediting the account reduces what that customer owes to the business.

Purchases returns journal

Businesses can return goods to the original suppliers. A purchases return will be authorised by the receipt of a credit note from the original supplier. When a credit note is received, an entry is made in the purchases returns journal. The monthly total of purchases returns is posted to the purchases returns account. An entry is made in the personal account of the relevant supplier each time a purchases return is authorised.

Key term

Purchases returns journal:
The book of prime entry used to record purchases returns.

Worked example 8

This is an extract from the purchases journal of the business in Worked example 6 for April 2018.

Purchases returns journal			
Date	Details	Credit note no.	Total
2018			$
13 April	Omar	3/100	23
17 April	Samir	3/101	10
30 April	Transferred to purchases returns account		33

Post the entries from the purchases returns journal to the correct ledger accounts, including the end of month total.

Nominal ledger				
Purchases returns				
		2018		$
		30 April	Purchases returns journal	33

Purchases ledger						
Samir						
2018			$	2018		$
17 April	Purchases returns	10		2 April	Purchases	34

Omar					
2018		$	2018		$
13 April	Purchases returns	23	5 April	Purchases	12
			11 April	Purchases	26

The total of purchases returns for the month is credited to the purchases returns account in the nominal ledger.

Notice that the original entries for purchases appear on the credit side of each account. The purchases returns entries are debited to the personal account of the supplier in the purchases ledger. Debiting the account reduces what the business owes to the supplier.

The general journal

Transactions involve a movement of money or a movement of goods into or out of the business. Most of these transactions appear in either the cash book, the sales and purchases journals or one of the returns journals. Any other transaction is entered in the **general journal.**

The general journal is used for transactions that occur less frequently. For example, it is used when recording accounting errors, as you will discover in Chapter 3, and when recording depreciation and irrecoverable debts, as you will discover in Chapter 4. The layout of the general journal is unlike the other journals and appears as follows:

General journal		Dr	Cr
Journal entry		$	$
Year			
Date	Name of account to be debited	Amount	
	Name of account to be credited		Amount
Narrative – a brief explanation of the transaction entered above			

Entries in the general journal must always follow the layout shown. The account to be debited must appear first, followed by the account to be credited. The name of the account to be credited is usually indented slightly.

A **narrative** explains the transaction in words. The narrative provides more details than appear in the main part of the entry. It should provide enough information for the transaction to be understood.

 4 What other transactions do you think would be entered in the general journal?

Worked example 9

On 16 April 2018, a business buys a machine for use within the business from Sharp Ltd on credit for $5000. This is the journal entry recording this:

General journal		Dr	Cr
Journal entry		$	$
2018			
16 April	Machinery	5000	
	Sharp Ltd		5000
Narrative:			

Write the narrative to explain this transaction.

Bought asset on credit.

Key terms

General journal: The book of prime entry used to record transactions not found in any other journal, sometimes referred to as the journal.

Narrative: A description of a transaction entered in the general journal.

The narrative does not have to repeat information already found in the journal entry. In this example, there is no need to say the value of the asset, what the asset is or who it was bought from. All this is already contained in the journal entry.

Worked example 10

On 21 April, a business owner introduces into the business a computer he previously used privately. The computer will now only be used in the business and is valued at $400.

Enter this transaction in the general journal.

General journal		Dr	Cr
Journal entry			
		$	$
21 April	Computer	400	
	Owner's equity		400
Asset introduced into the business by owner.			

> This type of transaction does not appear in any of the other books of prime entry.

Worked example 11

On 25 April 2018, Zhi, a customer who owes the business $800, agrees to return goods with a value of $350 and gives the business machinery in exchange for cancelling the remainder of the amount owing.

Enter this transaction in the general journal.

General journal		Dr	Cr
Journal entry			
2018		$	$
25 April	Sales returns	350	
	Machinery	450	
	Zhi		800
Asset accepted, along with the return of goods for full settlement of amount owing from customer.			

> This journal entry requires you to include two debit entries but only one credit entry. If the total of the debit entries equals the total of the credit entries then this is allowable. The amount owing by Zhi is settled by giving the business machinery of the same value as the remainder of the amount owing.

Applying

Discuss these questions in pairs.

1. What books of prime entry would be less useful for a business that sells services?

2. What would encourage a business to use a petty cash book as well as a cash book?

Complete this task in pairs.

Task

The following are transactions connected with the buying and selling of goods. Enter each transaction into the correct journal and post the relevant amounts to the ledger accounts affected for July 2018.

1 July	Inventory purchased on credit from Joseph for $45
4 July	Inventory purchased on credit from Markus for $54
5 July	Credit sales for $165 to Robert
8 July	Business returns inventory to Joseph worth $24
11 July	Robert returns inventory worth $31
16 July	Credit purchases from Olga for $81
18 July	Sales made on credit to Noah for $101
21 July	Inventory returned to Olga valued at $11
22 July	Inventory sold to Noah for $145
25 July	Noah returns inventory worth $32

Knowledge check

1   The sales journal contains:

   A   Sales made but not paid for at the time of sale
   B   Sales made for immediate cash settlement
   C   Sales of assets to be used within the business
   D   Returns of goods sold on credit

2   Where is the purchases returns account located?

   A   Purchases journal
   B   General ledger
   C   Purchases ledger
   D   Purchases returns journal

3   Goods are purchased from Adrianna on 13 April 2018 for $800. A cash discount of 2.5% is offered if the amount owing is settled within 14 days. Payment is made on 20 April 2018. Which is the correct double entry to record the discount?

	Debit	Credit
A	Adrianna $40	Discounts received $40
B	Discounts allowed $20	Adrianna $20
C	Discounts received $40	Adrianna $40
D	Adrianna $20	Discounts received $20

4 For each transaction, state in which book of prime entry the transaction would be recorded.

(a) Sales made on credit

(b) Goods previously sold by the business sent back to the business

(c) A computer used in business taken out of the business for personal use

(d) Cheque paid to settle an account relating to a previous purchase of goods

(e) Machinery sold with payment received by cheque

(f) Office furniture bought on credit specifically for resale

5 The following is a summary of the petty cash transactions for May 2018.

1 May	Received from petty cashier $100 as petty cash float
2 May	Rail fares $17
4 May	Petrol $8
8 May	Stationery purchases $4
10 May	Cleaning $11
18 May	Petrol $16
21 May	Cleaning $15
22 May	Bus fares $4
25 May	Cleaning $2

(a) Prepare a petty cash book with columns for expenditure on cleaning, travel expenses and stationery.

(b) Enter the month's transactions.

(c) Enter the receipt of the amount necessary to restore the imprest and carry down the balance for the commencement of the following month.

6 Prepare the journal entries necessary to record the following transactions for July 2018. Narratives are not required.

1 July	Equipment bought on credit from Tau for $900
8 July	The business owes $280 to Manuel but the debt is transferred to Sahar
13 July	Equipment worth $490 taken out of the business for personal use
19 July	Car bought on credit from Quality Cars Ltd for $2900
25 July	Computer accepted in return for outstanding debt of $325 owed to the business by Wei

7 From the following data, construct the cash book for the month of July 2018 and balance the cash book for the end of the month.

1 July	Balance at bank $860 (overdrawn) and $42 cash in the business cash register
4 July	Sale of machinery for $320 with payment received by cheque
7 July	Cash of $250 withdrawn from bank and placed into cash register.
11 July	Purchase of goods for resale $100 payment by cheque
14 July	Payment received by cheque from M Yang – a credit customer for $84
18 July	Wages paid by cheque $530
22 July	Payment of advertising $51 paid with cash
26 July	Sale of goods for cash $230

On 29 July, all cash held in the cash register, except for $40, was transferred into the bank account.

Check your progress

Read the unit objectives below and reflect on your progress in each

- Explain the advantage of using various books of prime entry

- Explain the use of, and process, accounting data in the books of prime entry – cash book, petty cash book, sales journal, purchases journal, sales returns journal, purchases returns journal and the general journal

 I struggle with this and need more practice.

 I can do this reasonably well.

I can do this with confidence.

- Post the ledger entries from the books of prime entry

- Distinguish between and account for trade discount and cash discounts

- Explain the dual function of the cash book as a book of prime entry and as a ledger account for bank and cash

- Explain the use of and record payments and receipts made by bank transfers and other electronic means

- Explain and apply the imprest system of petty cash.

1 Which is the correct double entry to record the return of goods to a credit supplier?

	Debit	Credit
A	Supplier account	Purchases
B	Supplier account	Sales returns
C	Supplier account	Purchases returns
D	Bank	Purchases returns

2 Which is the correct double entry to record receiving a cheque for rent received?

	Debit	Credit
A	Rent received	Bank
B	Rent received	Customer
C	Customer	Rent received
D	Bank	Rent received

3 The owner introduces her own laptop into the business for business use. Which is the correct double entry to record this?

	Debit	Credit
A	Owner's equity	Laptop
B	Drawings	Laptop
C	Laptop	Drawings
D	Laptop	Owner's equity

4 Which is the correct double entry to record the sale of goods on credit to A Gregory?

	Debit	Credit
A	Sales	A Gregory
B	Sales	Bank
C	A Gregory	Sales
D	Bank	Sales

5 A furniture retailer buys tables for cash for use in the business offices. Which is the correct double entry to record this?

	Debit	Credit
A	Purchases	Cash
B	Furniture	Cash
C	Cash	Purchases
D	Cash	Furniture

6 Which is the correct business document for making entries in the sales returns journal?

A A credit note

B A sales invoice

C A purchase invoice

D A paying-in slip

7 The purchases journal records

A Purchases made but not paid for at the time of purchase

B Purchases made for immediate cash settlement

C Purchases of assets to be used within the business

D Returns of goods purchased on credit

8 Where is the sales account located?

A The sales ledger

B The sales journal

C The nominal ledger

D The general journal

9 Which of the following is entered in the general journal?

A Purchase of equipment for business use for cash

B Credit purchase of machinery for business use

C Withdrawal of money from the business by the owner

D Sale of goods on credit to new customers

10 Goods are sold to Ariel on 7 July 2018 for $1200. The credit terms are for a 2.5% cash discount if payment is received within 14 days. Payment is received on 18 July. Which is the correct double entry to record the discount?

	Debit	Credit
A	Ariel $15	Discounts received $15
B	Ariel $30	Discounts received $30
C	Discounts allowed $30	Ariel $30
D	Discounts allowed $15	Ariel $15

11 Daniel is a trader who keeps full double entry records, including a three-column cash book. On 1 June 2018, his cash book showed the following debit balances:

Cash $218

Bank $5642

The business's transactions for the month of June 2018 included the following:

2 June	Goods sold to Nathan worth $900
5 June	Cheques paid totalling $2300 for new office furniture
9 June	Goods worth $300 returned by Nathan
15 June	Paid Thalia a cheque for $890 in full settlement of an amount owing totalling $920
17 June	Received a cheque from Nathan in settlement of his account of $600, after deducting a cash discount of 2.5%
21 June	Cash sales of $680 paid directly into bank
24 June	Office expenses of $150 paid by cash

(a) Prepare a cash book (with columns for discounts) for the business for June 2018. [12]
(b) Prepare the ledger account of Nathan for June 2018. [6]
(c) (i) Where would you find the account of Nathan? [1]
    (ii) In which book of prime entry would the transaction on 2 June be recorded? [1]

[Total 20]

12 Kate is a sole trader. The following transactions took place in August 2018.

5 August	The business exchanges its motorcycle worth $900 for a van of equivalent value with a friend
8 August	The business is owed $300 by Alysha. She is declared bankrupt and the business receives $50 in full settlement
13 August	Office equipment bought on credit from Sulaiman for $810
25 August	Goods taken out of business for personal use valued at $120
30 August	Fen owed the firm $50 but the debt is transferred to Uma

(a) Enter these transactions into the general journal. Narratives are not required. [12]
(b) From the following information, prepare the ledger account of Denys in the books of Kate. [6]

1 September	Denys owes the business $75
4 September	Goods sold on credit to Denys worth $855
18 September	Goods worth $114 returned by Denys
27 September	Cheque for $340 received from Denys in full settlement of an invoice totalling $355

(c) In which book of prime entry would the following transactions be entered?
    (i) Payment made for purchase of goods [1]
    (ii) Goods returned by a business to the original supplier. [1]

[Total 20]

13 The following is a summary of the pretty cash transactions for a small coffee bar for March 2018.

   1 Mar   Received from petty cashier $200 as petty cash float
   2 Mar   Newspapers $3
   4 Mar   Petrol $5
   8 Mar   Magazines $12
   10 Mar   Cleaning costs $14
   20 Mar   Petrol $22
   21 Mar   Cleaning costs $24
   22 Mar   Petrol $18
   25 Mar   Newspapers $7

   (a) Prepare a petty cash book with analysis columns for expenditure on cleaning, petrol and general expenses.

   Enter the month's transactions.

   Enter the receipt of the amount necessary to restore the imprest and carry down the balance for the commencement of the following month.   [12]

   (b) Explain what the following terms mean:

   (i) Imprest   [2]

   (ii) Float.   [2]

   (c) Explain two reasons why a business maintains a petty cash book in addition to the main cash book.   [4]

                                                                          [Total 20]

3 Verification of accounting records

3.1 The trial balance

3.2 Correction of errors

3.3 Bank reconciliation

3.4 Control accounts

With the large quantity of transactions recorded in the accounts, there is a risk that mistakes will be made. Apart from in very small businesses, it is difficult to locate errors in the accounting records. Verification of accounting records can be achieved using a variety of techniques and procedures that help identify errors by type and by location. The trial balance provides a check on the accuracy of the ledger accounts. If errors exist, a suspense account may be used to correct the errors. In correcting errors, control accounts for the sales and purchases ledgers can be used to check the accounts of customers and suppliers. Bank reconciliation is used to check the accuracy of the business cash book.

The trial balance

Learning objectives

By the end of this unit, you should be able to:

- understand that a trial balance is a statement of ledger balances on a particular date
- outline the uses and limitations of a trial balance
- prepare a trial balance from a given list of balances and amend a trial balance which contains errors
- identify and explain those errors which do not affect the trial balance – commission, compensating, complete reversal, omission, original entry, principle.

Starting point

Answer these questions in pairs.

1 Which accounts normally have:

(a) a debit balance

(b) a credit balance?

2 Which accounts could have either a debit or a credit balance?

Exploring

Discuss these questions in pairs.

1 Why might it be useful to prepare a list of all the balances from the ledger accounts?

2 Why do you think that the total of debit balances and the total of credit balances should be the same?

Developing

Preparing a trial balance

A **trial balance** is a list of all the balances from the double entry accounts at a specific date. The trial balance lists the balances in two columns. One column contains a list of the debit balances and the other column contains a list of the credit balances.

If the entries in the ledger accounts are correct and the accounts are correctly balanced, the total of the debit balances column will be the same as the total of the credit balances column. This is because every entry made in the double entry accounts always

Key term

Trial balance: A list of all balances from the double entry accounts.

consists of a debit entry and a credit entry of the same value. Even though the debit and credit entries are made in different accounts, the total of all the debit entries and the total of all the credit entries will be the same.

Key knowledge

If all the double entry transactions have been entered correctly and balanced correctly, the totals of the two columns of the trial balance will be the same.

Some types of account always have a debit balance, such as asset accounts. Other types of account always have a credit balance, such as owner's equity. It is important to know which accounts have debit balances and which accounts have credit balances.

This table shows the balances expected for different types of account.

Balances on double entry accounts	
Debit balances	Credit balances
Assets	Liabilities
Purchases	Revenue (sales)
Sales returns	Purchases returns
Drawings	Owner's equity (capital)
Expenses	Incomes
	Provisions*

*Provisions are covered in Chapter 4.

Notice that when preparing the trial balance, the term **revenue** is used to refer to the balance on the sales account. Revenue refers to the income generated from the sales made by the business.

Some accounts can have either a debit or a credit balance. For example, the bank balance can have either a debit or a credit balance depending on whether there is money in the bank or the bank balance is overdrawn.

An account of a person or other business can have either a debit or a credit balance depending on whether the business owes this other person or business money or is owed money by them. Knowing if a balance should be a debit balance or a credit balance is useful if the trial balance has been prepared incorrectly.

 1 What is the meaning of a credit balance on the cash account?

Key term

Revenue: Income generated by a business from its normal business activities, usually the sale of goods or services. Revenue may also be referred to as sales, sales revenue or turnover.

Worked example 1

The following are balances for Will as at 31 July 2018. Prepare a trial balance.

	$
Revenue	49000
Purchases	33000
Trade receivables	8750
Trade payables	2980
Bank	3213
Cash	131
Wages	6866
Equipment	21000
Owner's equity	20000
Rent received	980

Will		
Trial balance as at 31 July 2018		
	Dr	Cr
	$	$
Revenue		49000
Purchases	33000	
Trade receivables	8750	
Trade payables		2980
Bank	3213	
Cash	131	
Wages	6866	
Equipment	21000	
Owners' equity		20000
Rent received		980
	72960	72960

The title of a financial statement should always mention the business name, what the statement is and for what date it is for. Think of this as *Who? What? When?*

The two columns are placed side by side. The order of the balances listed in the trial balance is not important.

The totals of the two columns appear side by side. If the trial balance is correct, the totals will be the same.

Inventory and the trial balance

No single account exists for inventory. However, a balance for inventory appears in most trial balances. The value of any inventory is found by a stocktake. A stocktake is a manual count and valuation of the inventory (or stock) found within the business.

The value of inventory held at the end of the accounting period appears as a note underneath the trial balance.

The value for unsold inventory is recorded in an account in the nominal ledger. For example, if unsold inventory was valued at

Key term

Stocktake: A physical count and valuation of inventory held by a business.

$4500, this would appear as a note underneath the trial balance and would be entered in the inventory account as follows:

Inventory			
	$		$
Income statement	4500		

The value of closing inventory is transferred to the income statement as part of the end-of-period profit calculation.

The balance on the inventory account will appear within the trial balance for the next accounting period when it becomes the balance for opening inventory.

Inventory	Where in trial balance?
Inventory held at the start of the accounting period – Opening inventory	Appears as a debit balance in the trial balance
Inventory held at the end of the accounting period – Closing inventory	Appears as a note to the trial balance (usually underneath)

Worked example 2

The cash book shows an overdrawn balance. The following trial balance has been prepared but errors are present. Prepare a corrected trial balance for Mariam as at 31 December 2018.

Mariam		
Trial balance as at 31 December 2018		
	Dr	Cr
	$	$
Revenue		104000
Purchases	66750	
Bank	3108	
Premises	100000	
Wages and salaries		21300
Trade receivables		12313
Trade payables		8970
Owner's equity		88000
Drawings	15600	
Inventory at 1 January 2018	8452	
Rent	4910	
Sales returns		241
Purchases returns	488	
Bank loan	25000	
Inventory at 31 December 2018	9855	
	234163	234824

The balances entered incorrectly are moved and shown in **bold**.

Mariam		
Trial balance as at 31 December 2018		
	Dr	Cr
	$	$
Revenue		104 000
Purchases	66 750	
Bank	~~3108~~	3108
Premises	100 000	
Wages and salaries	21 300	~~21 300~~
Trade receivables	12 313	~~12 313~~
Trade payables		8970
Owner's equity		88 000
Drawings	15 600	
Inventory at 1 January 2018	8452	
Rent	4910	
Sales returns	241	
Purchases returns	~~488~~	488
Bank loan	~~25 000~~	25 000
Inventory at 31 December 2018	~~9855~~	
	229 566	229 566

Additional information:

Inventory at 31 December 2018 was valued at $9855.

The heading should always be **as at** or **at** – it is only for one date.

Bank can be a debit or a credit balance. A bank overdraft means the business owes the bank money and is a liability. It should be in the credit column.

Sales returns represents an increase in an asset so should be in the debit column.

Purchases returns represents a decrease in an asset so should be in the credit column.

Only 'opening' inventory should appear in the trial balance. 'Closing' inventory appears underneath the trial balance.

Uses and limitations of the trial balance

Producing a trial balance is helpful for a business.

- It provides an arithmetic check on the accuracy of the double entry book-keeping. If the totals of the debit and credit columns are not the same, at least one mistake has been made. A check can be performed to locate the mistake causing the difference in the totals of the balances before any further use of the balances is made.

- It makes it easier to prepare the financial statements of the business. The income statement and statement of financial position are constructed from the balances of the double entry accounts.

The trial balance does have limitations. These include:

- the time it takes to prepare

- the fact that even if the totals of the trial balance are the same, errors may exist in the accounts. Some types of error are not detected by the trial balance.

If the totals of the trial balance are not the same, at least one error must have occurred. Errors can be made in entering transactions into the double entry accounts. Errors can also be made when producing the trial balance.

2 Explain whether an income statement can be prepared without the use of a trial balance.

Errors and the trial balance

A difference in the totals of the trial balance indicates that errors have been made. However, even if the totals of the trial balance are the same, there may still be errors in the double entry accounts.

It is common to divide errors into two categories:

- Errors that do not affect the trial balance
- Errors that do affect the trial balance.

Key knowledge

'Errors that do not affect the trial balance' refers to errors that, if made, would still result in the totals of the debit and credit columns of the trial balance being the same. It does not mean the totals are correct. For example, missing out both the debit and credit entries for a cash sale would mean that the totals of the debit and credit columns of the trial balance are lower than their correct amounts. However, the trial balance columns would still have the same totals; each column would be lower than the correct total by the same amount.

Errors that do not affect the trial balance

Errors that do not affect the trial balance are classed according to the type of mistake that has been made.

Commission

An error of commission occurs when an entry is placed in the wrong personal account. All other aspects of the double entry (the amount, the entry in the other non-personal account and the side of entry in the wrong personal account) are correct. For example, a credit sale of $200 to Brown may be debited to the account of Browning by mistake.

Compensating

Compensating errors involve two or more separate errors. The combined effect of these errors is to affect the debit and credit columns of the trial balance in exactly the same way. For example, if the sales account and purchases account are both overstated by $1000 then the effect on each column of the trial balance is the same – the totals of both columns are the same but are both incorrect and $1000 too high.

Complete reversal

An error of complete reversal occurs when the entries for a transaction are made in the accounts on the wrong side of each account. The entries are made in the correct accounts and the

Key terms

Commission: An error caused by a transaction being entered into the wrong personal account.

Compensating: Two or more errors are made that affect the debit and credit columns of the trial balance by exactly the same amount. The totals of the debit and credit columns of the trial balance are the same but the totals are incorrect.

Complete reversal: A transaction is entered in the correct accounts and with the correct amount but the entries are on the wrong side of both double entry accounts. The totals of the debit and credit columns of the trial balance are the same but the totals are incorrect.

amounts are correct but the debit entry for the transaction is entered on the credit side of the account and the credit entry for the transaction is entered on the debit side. For example, a credit sale of $45 to Emma is debited to sales and credited to the account of Emma. The totals of the debit and credit columns of the trial balance will be the same and correct despite this being a mistake. This is because the same amount is added on the debit and credit side for the transaction.

Omission

An error of omission occurs when a transaction is not recorded in the double entry accounts. The totals of the trial balance are the same but are both too low. This is because the same amount is missing from the debit and credit totals.

Original entry

An error of original entry occurs when a transaction is entered in the correct accounts and is entered on the correct side of each account but the amount entered is incorrect. For example, a cash payment made for general expenses of $92 might be mistakenly entered in both accounts (cash and general expenses) as $39. The amount added to each account is different from the correct amount but the totals of the trial balance are still the same.

Principle

An error of principle occurs when one of the entries needed to record a transaction is made in the wrong type or class of account. For example, a business may sell a computer which was used by the business for cash. The correct entry would involve debiting the cash account. However, an error of principle is made if the sale of the computer is recorded in the sales account. This is an error as the sales account only records sales of inventory and not sales of assets used in the business. The totals of the trial balance will still be the same as the sale of an asset and the sale of inventory are both credit entries. In this case, the balance for revenue will be higher than the correct value and the balance for computers held by the business will also be higher than the correct value.

Errors of principle can also occur when entries are made in an expense account rather than an asset account. For example, payment of motor expenses is debited to the account of motor vehicles by mistake. The totals of the trial balance are still the same because the entries in motor expenses and motor vehicles are both debit entries.

 3 What would happen to the totals of the debit and credit columns of the trial balance if the amount debited to an account was different from the amount credited to the account when completing the double entry?

Key terms

Omission: The entries needed for a transaction are not entered in the accounts. The totals of the debit and credit columns of the trial balance are the same but the totals are incorrect.

Original entry: Entries are made in the correct accounts on the correct sides of each account but the amounts entered are not correct, although they are the same for the debit and credit entry. The totals of the debit and credit columns of the trial balance are the same but the totals are incorrect.

Principle: The correct amounts are entered for a transaction but they are entered in the wrong type or class of account.

Complete this task in pairs.

Task

The following trial balance has been prepared for Henwood Ltd for 2018. However, there are several errors within the trial balance. Prepare a corrected trial balance as at 31 December 2018.

Additional information: Henwood Ltd has a positive balance at the bank. It is not overdrawn.

	Dr	Cr
	$	$
Revenue	455000	
Purchases		252521
Sales returns	5451	
Purchases returns		4544
Premises		250000
Commission received		12312
Heating and lighting		8989
Machinery	26800	
Inventory at 1 January 2018		31313
Inventory at 31 December 2018	23288	
Trade payables	14519	
Trade receivables	18908	
Bank	11808	
Wages		39800
General expenses		8377
Owner's equity	19000	
Drawings	23408	
	770182	607856

Knowledge check

1   Which of the following statements about the trial balance is NOT correct?

   A   The trial balance provides a check on the accuracy of the ledger accounts.

   B   All errors are detected by the trial balance.

   C   The trial balance can be used to prepare the income statement.

   D   The totals of the two columns of the trial balance should be the same.

2   Which is the correct heading for the trial balance of Clayton Ltd prepared on 31 December 2018?

   A   Trial balance for Clayton Ltd as for the year ended 31 December 2018

   B   Trial balance as at 31 December 2018

   C   Clayton Ltd, Trial balance as at 31 December 2018

   D   Trial balance for Clayton Ltd for year as at 31 December 2018

3   What type of error has occurred when purchases of machinery are entered in the purchases account?

   A   Commission   **C**   Compensating

   B   Original entry   **D**   Principle

4   Which of the following errors is found by preparing a trial balance?

   A   An amount entered for a debit entry is double that made for the credit entry.

   B   A transaction is missed out of the accounts completely.

   C   A payment made to a supplier is entered in the wrong supplier account.

   D   A purchase of an asset on credit is debited to the supplier and credited to the asset accounts.

5   From the following balances, prepare a trial balance for Sara as at 31 December 2018.

	$
Revenue	45808
Sales returns	113
Purchases	32341
Purchases returns	242
Inventory as at 1 Jan 2018	2910
Inventory as at 31 Dec 2018	4150
General expenses	6306
Drawings	980
Owner's equity	18600
Assets	22000

6   State the type of error occurring in each of the following transactions:

   (a) Rent of $76 was entered in both accounts as $54

   (b) General expenses of $24 was actually a payment made for the owner's private expenses

   (c) Credit sales of $113 to Yan were debited to the account of Lei

   (d) Credit purchases of $32 from Iris were debited to Iris's account and credited to purchases

---

Check your progress

Read the unit objectives below and reflect on your progress in each.

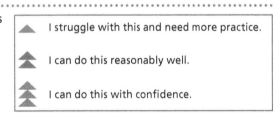

- Understand that a trial balance is a statement of ledger balances on a particular date

- Outline the uses and limitations of a trial balance

- Prepare a trial balance from a given list of balances and amend a trial balance which contains errors

- Identify and explain those errors which do not affect the trial balance – commission, compensating, complete reversal, omission, original entry, principle.

Correction of errors

Learning objectives

By the end of this unit, you should be able to:

- correct errors by means of journal entries
- explain the use of a suspense account as a temporary measure to balance the trial balance
- correct errors by means of suspense accounts
- adjust a profit or loss for an accounting period after the correction of errors
- understand the effect of correction of errors on a statement of financial position.

· ·

Starting point

Answer these questions in pairs.

1 What are the uses of a trial balance?

2 What types of error do not result in the totals of the debit and credit columns of the trial balance being different?

Exploring

Discuss these questions in pairs.

1 Which of the following types of error would also affect the profit for the year?

(a) Commission

(b) Original entry

(c) Omission.

2 What types of error result in the totals of the debit and credit columns of the trial balance being different?

Developing

Introduction

Many errors involve an incorrect amount being entered into the double entry account. Amounts entered may be wrong due to:

- **undercasting** – the amount recorded in the accounts is lower than the correct figure

- **overcasting** – the amount recorded in the accounts is higher than the correct figure

- **transposition** – the numbers (or parts of a larger number) are mixed up or reversed, e.g. $142 is written as $241.

Key terms

Undercasting: The amount recorded in the accounts is lower than the correct figure.

Overcasting: The amount recorded in the accounts is higher than the correct figure.

Transposition: Numbers (or parts of a larger number) are mixed up or reversed.

The errors will not affect the trial balance if the same amount is used for both the credit entry and the debit entry in the double entry accounts. You learned about errors that do not affect the trial balance in Unit 3.1. If the error is only made in one of the entries, the totals of the debit and credit columns of the trial balance will be different.

With a large number of transactions being entered in the ledgers every day it is likely that even the best book-keeper will occasionally make errors. Any error made in the ledger accounts means the accounting records do not represent an accurate financial record of the business. This means the financial statements constructed from the ledger accounts will be inaccurate and may provide misleading information about the financial performance of a business. As a result, on discovery of an error it is important to correct the mistake as soon as possible.

All errors are corrected by a combination of an entry into the appropriate book of prime entry (the general journal) and a correction in the double entry accounts.

Key knowledge

Procedure for the correction of errors:

1 Enter the correction into the general journal
2 Correct the accounting entries in the double entry accounts.

All corrections are made by adjusting the accounts so the result gives the same overall effect in the accounts as the original entry would have if it had been correct. For example, if a sale of $100 is mistakenly entered as $1000, the correction would be to debit the sales account by $900 as this adjustment will reduce the balance to the $100 credit entry that should have been recorded in the first place. The narrative in the general journal records the two accounts affected.

Key knowledge

The effect of an error is corrected by an adjustment to the account not a cancellation of the mistaken entry. Errors are **never** corrected by crossing out the mistake.

Correcting errors that do not affect the trial balance

Errors that do not affect the trial balance include the following types of errors:

- Commission
- Compensating
- Complete reversal
- Omission
- Original entry
- Principle

These errors were described in Unit 3.1.

Correcting an error of commission

Worked example 1

A sale of goods on credit to Yun for $78 is debited to the account of Maya by mistake. Prepare the entries in the books of the business to correct this error.

General journal (extract)		Dr	Cr
		$	$
Yun		78	
Maya			78
Credit sale of goods recorded in wrong personal account – now corrected			

Yun			
	$		$
Maya	78		

Maya			
	$		$
Sales	78	Yun	78

Correcting a compensating error

Worked example 2

Both the sales and purchases accounts were undercast by $150 due to the incorrect recording of credit transactions. Prepare the entries in the books of the business to correct this error.

General journal (extract)		Dr	Cr
		$	$
Purchases		150	
Sales			150
Accounts were both undercast but now corrected by adjustment			

The corrections in the double entry accounts:

Purchases			
	$		$
Credit supplier	150		

Sales			
	$		$
		Credit customer	150

This is an error of **commission**. The amounts entered are correct, and the entry in the sales account is correct, but the entry in the personal account of the credit customer in the sales ledger is incorrect.

The debit entry in Yun's account represents the correct entry for sales on credit to Yun. This entry is half of the correction.

Crediting Yun's account cancels the effect (but not the original entry) of the mistaken debit entry when the error is made. This entry is half of the correction. An equal amount on the opposite side of the account cancels out the effect of the original mistake.

This is a **compensating error**. The debit and credit balances are both undercast by $150.

The correction to the double entry accounts involves 'adding' $150 to both purchases (by debiting the account) and sales (by crediting the account). The details for each entry reference the personal accounts of the relevant credit supplier and credit customer for the original credit transaction.

If the errors had been one of both accounts being overcast, then the adjustment would take place on the opposite side of each account.

Complete reversal

Worked example 3

A business returns goods of $41 to Mariana. The entry was recorded by incorrectly debiting the purchases returns account and crediting the account of Mariana. Prepare the entries in the books of the business to correct this error.

General journal (extract)	Dr	Cr
	$	$
Mariana	82	
Purchases returns		82
Entries made on the wrong side of each account – now corrected		

Purchases returns			
	$		$
Mariana	41	Mariana	82

Mariana			
	$		$
Purchases returns	82	Purchases returns	41

This is an error of **complete reversal**. The amounts entered are correct and in the correct accounts, but both are on the incorrect side of the account.

Crediting the account with $82 (double the amount of the original error) cancels out the error (the debit entry) and restores the correct entry of $41 on the credit side.

Debiting this account with $82 (again, double the amount) cancels out the mistaken credit entry and restores what should have been the correct debit entry of $41.

Correcting an error of omission

Worked example 4

A payment of $45 for telephone expenses was made by cheque but not recorded in the accounts. Prepare the entry in the general journal for the correction of this error.

General journal (extract)	Dr	Cr
	$	$
Telephone expenses	45	
Bank		45
Original transaction not recorded in ledger accounts – transaction now entered		

This is an **error of omission**. The correction to the double entry accounts (not shown here) involves making the entries that should have been made originally.

You use the general journal to correct the mistake and also update the cash book, where the transaction would have been recorded if it had not been omitted.

Correcting an error of original entry

Worked example 5

A cash payment of $45 for advertising was entered in both accounts mistakenly as $54. Prepare the entries in the books of the business to correct this error.

General journal (extract)	Dr	Cr
	$	$
Cash	9	
Advertising		9
Error of original entry – accounts corrected by adjustment of $9 in each account		

Cash			
	$		$
Advertising	9	Advertising	54

Advertising			
	$		$
Cash	54	Cash	9

This is an error of **original entry**. In this case, the numbers of the amount have been transposed, resulting in both accounts being overcast. Correcting the error requires an adjustment in each account to restore the correct amount. Here, reducing the balance on the account requires an entry of $9 on the opposite side of each account to the entry made in error.

Debiting the account with $9 reduces the balance on the account by this amount which is the adjustment needed to restore the correct entry of $45.

Crediting the account with $9 reduces the balance on the account and this adjustment restores the correct entry of $45.

Correcting an error of principle

Worked example 6

A van was serviced and payment was made by cheque. In error, these motor expenses of $200 are debited to the motor vehicles account. Prepare the entries in the books of the business to correct this error.

General journal (extract)	Dr	Cr
	$	$
Motor expenses	200	
Motor vehicles		200
Motor expenses classed as purchase of motor vehicles – now corrected		

Motor expenses			
	$		$
Motor vehicles	200		

This is an error of **principle**. An entry has been made in the wrong type or class of account. In this case the motor vehicles account was debited by mistake; the correct entry would have been in the motor expenses account.

Debiting the account with $200 restores the correct entry to this account.

Motor vehicles			
	$		$
Bank	200	Motor expenses	200

Crediting the account with $200 reduces the balance on this account by that amount. This entry, in effect, cancels out the mistaken entry. The details of the entry record the account where the entry should have been made.

 1 How do you think an error of commission would be discovered by the business?

Correcting errors that do affect the trial balance

Some errors cause the total of the debit column and the total of the credit column of the trial balance to differ. The correction of errors that *do* affect the trial balance requires a new double entry account to be used. This new account is the **suspense account**.

Errors should always be corrected as soon after they are detected as possible. When errors cause the totals of the trial balance to differ, you open a suspense account and use it to make the trial balance totals the same. Using the suspense account is a temporary measure to allow the business to prepare the financial statements for the period.

For example, the trial balance shown here does not balance.

Key term

Suspense account: A temporary account used when the trial balance totals differ. It is used to ensure that the totals of the trial balance are the same.

Trial balance as at 31 March 2018		
	Dr	Cr
	$	$
Totals	25 400	26 000

Until errors are found and corrected, a suspense account is opened with a balance equal to the difference in the trial balance columns ($26 000 − $25 400 = $600).

Suspense				
2018		$	2018	$
31 Mar	Trial balance difference	600		

With the suspense account balance included in the trial balance, the totals of the debit and credit columns will be the same.

Trial balance as at 31 March 2018		
	Dr	Cr
	$	$
Totals	25 400	26 000
Suspense account	600	
	26 000	26 000

The suspense account balance remains until the errors are located and corrected. Correcting any error that affects the trial balance requires an entry in the suspense account. Once all the errors have been located and corrected, there should be no outstanding balance on the suspense account.

Worked example 7

A trial balance prepared on 31 March 2018 does not balance. The difference is a shortage of $600 on the debit column. During April 2018, the following errors are discovered:

- The insurance account had been undercast by $220.
- The sales returns account had been overcast by $170.
- A credit sale of $180 to Jon had been credited to the sales account and also credited to the account of Jon.
- The purchases account was undercast by $190.

Prepare the entries in the general journal and the suspense account to correct these errors.

General journal (extract)		Dr	Cr
		$	$
Insurance		220	
Suspense			220
Expense originally undercast – now corrected			
Suspense		170	
Sales returns			170
Account overcast – now corrected			
Jon		360	
Suspense			360
Two credit entries made – now corrected			
Purchases		190	
Suspense			190
Account undercast – now corrected			

	Suspense				
2018		$	2018		$
1 Apr	Balance b/d	600	30 Apr	Insurance	220
30 Apr	Sales returns	170	30 Apr	Jon	360
			30 Apr	Purchases	190
		770			770

The insurance account needs debiting by the undercast amount of $220. The credit entry is in the suspense account.

To correct the overcasting of the account, you credit the sales returns account by the overcast amount to reduce the balance on the account. The debit entry is in the suspense account.

The account of Jon needs debiting by double the amount to cancel out and restore the correct debit entry required – with an equal credit entry made in the suspense account.

Purchases has been undercast. Debiting the account with the shortfall corrects this error and a credit entry is made in the suspense account.

The opening balance in the suspense account is the shortage in the debit column from the trial balance.

Each error correction requires an entry in the suspense account. After correction, there is no outstanding balance on the suspense account. This means it is likely that all the errors have been found and corrected. The trial balance totals should now be the same.

3.2

2 Could errors still exist in the accounts even if the suspense account has no outstanding balance?

Adjusting profit and loss after the correction of errors

Errors may also affect the profit for the year. Profit should be adjusted as errors are located and corrected. Errors affect the profit or loss if the error's correction involves adjustments to items in the income statement of the business. An error that affects either income or expenses will affect the profit of the business.

Worked example 8

Harper's calculated profit for the year ended 31 December 2018 is $9100. However, she discovers the following errors:

- The sales returns journal was undercast by $18.

- Advertising of $40 paid for by cheque was credited to the bank account and also credited to the advertising account.

- A credit purchase of $100 from Jesse was mistakenly credited to the account of Leo.

- A sale of a laptop used by the business for $240 was credited to the sales account by mistake.

Prepare a statement of corrected profit for Harper once all errors have been corrected.

Harper Statement of corrected profit for the year ended 31 December 2018		
	$	$
Profit before adjustment		9100
Less sales returns	18	
Less advertising	80	
Less sale of asset	240	338
Corrected profit for the year		8762

You must decide if each error affects the profit – does it affect income or expenses?

Errors of commission (in this example, entering a credit purchase in the account of Leo rather than Jesse) do not affect income or expenses and therefore do not affect profit.

Sales returns should be increased by $18. This will reduce net sales for the period and will therefore reduce overall profits by $18.

To correct this error, advertising is debited by $80. This increases the debit balance on an expense account by $80 and so $80 is subtracted from profit.

The effect of correction of errors on a statement of financial position

When all errors are located and corrected, the balance on the suspense account is cleared. Until that happens, the balance on the suspense account will appear on the statement of financial position.

Where it appears on this statement depends on the suspense account balance.

Sales of inventory count towards the revenue for a period but not the amount received from the sale of the laptop as this is an asset. (See Unit 4.1 for more detail.) You subtract the income from the sale of the laptop from the profit for the period.

Suspense account balance	Appears on statement of financial position as:
Debit balance	Asset
Credit balance	Owner's equity and liabilities

When errors are corrected, adjustments to the statement of financial position may be required.

Worked example 9

The following errors were discovered as at 31 December 2018:

1 A sale of office furniture for $550 was credited to the sales account.

2 A purchase of equipment on credit for $890 was entered in both the equipment account and the credit supplier's account as $980.

3 $120 in cash was taken from the business by the owner but was not recorded in the accounts.

How would the correction of each error affect the statement of financial position?

---

1 The value of assets for office furniture is reduced by $550. Profit is also reduced by $550 and, in turn, this reduces the value of owner's equity.

2 The value of assets for equipment is reduced by $90. The value of trade payables, a liability, is reduced by the same amount, $90.

3 The value of assets for cash is reduced by $120.

The value of the owner's equity is also reduced by $120 as the cash taken will be included in drawings which is subtracted from the owner's equity on the statement of financial position.

Applying

Complete this task in pairs.

Task

Profit for the year ended 31 December 2018 for Wrightson Ltd is calculated as $750. However, the following errors are discovered:

1 The purchases returns journal had been overcast by $52

2 Motor expenses of $230 paid for by cheque included a private motor expense payment of $50

3 Wages of $68 were credited to the wages account by mistake

4 A credit sale of $32 to Jana was entered in both accounts as $23.

Prepare the entries in the general journal needed to correct these errors.

Open a suspense account and prepare appropriate entries to correct the errors. You will need to calculate the opening balance.

Prepare a statement of corrected profit for the year.

Knowledge check

1 Which of the following errors do not affect the trial balance?

(a) Entry for discounts received only entered into the personal account of the credit supplier.

(b) Payment of $87 for advertising entered in both accounts as $78.

(c) Cheque of $112 paid to Durga credited to the account of Maxim.

(d) Motor car purchased debited to maintenance expenses by mistake.

A (a) and (b)   **C** (b), (c) and (d)

B (b) and (d)   **D** (a) and (d)

2 A computer used by the business is sold but credited to the sales account. Which of the following pairs of entries would correct this error?

	Account to be debited	Account to be credited
A	Computer	Sales
B	Computer	Bank
C	Sales	Owner's equity
D	Sales	Computer

3 Which of the following errors would affect the level of profit?

A Entering a payment in the personal account of the wrong credit supplier.

B Failing to record a cash withdrawal taken by the owner for private use.

C Entering a receipt from a credit customer on the debit side of their personal account.

D Overcasting the value of sales returns

4 Decide whether the following errors affect the trial balance:

(a) A purchase on credit is only entered into the supplier's personal account.

(b) A transaction is not recorded in the accounts.

(c) The amounts for the debit and credit entries for a transaction are different.

(d) A sale of a piece of equipment is credited to the sales account by mistake.

(e) Payment of an electricity bill by cheque is credited to both accounts.

5 **(a)** Prepare journal entries to correct the following errors. Narratives are not required.

- A payment of $98 made by cheque to Mandeep is entered in both accounts as $89.
- Sales returns by Ahmet valued at $55 were debited to Ahmet's account and credited to the sales returns account.
- Office equipment sold for $450 was credited to the sales account by mistake.

- Purchases returns to Bibek of $14 were entered by mistake in the account of Lili.
- The owner contributed $400 to the business by cheque but this was not recorded.

(b) Calculate the overall change to the assets of the business after the errors are corrected.

6   Ander is a sole trader and has just completed his accounts for the first year of trading. His profit for the year was calculated as $2114. However, during the following month the following errors were discovered that affect the profit:

- The purchases journal was undercast by $220.
- Sales of $70 to Tamir on credit were entered in the sales account as $700.
- Ander decided to bring his own car, valued at $1000, into the business for business use only. This was not recorded.
- Office expenses of $231 paid for by cheque were credited to both accounts.

    (a) Prepare the journal entries to correct these errors (narratives are not required).

    (b) Open a suspense account. Calculate the opening balance after entering all the necessary entries.

    (c) Prepare a statement of corrected profit.

    (d) Explain the overall effect on the value of assets in the statement of financial position after the errors have been corrected.

Check your progress

Read the unit objectives below and reflect on your progress in each.

- Correct errors by means of journal entries

- Explain the use of a suspense account as a temporary measure to balance the trial balance

- Correct errors by means of suspense accounts

- Adjust a profit or loss for an accounting period after the correction of errors

- Understand the effect of correction of errors on a statement of financial position.

 I struggle with this and need more practice.

 I can do this reasonably well.

 I can do this with confidence.

Bank reconciliation

Learning objectives
By the end of this unit, you should be able to:
- understand the use and purpose of a bank statement
- update the cash book for bank charges, bank interest paid and received, correction of errors, credit transfers, direct debits, dividends, and standing orders
- understand the purpose of, and prepare, a bank reconciliation statement to include bank errors, uncredited deposits and unpresented cheques.

Starting point

Answer these questions in pairs.

1 What is the cash book of a business?

2 What information is contained on a bank statement?

Exploring

Discuss these questions in pairs.

1 How can the cash book have a debit balance but the bank statement shows a credit balance if no mistakes have been made?

2 Why is the cash book likely to contain more errors than other ledger accounts?

Developing

The use and purpose of a bank statement

The bank column of the business cash book and the bank statement issued by the bank should be the same as they are a record of the same set of transactions.

The cash book is prepared from the point of view of the business. This means any payments received are debited to the cash book and payments made are credited to the cash book. However, the bank statement is prepared from the bank's point of view so items that appear as a debit on the cash book will appear as a credit on the bank statement.

Key knowledge

The cash book balance (bank column) is from the business's point of view.

The bank statement balance is from the bank's point of view.

Key term

Bank reconciliation: The process of checking why the cash book bank balance and the bank statement balance are different from each other (as they should be the same in theory).

Uses of the bank statement include:

- obtaining a correct balance on the bank account
- identifying errors in the cash book
- identifying errors on the bank statement
- identifying amounts not yet credited or debited by the bank (due to the time taken to clear amounts)
- checking for fraud or embezzlement – where someone has taken money from the bank account without permission.

A difference between the balances in the cash book and on the bank statement can be explained by one or more of the following:

- **Automated transactions** – payments into and out of the bank account that have happened automatically and have not yet been entered in the business's cash book.
- **Timing differences** – payments and receipts entered in the cash book that have not yet been paid into or out of the bank account.
- **Errors** have been made (either by the bank or, more likely, by the business). For example, a business may have incorrectly entered an amount deposited in the bank account.
- **Fraud** or **embezzlement** has occurred.

Bank reconciliation is the process of explaining why the bank statement balance and the cash book bank balance are different. To find out if errors are present or fraud has occurred, the business will need to ensure that automated transactions and timing differences can be accounted for.

Automated transactions

As technology has advanced over time, increasingly many bank transactions are automated. This is where money is paid into and out of a bank account without the payee or payer having to take direct action. Instead, they have authorised the transaction at some point in the past, for example by setting up a regular standing order or authorising a bill to be paid by direct debit.

 How would contactless transactions appear in the cash book of a business?

It is increasingly likely that the cash book bank balance and the bank statement balance will not be the same because of automated transactions.

Automated transactions occur without the business having to authorise each transaction individually. The most common types of automated transactions include bank charges, interest (paid or received), **credit transfers**, **direct debits**, dividends and **standing orders**.

Key terms

Credit transfer: An automated payment of money into a bank account.

Direct debits: A regular automated payment of varying amounts made from a bank account (usually for utility bills).

Standing orders: A regular automated payment of a fixed amount made from a bank account.

Updated cash book: A cash book brought up to date by the business by the addition of automated transactions and other transactions the business has yet to enter into the cash book.

Automated transaction	Description
Bank charges	Banks usually charge businesses for the services they provide. These include regular charges, for example for depositing cash and cheques, and penalty charges, for example for exceeding the agreed overdraft limit.
Interest paid	Borrowing from the bank (e.g. loans and overdrafts) will mean the business is charged interest. This is based on the interest rate and the amount borrowed. Interest on overdrafts is paid in addition to the fees charged by the bank for the use of an overdraft facility.
Interest received	Some banks pay interest on money kept in a bank account. This is based on the balance in the bank account as well as the interest rate. Interest is more likely to be received from balances in savings accounts rather than the main bank account of the business.
Credit transfer	A credit transfer is the receipt of money directly into the bank.
Standing order	A regular fixed amount of money paid out of the bank account.
Direct debit	A regular payment of varying amounts paid out of the bank account (usually for expenses that vary monthly).
Dividends	Dividends are paid to those holding shares in other companies and these may be directly paid into the bank account.

2 What is a standing order used for?

Updating the cash book

One way to discover if errors exist in the cash book entries (or on the bank statement) is to first update the cash book. This involves adding items that appear on the bank statement but have not yet been entered into the cash book.

Reasons why the cash book needs bringing up to date include errors made by the business or by the bank, and automated payments and receipts into the bank account.

Worked example 1

The following cash book is for July 2018:

Cash book (bank columns only)					
2018		$	2018		$
1 Jul	Balance b/d	26	9 Jul	Olivia	217
8 Jul	Markus	350	19 Jul	Noah	370
26 Jul	Mikhail	323	31 Jul	Balance c/d	112
		699			699
1 Aug	Balance b/d	112			

The following items appeared on the bank statement for July 2018, but do not appear yet in the cash book.

	$
Interest paid	21
Standing order: Mehmet	45
Direct debit: Eastern Water	110
Dividends received	34

Bring the cash book up to date with the above items.

Cash book (bank columns only)					
2018		$	2018		$
1 Aug	Balance b/d	112	1 Aug	Interest	21
1 Aug	Dividends received	34	1 Aug	Standing order: Mehmet	45
1 Aug	Balance c/d	30	1 Aug	Direct debit: Eastern Water	110
		176			176
			1 Aug	Balance b/d	30

The items not yet in the cash book are entered either as receipts or payments. Notice that all these appear on the same date – the start of the following month.

An alternative approach to updating the cash book is to add all the new entries onto the original cash book and to rebalance that at the end of the previous month. Based on Worked example 1, this would appear as follows:

Cash book (bank columns only)					
2018		$	2018		$
1 Jul	Balance b/d	26	9 Jul	Olivia	217
8 Jul	Markus	350	19 Jul	Noah	370
26 Jul	Mikhail	323	31 Jul	Interest	21
31 Jul	Dividends received	34	31 Jul	Standing order: Mehmet	45
31 Jul	Balance c/d	30	31 Jul	Direct debit: Eastern Water	110
		763			763
			1 Aug	Balance b/d	30

Both approaches give the same updated balance.

Bank reconciliation statements

Once the cash book has been updated the business can prepare a bank reconciliation statement.

The bank reconciliation statement shows any differences that exist between the cash book bank balance and the bank statement balance due to timing differences. Timing differences arise because there is a delay between entering a payment or receipt into the cash book and the movement of money into and out of the bank account. These delays are caused by:

Key term

Bank reconciliation statement: A statement explaining the differences between the cash book bank balance and the balance on the bank statement.

- the time taken to post a cheque to the payee
- the time taken for the payee to deposit a cheque in their bank account
- the time taken for a cheque or other deposit to be cleared by the bank once deposited (banks typically take a few days before the money is placed into the account of the payee).

These delays will affect both payments from and receipts into the bank account.

An unpresented cheque is a cheque which has been issued but the payment has not yet appeared on the bank statement. The payment will have been credited to the business cash book when the cheque was issued. The delay will depend on how quickly the payee deposits the cheques. Unpresented cheques mean the bank statement balance will be higher than the cash book balance.

An uncredited deposit is an amount which has been received but the receipt has not yet appeared on the bank statement. The receipt will have been debited to the business cash book when the payment was received. The delay will be shorter if the deposit consists of cash rather than a cheque.

These delays can explain why the cash book bank balance is different from the bank statement balance. A bank reconciliation statement adjusts the balances to take these timing differences into account.

If the updated cash book bank balance and bank statement balance cannot be reconciled (i.e. shown to be the result of timing differences) then something has gone wrong and investigation is needed.

 If cheques are no longer used for payments, will the timing delays between entering an item in the cash book and it appearing on the bank statement disappear?

Key terms

Unpresented cheque: A cheque which has been issued but the payment has not yet appeared on the bank statement. The payment will have been credited to the business cash book when the cheque was issued.

Uncredited deposit: An amount which has been received but the receipt has not yet appeared on the bank statement. The receipt will have been debited to the business cash book when the payment was received.

Preparing a bank reconciliation statement

There are two approaches to preparing a bank reconciliation statement. Either the statement will use the updated cash book bank balance and make adjustments for both unpresented cheques and uncredited deposits. Or it will start with the bank statement balance and make adjustments to arrive at the updated cash book balance.

The adjustments are as follows:

Bank reconciliation statement	
Starting with updated cash book bank balance:	*Starting with bank statement balance:*
Updated cash book balance	Bank statement balance
Add Unpresented cheques	*Less* Unpresented cheques
Less Uncredited deposits	*Add* Uncredited deposits
Equals bank statement balance	*Equals* updated cash book balance

If the balances can be reconciled, then this means there are no errors or fraudulent activity within the cash book or bank statement.

Worked example 2

The following are the cash book and the bank statement of Nadia.

Cash book (bank columns only)						
		$				$
1 Aug	Balance b/d	87	8 Aug	Jian		171
8 Aug	Elias	65	21 Aug	Batkhaan		34
14 Aug	Hunter	423	28 Aug	Rebekah		124
27 Aug	Shu	431	31 Aug	Balance c/d		677
		1006				1006
1 Sep	Balance b/d	677				

Bank statement		Dr	Cr	Balance
		$	$	$
1 Aug	Balance b/d			87
11 Aug	Elias		65	152
12 Aug	Jian	171		19 O/D*
18 Aug	Hunter		423	404
24 Aug	Batkhaan	34		370
31 Aug	Balance c/d			370

*O/D means overdrawn balance. An overdrawn balance can also be shown as DR – indicating a debit balance on the account from the viewpoint of the bank.

Prepare a bank reconciliation statement as at 31 August.

Nadia Bank reconciliation statement as at 31 August	
	$
Balance as per cash book	677
Add unpresented cheques (Rebekah)	124
	801
Less uncredited deposits (Shu)	431
Balance as per bank statement	370

Notice that the statement contains the Who? What? When? format for the title.

Starting with the cash book bank balance, unpresented cheques are added and uncredited deposits are subtracted.

There are no items on the bank statement that are not on the cash book. This means the cash book does not need updating.

These two transactions do not appear on the bank statement. This is probably because they occurred near the end of the month. After adjusting for the unpresented cheque (Rebekah) and the uncredited deposit (Shu) the final figure matches the balance on the bank statement. This means the two balances are reconciled and there are no errors or fraud present in the cash book or bank statement.

Other entries to include in the cash book

The cash book may need adjusting for other items. These include:

Stale cheques

A cheque becomes a stale cheque when it is unpresented for six months from the date written on the cheque. Some banks will allow older cheques to be processed but six months is a common time limit. In this case, the bank will not process the cheque and the money will not be transferred from the payer to the payee. These would appear on the credit side of the cash book of the payer (the business issuing the cheque) when the cheque was issued but then would not appear on the bank statement so the cash book would need adjusting when it is updated.

Dishonoured cheques

When a cheque is received and deposited into the business bank account, the money is paid into the bank account of the business within a few days. However, if the payer of the cheque has insufficient funds in their account to make the payment then the bank may dishonour the cheque. In this case, the money added to the account when the cheque was deposited will be cancelled. The cash book entry which records a cheque being debited to the cash book will have to be amended if the cheque is dishonoured. Dishonoured cheques are sometimes referred to as bouncing cheques.

Errors

Errors may have been made when producing the cash book. If these are discovered, then they can be corrected when the cash book is updated. When correcting these errors, an entry is made on the other side of the account to adjust the total.

Key terms

Stale cheque: A cheque that a bank will not process because it is more than six months old.

Dishonoured cheque: A cheque presented to the bank which the payer has insufficient funds in their account for the bank to transfer money to make payment.

Worked example 3

Ella received a bank statement for May 2018 showing a credit balance of $134 at the end of the month. The bank column of her cash book had a debit balance of $114 on 1 June. A comparison of the cash book and the bank statement revealed the following.

1 Items appearing only on the bank statement:

   Direct debit to Kalim $91

   Cheque received from Julia, a credit customer, for $214 was dishonoured

   Electricity bill paid by standing order $65

   Dividends received $50

2 Items appearing only in the cash book:

Cheque paid to Loukas, a credit supplier $335

Cash sales paid directly into the bank on 24 May $95

3 The total of the credit side of the cash book had been overcast $100

Update the cash book of Ella as at 1 June 2018. Once updated, prepare a bank reconciliation statement for the same date.

The cash book is updated with items appearing on the bank statement but not in the cash book.

		Ella				
		Cash book as at 1 June 2018				
2018			$	2018		$
1 June	Balance b/d		114	1 June	Kalim	91
1 June	Dividends		50	1 June	Dishonoured cheque: Julia	214
1 June	Error correction		100	1 June	Electricity (S.O)	65
1 June	Balance c/d		106			
			370			370
				1 June	Balance b/d	106

The cash book credit column was overcast by $100. The debit entry here adjusts the balance to correct the error.

In the case of the dishonoured cheque from Julia, a credit entry is made in the cash book to reflect the cancellation of the income that the cash book had initially recorded on the debit side.

Ella	
Bank reconciliation statement as at 1 June 2018	
	$
Balance on updated cash book	106 (O/D)
Add unpresented cheque (Loukas)	335
	229
Less uncredited deposit (cash sales)	95
Balance on bank statement	134

The bank reconciliation statement starts with the updated cash book balance which is an overdrawn balance after its update.

The unpresented cheque is added and the uncredited deposit is subtracted. The two balances are reconciled. This means there are no further errors on the cash book.

What happens if the balances cannot be reconciled?

After updating the cash book, it should be possible to reconcile the cash book bank balance and bank statement balance. If they cannot be reconciled then this means one of the following has occurred:

- An error has been made by the business which has not been discovered. Investigation into where the error is located will be undertaken.

- An error has been made by the bank. The bank should be contacted to resolve the issue.

- Fraud or embezzlement has occurred. Someone has taken money out of the business without permission. Checks on who was responsible for handling money will probably be needed.

Applying

Complete this task in pairs.

Task

From the following bank statement and cash book for July, prepare an updated cash book and a bank reconciliation statement for 1 August.

		Dr ($)	Cr ($)	Balance ($)
1 Jul	Balance			542
6 Jul	Marios	312		230
8 Jul	Althea		635	865
9 Jul	Interest	44		821
10 Jul	Standing order: Baatar	275		546
13 Jul	Direct debit: Insurance	112		434
17 Jul	Credit transfer		180	614
20 Jul	Cheque dishonoured: Althea	635		21
22 Jul	Ivan		87	66
25 Jul	Bank charges	11		55
26 Jul	Ranjit	143		88
28 Jul	Hao		190	102
31 Jul	Balance			102

Cash book (bank columns only)		Dr ($)				Cr ($)
1 Jul	Balance b/d	542	2 Jul	Marios		312
4 Jul	Althea	635	22 Jul	Ranjit		143
18 Jul	Ivan	87	27 Jul	Carlos		240
20 Jul	Hao	190	31 Jul	Balance c/d		1090
29 Jul	Leyla	331				
		1785				1785

Knowledge check

1 When bringing the cash book up to date, which of the following does not appear as a debit entry?

   A Credit transfer   C Dividends received

   B Interest received   D Standing order

2 Look at the cash book

Cash book			
	$		$
Kasi	250	Padma	53
Yusuf	76	Banele	111

The following two items are on the bank statement but not yet in the cash book:

Interest charged $3

Credit transfer $88

What is the balance on the cash book after it has been updated?

   A $77 debit   C $247 debit

   B $162 debit   D $77 credit

3 Which of the following is a correct procedure for bank reconciliation?

   A Updated cash book balance + unpresented cheques + uncredited deposits

   B Bank statement balance – unpresented cheques – uncredited deposits

   C Updated cash book balance – unpresented cheques + uncredited deposits

   D Bank statement balance – unpresented cheques + uncredited deposits

4 The cash book was balanced on 31 August.

Cash book					
2018		$	2018		$
2 Aug	Simona	64	1 Aug	Balance b/d	113
6 Aug	Mustafa	344	7 Aug	Rabina	423
11 Aug	Reem	123	9 Aug	Hania	543
16 Aug	Hasim	165	17 Aug	Yannick	312
31 Aug	Balance c/d	695			
		1391			1391

The following entries appear on the bank statement for August but have yet to be entered in the cash book:

	$
Standing order: Rachid	250
Direct debit: Faisal	89
Interest received	8
Credit transfer: Somchi	430
Dishonoured cheque	121
Bank charges	11
Dividends received	85

Bring the cash book up to date with these entries.

5 The bank columns in the cash book for November 2018 and the bank statement for that month for Chun are:

Cash book (bank columns only)		$			$
5 Nov	Mandeep	131	1 Nov	Balance b/d	89
14 Nov	Marios	312	4 Nov	Petar	433
18 Nov	Amanda	121	21 Nov	Ahmet	231
25 Nov	Rajab	56	24 Nov	Salma	199
30 Nov	Balance c/d	332			
		952			952
			1 Dec	Balance b/d	332

Bank statement		Dr	Cr	Balance
2018		$	$	$
1 Nov	Balance b/d			89 (O/D)
9 Nov	Petar	433		522 (O/D)
11 Nov	Mandeep		131	391 (O/D)
12 Nov	Bank charges	25		416 (O/D)
18 Nov	Direct debit: Telephone bill	95		511 (O/D)
19 Nov	Marios		312	199 (O/D)
26 Nov	Ahmet	231		430 (O/D)
27 Nov	Amanda		121	309 (O/D)
29 Nov	Dividends		44	265 (O/D)
30 Nov	Balance			265 (O/D)

(a) Bring the cash book up to date as on 30 November 2018.

(b) Prepare a bank reconciliation statement as on 30 November 2018.

Control accounts

Learning objectives

By the end of this unit, you should be able to:

- understand the purposes of purchases ledger and sales ledger control accounts
- identify the books of prime entry as sources of information for the control account entries
- prepare purchases ledger and sales ledger control accounts to include credit purchases and sales, receipts and payments, cash discounts, returns, irrecoverable debts, dishonoured cheques, interest on overdue accounts, contra entries, refunds, and opening and closing balances (debit and credit within each account).

Starting point

Answer these questions in pairs.

1. What does the sales ledger contain?

2. Why does a business allow trade credit?

Exploring

Discuss these questions in pairs.

1. What accounting entries appear in a purchases ledger?

2. What happens to the sales and purchases ledgers if the business does not allow credit transactions?

Developing

Introduction

It is important that any errors are corrected as soon as possible. This can be achieved if the errors are located quickly. The trial balance highlights arithmetic errors in the ledger accounts – though it will not uncover all errors. Bank reconciliation highlights errors in the cash book (or errors made by the bank). Control accounts are another technique used for locating errors.

Control accounts are used to check the accuracy of the personal accounts of credit customers and credit suppliers in the sales and purchases ledgers. The following control accounts are used:

- Sales ledger control account – to check the accuracy of the sales ledger

- Purchases ledger control account – to check the accuracy of the purchases ledger.

For a small business or one that deals with a small number of suppliers and customers, the purchases and sales ledgers will be small. However, larger businesses may have many personal accounts to maintain. The sales and purchases ledgers are used frequently and errors are difficult to find.

Checking the accuracy of all the accounts of credit customers and credit suppliers takes a long time. Control accounts provide an arithmetical check on the accuracy of personal ledgers. This makes spotting errors easier and quicker.

Although control accounts look like double entry accounts, control accounts are memorandum accounts and are not part of the double entry system.

Sales ledger control account

Checking the accuracy of the sales ledger involves comparing the opening and closing balances for trade receivables. The opening balance for trade receivables is the total of the opening balances on all the personal accounts of the credit customers of the business. The closing balance for trade receivables is the total of the closing balances on the same accounts.

The change in the balances is checked against information from the books of prime entry to see if there are any discrepancies. Discrepancies would indicate errors are present.

Key terms

Sales ledger control account: A memorandum account used to check the accuracy of the sales ledger.

Purchases ledger control account: A memorandum account used to check the accuracy of the purchases ledger.

Memorandum accounts: Accounts which are not part of the double entry system.

Worked example 1

A business has three credit customers. Their accounts (as found in the sales ledger), the cash book entries relevant to these customers and the entries in sales and sales returns journals are as follows:

Sales ledger accounts:

Nazar		$			$
1 Apr	Balance b/d	240	14 Apr	Sales returns	115
7 Apr	Sales	1050	16 Apr	Bank	850
			30 Apr	Balance c/d	325
		1290			1290
1 May	Balance b/d	325			

Jie

		$			$
1 Apr	Balance b/d	85	17 Apr	Discounts allowed	40
9 Apr	Sales	980	17 Apr	Bank	760
			30 Apr	Balance c/d	265
		1065			1065
1 May	Balance b/d	265			

Erwan

		$			$
1 Apr	Balance b/d	450	16 Apr	Sales returns	125
11 Apr	Sales	1750	22 Apr	Bank	1370
			22 Apr	Discounts allowed	30
			30 Apr	Balance c/d	675
		2200			2200
1 May	Balance b/d	675			

Balance for trade receivables on 1 April is:
$240 + $85 + $450 = $775

Balance for trade receivables on 30 April is:
$325 + $265 + $675 = $1265

Books of prime entry:

Sales journal

		$
7 Apr	Nazar	1050
9 Apr	Jie	980
11 Apr	Erwan	1750
Total transferred to sales account		3780

Sales returns journal

		$
14 Apr	Nazar	115
16 Apr	Erwan	125
Total transferred to sales returns account		240

Cash book (extract)

Date		Discount $	Cash $	Bank $	Date		Discount $	Cash $	Bank $
16 April	Nazar			850					
17 April	Jie	40		760					
22 April	Erwan	30		1370					
Totals		70		2980					

Construct the sales ledger control account for April.

Sales ledger control account					
		$			$
1 Apr	Balance b/d	775	30 Apr	Sales returns	240
30 Apr	Sales	3780	30 Apr	Bank	2980
			30 Apr	Discounts allowed	70
			30 Apr	Balance c/d	1265
		4455			4455
1 May	Balance b/d	1265			

The opening balance for trade receivables is the total of the opening balances from the personal accounts in the sales ledger. On 1 April this is $240 + $85 + $450 = $775, as calculated above.

In Worked example 1, the sales ledger control account balances are as expected – the closing balance found in the sales ledger accounts is equal to the balance needed for the control account to balance.

The sales figure is from the sales journal for April.

Errors may still exist even if the sales ledger control account balances but many errors have been avoided. For example, entering different amounts for a sales ledger transaction for the debit and credit entries would be highlighted by the control account not balancing. However, an error of commission would not be detected by a control account that balances.

The bank entry is from the debit column for bank in the cash book extract.

1 What different methods can a customer use to settle amounts owing to a business?

The discounts entry is from the discounts column on the debit side of the cash book.

Information used in the sales ledger control account

The closing balance on the sales ledger control account should be the same as the closing balance for trade receivables, found by adding the closing balances on all the personal accounts in the sales ledger. If these are not the same then errors exist in the accounting entries.

The information used to construct the sales ledger control account is contained in the various ledgers and books of prime entry. The main sources of information are:

The closing balance for trade receivables is the total of the closing balances from the personal accounts in the sales ledger. On 30 April this is $325 + $265 + $675 = $1265.

Information used in the sales ledger control account	
Item in the sales ledger control account	Location of information
Opening balance	Personal accounts in the sales ledger
Credit sales	Sales journal
Payments received	Cash book (bank column – debit side)
Discounts allowed	Cash book (discounts column – debit side)
Sales returns	Sales returns journal
Closing balance	Personal accounts in the sales ledger

Irrecoverable debts

Occasionally a business does not receive an amount owing from a customer. This can be classed as an irrecoverable debt and the amount owing may be written off from the trade receivables total.

The amount is credited to the personal account of the customer and this cancels the amount owing.

Irrecoverable debts are a credit entry in the sales ledger control account.

Dishonoured cheques

A business receiving a cheque that is dishonoured means the credit customer still owes money to the business.

Dishonoured cheques are debited to the personal account of the customer who sent the cheque. The customer's debt to the business is not reduced so debiting the account restores the amount owing.

Dishonoured cheques are a debit entry in the sales ledger control account.

Refunds

If a credit customer has overpaid or has returned goods after already paying for them, the business may refund the customer.

The refund is debited to the customer's account to cancel the amount that they have overpaid by and the refund is credited to the cash book.

Refunds are a debit entry in the sales ledger control account.

Interest due on overdue accounts

Businesses can charge customers interest if payment of an amount owing to the business is late.

The interest due increases what is owed to the business and is debited to the customer's account.

Interest due on overdue trade receivables is a debit entry in the sales ledger control account.

Other entries in the control account

There are other entries found in the trade receivables accounts. Any entries in the credit customers' personal accounts also appear in the sales ledger control account.

Other entries include those shown in Worked example 2.

Worked example 2

The following information is for February 2018:

		$
1 Feb	Balance for trade receivables	5432
28 Feb	Total from sales journal for month	236707
28 Feb	Bank receipts from customers in respect of credit sales	229808
28 Feb	Total from sales returns journal for month	4112
28 Feb	Discounts allowed	2341
28 Feb	Interest on overdue trade receivables	53
28 Feb	Irrecoverable debts	441
28 Feb	Dishonoured cheques	129
28 Feb	Refunds to credit customers	98
28 Feb	Balance for trade receivables	5717

Key terms

Irrecoverable debt: An amount owed to a business by a credit customer that cannot pay or will not pay the money that is owed. The amount is written off.

Written off: Cancelling a debt owed to the business due to the failure to collect the amount owing.

Prepare a sales ledger control account for February 2018.

Sales ledger control account					
2018		$	2018		$
1 Feb	Balance b/d	5 432	28 Feb	Sales returns	4 112
28 Feb	Credit sales for month	236 707	28 Feb	Discounts allowed	2 341
28 Feb	Dishonoured cheques	129	28 Feb	Bank	229 808
28 Feb	Interest on overdue trade receivables	53	28 Feb	Irrecoverable debts	441
28 Feb	Refunds to customers	98	28 Feb	Balance c/d	5 717
		242 419			242 419
1 Mar	Balance b/d	5 717			

The amount owing to the business increases because some of the payments received were dishonoured cheques.

The amount owing to the business increases due to the interest charged on overdue amounts.

This indicates the total amount owing from all credit customers at the start of the month.

The amount owing as trade receivables increases by the credit sales made during the month.

The sales returns, discounts allowed, bank receipts and irrecoverable debts all reduce the amounts owing to the business.

Purchases ledger control account

The accuracy of the purchases ledger is checked using a similar process to that used to check the accuracy of the sales ledger. The check involves comparing the opening and closing balances for trade payables. The opening balance for trade payables is the total of the opening balances on all the personal accounts of the credit suppliers of the business. The closing balance for trade payables is the total of the closing balances on the same accounts.

This amount is what is owed by credit customers at the end of the month.

The sales ledger control account balances. This means that there is a reduced risk of errors existing in the sales ledger.

Information used in the purchases ledger control account

You can check the accuracy of the purchases ledger against the information from the books of prime entry to see if there are errors. If the purchases ledger control account does not balance then errors must exist.

Information used in the purchases ledger control account	
Item in the purchases ledger control account	Location of information
Opening balance	Personal accounts in the purchases ledger
Credit purchases	Purchases journal
Payments made to suppliers	Cash book (bank column – credit side)
Discounts received	Cash book (discounts column – credit side)
Purchases returns	Purchases returns journal
Interest due on overdue accounts owing to suppliers	Nominal ledger account for interest due
Closing balance	Personal accounts in the purchases ledger

 2 Why do you think a business might charge interest on an overdue account?

Worked example 3

The following data relates to the accounts of trade payables for January 2018.

	$
Balance for trade payables at 1 January	4223
Balance for trade payables at 31 January	3636
Interest owing on overdue accounts to trade payables	870
Totals for books of prime entry:	
Purchases journal	201800
Purchases returns journal	9807
Cash book entries in respect of payments of trade payables:	
Bank	191000
Discounts received	2450

Prepare a purchases ledger control account for January 2018.

Purchases ledger control account					
2018		$	2018		$
31 Jan	Purchases returns	9807	1 Jan	Balance b/d	4223
31 Jan	Cash book	191000	31 Jan	Credit purchases for January	201800
31 Jan	Discounts received	2450	31 Jan	Interest owing on overdue trade payables	870
31 Jan	Balance c/d	3636			
		206893			206893
			1 Feb	Balance b/d	3636

Contra entries

A business may buy from and sell to the same business. There will be an account for the other business in both the sales ledger and the purchases ledger – that is, it will be included in both trade receivables and trade payables.

The debts between the two businesses can be offset against each other so that only one transaction is needed to clear the outstanding balance. For example, if you owe a person $10 and they owe you $5, then to clear the debt you would offset one debt against the other. In this example, you would pay the other person $5 to clear both debts.

This process of offsetting reduces amounts owing by the business and the amount owed to the business. Entries appear in the personal account of the other business in both the sales ledger and the purchases ledger. The amount to be offset will then appear in both control accounts and is known as a contra entry.

This is the total amount owed by the business to all its credit suppliers at the start of the month.

The amount owed by the business as trade receivables increases by the credit purchases made during the month.

The business owes money as a result of not paying trade payables on time – this adds to the amount the business owes.

Payment made to the business's credit suppliers is debited here (and credited to the cash book) as it reduces the liabilities of the business.

The balance of trade payables at the end of January is the same as the balance on the purchases ledger control account. This means that there is a reduced risk of errors existing in the purchases ledger.

Discounts received (given by the credit suppliers of the business) reduce the liabilities.

Purchases returns reduce the amount owed by the business and are debited here (as they reduce the total of liabilities).

Key terms

Contra entry: A double entry where both the debit and credit entries are in the same account.

3. In your study of cashbooks, you also made contra entries. Can you state what these were?

Worked example 4

The business owes Irina $43 and Irina owes the business $21. Prepare the contra entries needed to offset the debts against each other in both ledger accounts.

Purchases ledger Irina				Sales ledger Irina			
	$		$		$		$
Irina (SL)	21	Balance b/d	43	Balance b/d	21	Irina (PL)	21
Balance c/d	22						
	43		43				
		Balance c/d	22				

> By offsetting the debts against each other, the amount owed to Irina is reduced by $21.

> The amount owed by Irina is cancelled by the offsetting.
>
> The offsetting will appear in both control accounts when they are prepared and are contra entries.

Credit and debit balances in the same control account

The opening debit balance on the sales ledger control account shows the total amount owing to the business as trade receivables at the start of the period. Similarly, in the purchases ledger control account, the opening credit balance shows the total amount that the business owes as trade payables at the start of the period.

There can also be an opening balance on the credit side of the sales ledger control account and an opening balance on the debit side of the purchases ledger control account. These opening balances appear on the opposite side of what is normally expected.

Reasons for a credit balance in the sales ledger

A credit balance in the sales ledger means the business owes money to one or more credit customers. This is unusual and is likely to be because of one of the following:

- A customer has returned goods after paying for them in full. This means the customer is due a refund.

- A customer has overpaid an amount it owes the business. This could be a mistake or because the customer wasn't aware of a discount it qualified for.

- A customer has prepaid the amount or part of the amount of an invoice. For example, a business may have paid for an item that was out of stock and the delivery date is uncertain.

Reasons for a debit balance in the purchases ledger

A debit balance in the purchases ledger means that one or more of the credit suppliers owes the business money. This is unusual and is likely to be because of one of the following:

- The business has returned goods it has already paid for. This means the business should receive a refund from the supplier.

- The business has overpaid an amount it owes a supplier. For example, a business may not have realised that it qualified for a discount.

- The business has prepaid for goods purchased on credit. For example, a business may have paid for items that it intends to purchase in the future but for which it has not yet placed an order.

4 Why might a business pay in advance for goods it intends to purchase in the future but for which it has not yet placed an order?

Uses of control accounts

1 Control accounts can be used to check the arithmetical accuracy of the ledgers. If the ledger account balances are different from the balances in the control accounts, errors are present. The preparation of a control account will help detect and locate these errors. This only highlights errors that affect the trial balance.

2 Control accounts can be used to calculate missing figures. For example, the closing balance on a control account can be calculated if the other entries in the control account are available. This is very useful when the records of a business are incomplete.

3 The preparation of control accounts can detect business transactions which are unauthorised or not recorded properly as part of fraudulent activity.

Worked example 5

The following are items taken from the books of a business for March 2018.

	$
Trade receivables balance as at 1 March 2018	1119
Trade payables balance as at 1 March 2018	697
Credit balances in sales ledger as at 1 March 2018	98
Credit sales	54543
Cash sales	2123
Credit purchases	41499

Cash purchases	1123
Cash book receipts in respect of credit sales	51999
Cash book payments for credit purchases	39534
Dishonoured cheques	456
Contra entries	414
Sales returns	534
Purchases returns	724
Irrecoverable debts	842
Refunds to customers	56
Interest on overdue trade payables	22
Discounts allowed	876
Discounts received	641
Trade receivables balance as at 31 March 2018	1411
Trade payables balance as at 31 March 2018	805

The senior book-keeper believes that the purchases ledger is incorrect. He suspects the purchases journal has been undercast by $100 and is worried there may be other errors in the sales ledgers.

Construct both the sales ledger control account and the purchases ledger control account for March 2018.

Comment on the accuracy of the purchases and sales ledgers.

Sales ledger control account					
2018		$	2018		$
1 Mar	Balances b/d	1119	31 Mar	Balance b/d	98
31 Mar	Credit sales	54543	31 Mar	Cash book for credit sales	51999
31 Mar	Dishonoured cheques	456	31 Mar	Discounts allowed	876
31 Mar	Refunds to customers	56	31 Mar	Irrecoverable debts	842
			31 Mar	Sales returns	534
			31 Mar	Contra entries	414
			31 Mar	Balances c/d	1411
		56174			56174

Purchases ledger control account					
2018		$	2018		$
31 Mar	Cash book for credit purchases	39534	1 Mar	Balances b/d	697
31 Mar	Discounts received	641	31 Mar	Credit purchases for March	41499
31 Mar	Purchases returns	724	31 Mar	Interest on overdue trade payables	22
31 Mar	Contra entries	414			
31 Mar	Balances c/d	905			
		42218			42218

The closing balance on the purchases ledger should be $805 but appears in the control account as $905. This book keeper's suspicion is correct. An undercasting of the purchases journal of $100 would explain the discrepancy.

The sales ledger control account balances correctly which indicates no errors are present.

Note that the contra items in worked example 5 appear in both the sales ledger and the purchases ledger control accounts as they are offsetting one debt against another. All other items appear in only one account of the control accounts. Note that the cash sales and cash purchases do not appear at all. Cash transactions do not affect trade receivables or trade payables and do not appear in the sales and purchases ledgers. However, cash received in payment from credit customers and cash paid to credit suppliers *is* recorded in the control accounts.

Applying

Discuss these questions in pairs.

1. What errors are not detected by a control account?

2. Which types of business (e.g. retail, manufacturing, large, small, etc.) do you think benefit most from the preparation of control accounts?

3. Would using accounting software packages make the preparation of control accounts less useful?

Knowledge check

1. Which of the following appears in a sales ledger control account?

   A Cash sales   C Sales returns

   B Discounts received   D Payments to credit suppliers

2. Based on the following information, what is the value of credit sales for the month?

	$
Trade receivables balance b/d	1231
Trade receivables balance c/d	564
Payments received	18980

   A $19647   C $18313

   B $18980   D $20775

3 Which of the following does NOT appear in a purchases ledger control account?

    A Discounts given to the business by suppliers

    B Cash purchases

    C Opening balance for trade receivables

    D Goods returned to original suppliers by the business

4 Prepare a sales ledger control account from the following data.

	$
Balance b/d	6546
Balance c/d	5453
Payments received	43431
Credit sales	44205
Sales returns	877
Discounts allowed	990

5 Prepare a purchases ledger control account from the following data.

	$
Balance b/d	2230
Balance c/d	898
Payments made to credit suppliers	18711
Credit purchases	20131
Purchases returns	1986
Discounts received	766

6 Use the following data to prepare control accounts for both the purchases and sales ledgers for March 2018. The closing balance on each account is unknown and is for you to calculate.

	$
Purchases ledger balances at 1 March	3123
Sales ledger balances at 1 March	6225
Credit sales for March	74554
Credit purchases for March	43545
Payments made to credit suppliers during March	39040
Discounts allowed for March	651
Discounts received for March	333
Sales ledger balances offset against purchases ledger balances	290
Irrecoverable debts	291
Purchases returns for March	1112
Sales returns for March	2314
Cash and cheques received from credit customers	72010

7 From the following data, prepare control accounts for both the purchases and sales ledgers for July 2018. The closing balance on each account is unknown and is for you to calculate.

	$
Purchases ledger balances at 1 July	4370
Sales ledger balances at 1 July	10141
Sales journal for July	131322
Purchases journal for July	98697
Payments made to credit suppliers during July	90020
Cash sales for July	6757
Refunds to credit customers in July	310
Discounts allowed for July	3423
Sales ledger balances offset against purchases ledger balances	890
Irrecoverable debts	445
Interest on overdue trade payables	27
Discounts received for July	2311
Purchases returns journal for July	1980
Sales returns journal for July	5690
Cash and cheques received from customers	125101

Check your progress

Read the unit objectives below and reflect on your progress in each.

- Understand the purposes of purchases ledger and sales ledger control accounts

- Identify the books of prime entry as sources of information for the control account entries

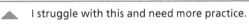 I struggle with this and need more practice.

 I can do this reasonably well.

 I can do this with confidence.

- Prepare purchases ledger and sales ledger control accounts to include credit purchases and sales, receipts and payments, cash discounts, returns, irrecoverable debts, dishonoured cheques, interest on overdue accounts, contra entries, refunds, and opening and closing balances (debit and credit within each account).

Chapter review

1 Which of the following should be in the debit column of a trial balance?

   A   Inventory at the end of the accounting period

   B   Inventory at the start of the accounting period

   C   Owner's equity

   D   Trade payables

2 By how much would the following entries add to the debit column of the trial balance?

	$
Machinery	544 334
Motor expenses	4 433
Sales	112 901
Purchases returns	875
Owner's equity	99 000

   A $549 642

   B $761 543

   C $647 767

   D $548 767

3 Which of the following errors do not affect the trial balance?

   A   Entering the debit and credit entries of a transaction on the wrong side

   B   Entering an amount received from a credit customer on the debit side of the wrong customer's account

   C   Entering only two debit entries for one transaction

   D   Property improvements are credited to property maintenance by mistake

4 A business debits and credits an account with double the correct amount. What type of error has occurred?

   A   Complete reversal

   B   Transposition

   C   Principle

   D   Original entry

5 Which of the following statements are true about errors and suspense accounts?

   (a) All corrections require an entry in the suspense account.

   (b) A trial balance that balances guarantees no errors are present.

   (c) To correct an error of reversal requires that double the amount is entered on the correct side of each account.

   A   (a) and (b)

   B   (a) and (c)

   C   (c) only

   D   (a), (b) and (c)

6 Which of the following errors affect profit?

   A   Entering purchases returns on the wrong side of the credit supplier's account

   B   Overcasting the value of discounts received

   C   Failing to record the receipt of a payment from a credit customer in the accounts

   D   Entering an addition to owner's equity on the wrong side of both accounts

7 Which of the following would not appear as a credit entry when bringing the cash book up to date?

A   Credit transfer   C   Bank charges

B   Interest paid   D   Dishonoured cheque

8 Which of the following would not appear in a bank reconciliation statement?

A   An item in the cash book that does not appear on the bank statement

B   Unpresented cheques

C   Deposits not yet credited by the bank

D   A payment made to a credit supplier which appears in the cash book and on the bank statement

9 Based on the following, calculate the value of credit sales for the month.

	$
Balance of trade receivables at the start of the month	434
Balance of trade receivables at the end of the month	813
Payments received from credit customers	8781

A $8402   C $9160

B $9215   D $9594

10 Which of the following would appear on the credit side of the purchases ledger control account:

(a) cash purchases

(b) interest on overdue trade payables

(c) credit purchases

A   (b) and (c)   C   (a) and (c)

B   (a) and (b)   D   (a), (b) and (c)

11 The book-keeper of Bibek has prepared a trial balance for the most recent accounting period. There are several mistakes.

Bibek Trial balance for year ended 31 December 2018	Dr	Cr
	$	$
Revenue	87588	
Purchases		48998
Sales returns	541	
Purchases returns		4323
Machinery		21000
Discounts received	898	
General expenses		14500
Equipment	18500	
Inventory at 1 January 2018	4342	
Inventory at 31 December 2018	6544	
Trade payables		6456
Trade receivables	8787	

	Dr	Cr
Bank	2466	
Office salaries		23000
Discounts allowed		1131
Owner's equity	55000	
Drawings	11000	
Suspense		76258
	195666	195666

(a) Prepare a corrected trial balance from the above information. [11]

(b) Explain two uses of the trial balance for a business. [4]

(c) It was noticed that in addition to the errors in the trial balance, the book-keeper had also entered transactions into the accounts of incorrect customers and suppliers.

   (i)   State the name of the error described. [1]

   (ii) Explain why this error does not affect the trial balance. [2]

   (iii) Name and explain one other error that does not affect the trial balance. [2]

[Total 20]

12 A bank statement is available for the account of Bintu for September 2018.

		Dr	Cr	Balance
		$	$	$
1 Sep	Balance			201 (O/D)
4 Sep	Sara		414	213
5 Sep	Interest	22		191
10 Sep	Standing order: Jian	335		144 (O/D)
11 Sep	Direct debit: Council tax	89		233 (O/D)
15 Sep	Credit transfer		150	83 (O/D)
18 Sep	Dishonoured cheque: Sara	414		497 (O/D)
25 Sep	Dividends		22	475 (O/D)
27 Sep	Keiko	410		885 (O/D)
29 Sep	George		290	595 (O/D)
30 Sep	Balance			595 (O/D)

(a) Explain the following terms found on the bank statement:

   (i)   credit transfer [2]

   (ii) direct debit [2]

   (iii) dishonoured cheque [2]

(b) In which ledger would the account for Council tax be found? [1]

(c) The cash book for Bintu for September 2018 appears here:

		$			$
2 Sep	Sara	414	1 Sep	Balance b/d	201
22 Sep	George	290	20 Sep	Keiko	410
29 Sep	Beatriz	287	28 Sep	Irina	146
			30 Sep	Balance c/d	234
		991			991

Using the bank statement, bring the cash book up to date for 1 October 2018. [8]

(d) Prepare a bank reconciliation statement for Bintu as at 1 October 2018. [5]

[Total 20]

13 The following balances are from the books of Gabriel for April 2018.

	$
Balance of trade payables at 1 April	6670
Balance of trade payables at 30 April	?
Credit purchases for month	404 524
Cash purchases for month	24 809
Payments in respect of trade payments	396 987
Purchases returns for month	2311
Discounts received in month	1101
Contra entries in purchases ledger	765
Discounts allowed for month	786
Interest on overdue trade payables	175

(a) No errors are present in the books of Gabriel. Prepare a purchases ledger control account for April 2018 and balance it. [8]

(b) State in which book of prime entry each of the following entries would be located:

    (i) Credit purchases for month [1]

    (ii) Discounts received. [1]

(c) Explain the term 'contra entries in the purchases ledger'. [2]

(d) Explain two uses of control accounts. [4]

(e) Outline two limitations of using control accounts. [4]

[Total 20]

14 Hruday has produced a trial balance for 31 December 2018. The totals of the two columns are not the same. There is a shortage on the debit column of the trial balance of $120. Hruday quickly discovers a number of errors in the accounts. The errors discovered are as follows:

1 The purchases account was undercast by $282.

2 Insurance paid in cash of $120 was correctly entered in the insurance account but the cash book entry for insurance was for $30.

3 Interest charged to Hruday on an overdue payment by Ester, a supplier, for $11 was entered in the interest charged account but was not entered in the supplier's account.

4 Cash drawings of $114 taken by Hruday were entered in both accounts as $411.

5 A dishonoured cheque for $42 from Nelu was not recorded in the accounts at all.

An estimate of the profit for the year before these errors were discovered was $990.

(a) Prepare the journal entries required to correct errors 1–5 listed above [10]

(b) Prepare a suspense account to correct these errors. [4]

(c) State one reason why a supplier may charge interest on overdue payments. [1]

(d) State three errors that affect the trial balance. [3]

(e) Calculate a new estimate of the profit for the year after the errors have been corrected. [2]

[Total 20]

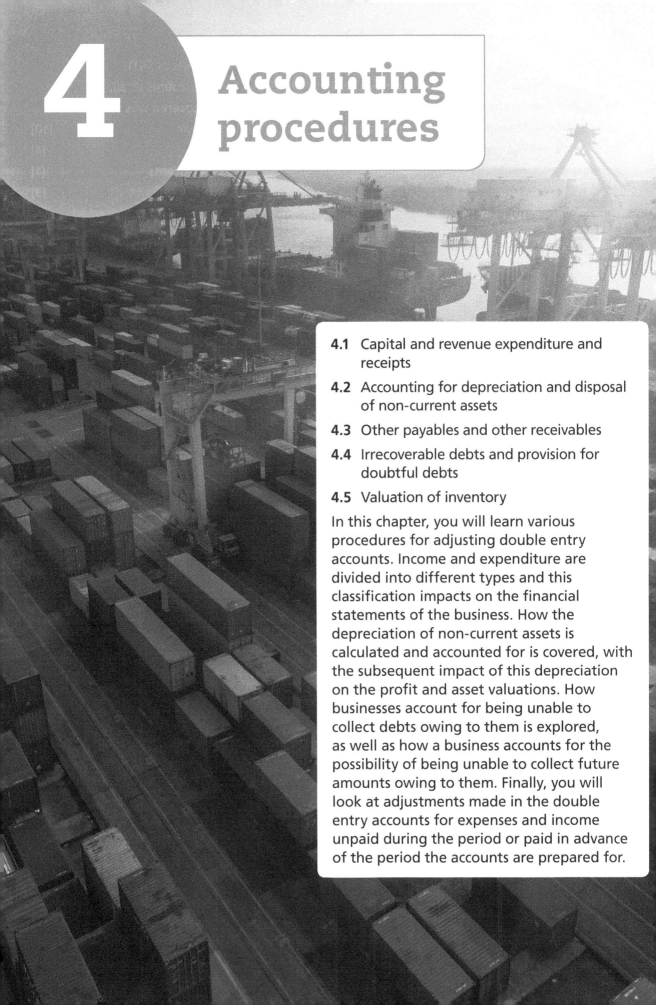

4 Accounting procedures

4.1 Capital and revenue expenditure and receipts

4.2 Accounting for depreciation and disposal of non-current assets

4.3 Other payables and other receivables

4.4 Irrecoverable debts and provision for doubtful debts

4.5 Valuation of inventory

In this chapter, you will learn various procedures for adjusting double entry accounts. Income and expenditure are divided into different types and this classification impacts on the financial statements of the business. How the depreciation of non-current assets is calculated and accounted for is covered, with the subsequent impact of this depreciation on the profit and asset valuations. How businesses account for being unable to collect debts owing to them is explored, as well as how a business accounts for the possibility of being unable to collect future amounts owing to them. Finally, you will look at adjustments made in the double entry accounts for expenses and income unpaid during the period or paid in advance of the period the accounts are prepared for.

Capital and revenue expenditure and receipts

Learning objectives
By the end of this unit, you should be able to:
- distinguish between and account for capital expenditure and revenue expenditure
- distinguish between and account for capital receipts and revenue receipts
- calculate and comment on the effect on profit of incorrect treatment
- calculate and comment on the effect on asset valuations of incorrect treatment.

Starting point

Answer these questions in pairs.

1. Assets are bought on credit. What happens to the accounting equation?

2. How is profit calculated for an accounting period?

Exploring

Discuss these questions in pairs.

1. A business buys a lot of expensive assets. What happens to profit?

2. Can a business increase profits by selling assets?

Developing

Capital expenditure and revenue expenditure

Businesses spend money on many things. These include the running costs of the business, repaying debts and buying assets. Expenditure in the accounting system is classified by type. There are two types of expenditure: capital expenditure and revenue expenditure.

Capital expenditure is expenditure used to purchase assets to be used in the business for more than a year. Capital expenditure also includes the cost involved in getting these assets ready for business use, such as:

Key terms

Capital expenditure:
Business expenditure used to purchase or improve assets that are expected to be used in the business for more than one year. It also includes the cost of getting those assets ready for use. Capital expenditure is not classed as an expense on the income statement of a business.

Revenue expenditure:
Expenditure on running the business. It is clearly linked to a specific time period. Revenue expenditure is classed as an expense on the income statement of a business.

- cost of delivering the asset to the business

- installation cost

- any legal costs incurred in order to buy the asset.

Capital expenditure also includes expenditure on *improving* assets, such as upgrades to an existing machine.

When calculating profit, capital expenditure is not subtracted from income as an expense. Instead, capital expenditure is shown on the statement of financial position. (You will learn more about this in Unit 5.1).

Revenue expenditure is expenditure incurred in the running of the business on an everyday basis. It includes expenses that can be linked to a particular time period. These include:

- the costs of operating the assets purchased

- any repair and maintenance costs of assets (but only if the repairs and maintenance do not improve the asset)

- expenses generated in running the business

- purchases of inventory.

Examples of assets	Capital expenditure	Revenue expenditure
Machinery	Cost of buying assets	Maintenance and repairs
Premises	Delivery costs	Replacement parts
Motor vehicles	Import costs (if applicable)	Power costs (electricity, gas, fuel)
Fixtures and fittings	Cost of installation	Wages of the operators
	Initial testing and safety certificate	Operating costs
	Initial training of employees	Insurance
	Legal costs of buying assets (e.g. solicitors fees for buying premises)	Rent

The distinction between capital and revenue expenditure is important. When calculating profit, only revenue expenditure is subtracted from the income earned by the business. Therefore, profit will be lower if an item of capital expenditure is included. Some expenditure might include portions of both capital and revenue expenditure. It is important to separate the two wherever possible.

Key knowledge

Capital expenditure includes the one-off costs linked with buying assets and improving existing assets. This usually involves expenditure that benefits the business for more than one accounting period, that is, it is *long-term* expenditure that improves the business.

Revenue expenditure includes costs associated with a specific time period, for example wages and other costs paid for a specific period of time. It includes the costs associated with keeping the business trading.

Worked example 1

Steve owns a garage for repairing cars. In the last financial year, he spent the following on the purchase and use of a truck used to recover broken-down cars.

	$
Cost of purchasing truck	20 000
Painting business sign on side of truck	600
Replacing worn tyres	500
Fuel costs for year	2000
Insurance for year	1000
Purchase of new engine for truck	3800

From this information, calculate the value of capital expenditure.

Capital expenditure	
	$
Cost of purchasing truck	20 000
Painting business sign on side of truck	600
Purchase of new engine for truck	3800
Total capital expenditure	24 400

This is the cost of buying a new asset so it is capital expenditure.

This is a cost of getting the truck ready for business usage so it is capital expenditure.

This is a cost of maintaining the asset in current use so it is revenue expenditure.

This is a cost of using the asset for a period of time so it is revenue expenditure.

This is a cost of using the asset for a period of time so it is revenue expenditure.

This is a cost of improving the asset so it is capital expenditure.

1 Explain how a decision on classifying expenditure as capital or revenue expenditure may be subjective.

Capital receipts and revenue receipts

Business income can be divided into two types:

- Capital receipts
- Revenue receipts

One-off items of income received by the business are known as capital receipts. This includes income that is unlikely to be repeated regularly. An example of a capital receipt is the money received when an asset is sold because it is no longer used or is surplus to requirements.

Capital receipts are **not** included as income for the business when calculating profit.

Examples of capital receipts include:

- additions of money to the business from the owner
- sales of non-current assets
- loans and other long-term borrowing taken out by the business
- issue of shares (only for a limited company).

A revenue receipt is income from the running of the business. Revenue receipts are normally linked to a particular time period,

Key terms

Capital receipts: Business income that is not part of the day-to-day operations of the business. Capital receipts are **not** classed as income on the income statement of the business.

Revenue receipts: Business income that comes from the day-to-day business operations. Revenue receipts are classed as income on the income statement of the business.

such as interest earned for a year. Examples of revenue receipts include:

- sale of inventory
- commission received
- rent received
- profit on disposal of non-current assets.

Revenue receipts are included as income in the calculation of profit.

Worked example 2

The following is a list of income and expenses for a small community sports club. Classify these as capital expenditure, revenue expenditure, capital receipts or revenue receipts.

(a) Sale of club house equipment

(b) Purchase of supplies for the club house

(c) Wages paid to workers in the club house

(d) Purchase of a new television for the club house

(e) General expenses for the club house

(f) Annual subscription fees received from club members

(g) Grant received from government to develop the club house

(h) Delivery costs for a new television used in the club house

(i) Sale of refreshments in the club house snack bar.

Capital expenditure: (d), (h)

Revenue expenditure: (b), (c), (e)

Capital receipts: (a), (g)

Revenue receipts: (f), (i)

> Expenditure on assets used in the club and the costs connected with getting them ready for use are classified as capital expenditure.

> Revenue expenditure items are costs involved in the running of the club.

> One-off incomes, such as the grant, are capital receipts.

> Incomes earned running the sports club are revenue receipts. They are clearly linked to the activities of the club.

2 Explain why profits and cash receipts are not the same thing.

The effect of incorrect treatment of expenditure

Key knowledge

You have already met incorrect treatment of expenditure when you studied errors of principle.

If errors are made in the classification of expenditure between capital expenditure and revenue expenditure then the profit calculated will be incorrect. Revenue expenditure is subtracted from revenue receipts when calculating profit. Incorrect classification of either means profit is also incorrectly calculated.

Key knowledge

Profit = revenue receipts – revenue expenditure

For example, if a business purchases equipment to be used in the business, this is classified as capital expenditure. If it is mistakenly classed as revenue expenditure, this will be higher than the correct level. This will result in lower profit recorded in error.

Incorrect classification of expenditure and receipts also affects asset valuations. For example, incorrectly including an item of revenue expenditure as capital expenditure means that the assets of the business will be overvalued.

In fact, an incorrect classification leads to both incorrect profit and incorrect assets valuation. For example, a business that incorrectly classifies building maintenance expenses as capital expenditure will find that profits for the period are higher than their true value. This is because revenue expenditure is lower than the correct value. At the same time, asset values will be higher than their true value. This is because by classifying building maintenance expenses as capital expenditure, this is added to the value of the business's assets.

Worked example 3

A new business has the following incomes and expenses for its first year of trading:

	$
Sales	33 000
Purchases (of inventory)	18 000
Purchases (of equipment)	10 000
Other expenses	8 000

The purchase of equipment is bought to be used in the business but is incorrectly treated as revenue expenditure.

What is the effect on business profit and asset valuations?

The correct level of profit for the first year should be:

    sales revenue less revenue expenditure:
    $33 000 – ($18 000 + $8000) = $7000

The incorrect treatment means that profit is calculated as:
    $33 000 – ($18 000 + $8000 + $10 000) = a loss of $3000

The value of the equipment ($10 000) should be included in the valuation of assets for the business.

> The inclusion of capital expenditure (the purchase of equipment) with the revenue expenditure means that the business appears to make a loss. With correct treatment of expenditure, the business makes a profit.

> When capital expenditure is treated as revenue expenditure, asset values are understated.

Incorrect treatment of expenditure can have serious implications. Investors or lenders may be unwilling to invest in or lend money to a business that appears to be making a loss. Decisions to expand may be postponed if profits seem low.

Worked example 4

A business purchases new premises. The following expenses are paid.

	$
Premises	85000
Repairing premises	2200
New improved windows and door	6600
Legal costs associated with purchase of premises	1900
Annual business rates on premises	3000

All of the expenses are classed as capital expenditure.

What is the impact on profit and asset valuation?

The amount included as capital expenditure is:

$$\$85\,000 + \$2200 + \$6000 + \$1900 + \$3000 = \$98\,700$$

The correct value for capital expenditure is:

	$
Premises	85000
New improved windows and door	6600
Legal costs associated with purchase of premises	1900
	93500

The correct value for revenue expenditure is:

	$
Repairing premises	2200
Annual business rates on premises	3000
	5200

Repairing premises is classed as revenue expenditure as it is maintaining but not adding value to the asset.

Annual business rates are a regular expense, so are classed as revenue expenditure.

The incorrect treatment means the following:

- Profit is overstated. Profit should be $5200 lower than originally calculated. (Revenue expenditure is higher than it was).

- Asset values are overstated. Assets should be valued $5200 lower than originally calculated.

Applying

Discuss these questions in pairs.

1. A business buys paper for the office printer. Would you treat any unused paper as capital expenditure and include it as an asset?

2. A business replaces the computers used within the business with updated ones most years. How would you class the purchase of a computer to be used within this business?

Knowledge check

1 Which of the following would be included as capital expenditure?

    A Repainting old premises

    B Rewiring an old building

    C Installation of the latest efficient heating systems

    D Plastering a building which needs repair

2 Which of the following would not count as revenue expenditure for a motor trader?

    A Purchase of cars for resale

    B Extension to a garage workshop

    C Delivery costs of cars for resale

    D Wages paid to mechanics

3 Which of the following is treated as a capital receipt by a computer retailer?

    A Sale of computers

    B Purchase of new office furniture

    C Sale of some fixtures no longer needed

    D Rent received on surplus property of computer retailer

4 What is the effect of including capital expenditure within revenue expenditure?

    A Reported profits are lower

    B Assets are overvalued

    C Reported profits are higher

    D Liabilities are undervalued

5 Ghufran owns and runs a bowling alley. The following list includes his costs for the month of October. Classify these items as either capital or revenue expenditure:

    A Purchase price of new electronic scoreboards

    B Heating costs in running bowling alley

    C Wages paid to temporary staff during peak season

    D Installation costs of new computer system

    E Rent for bowling alley premises

6 The following costs were generated by the purchase and running of a new machine. Originally, all of these costs were included in the income statement as revenue expenditure.

    (a) Calculate the correct amounts to be included as capital expenditure and as revenue expenditure.

    (b) Calculate the overall change to profit for the year once expenditure has been correctly allocated.

    (c) Calculate the change to the assets of the business once expenditure has been correctly allocated.

	$
Buying new machine	24 000
Legal costs involved in buying machine	910
Operational costs for machine for financial year	2 313
Installation costs of machine	430
Maintenance of machine	299

Check your progress

Read the unit objectives below and reflect on your progress in each.

- Distinguish between and account for capital expenditure and revenue expenditure

- Distinguish between and account for capital receipts and revenue receipts

- Calculate and comment on the effect on profit of incorrect treatment

- Calculate and comment on the effect on asset valuations of incorrect treatment.

 I struggle with this and need more practice.

 I can do this reasonably well.

I can do this with confidence.

Accounting for depreciation and disposal of non-current assets

Learning objectives

By the end of this unit, you should be able to:

- define depreciation
- explain the reasons for accounting for depreciation
- name and describe the straight line, reducing balance and revaluation methods of depreciation
- prepare ledger accounts and journal entries for the provision of depreciation
- prepare ledger accounts and journal entries to record the sale of non-current assets, including the use of disposal accounts.

Starting point

Answer these questions in pairs.

1 Where do assets purchased for business use appear in the financial statements?

2 Why do businesses purchase assets?

Exploring

Discuss these questions in pairs.

1 Why would a business want to use the original cost for valuing an asset held for more than one year?

2 How does a business decide how long an asset will be used in the business?

Developing

What is depreciation?

Non-current assets are bought for long-term use in the business. They are used within the business to generate income and are not purchased for resale. The purchase of non-current assets is classed as capital expenditure and non-current assets appear on the statement of financial position. Non-current assets are long-term assets and are assumed to last more than one full year, though their lifespan may vary depending on the type of asset. The cost of any purchased non-current asset is accounted for through depreciation.

Key terms

Non-current asset: An asset bought for use within the business and normally kept for more than one year.

Depreciation: An estimation of how the cost of an asset should be allocated over its useful life.

Depreciation involves an estimation of how long an asset will be used. The cost of the asset is then allocated across the number of years of its expected life. The allocated cost each year is recorded in expenses in the income statement. (You will learn about this in Unit 5.1). Although depreciation is placed in expenses and therefore reduces profit, there is no movement of cash – no bills are being settled and no one is being paid. Depreciation is a book-keeping entry only. It is a provision and records the amount to be set aside. For example, if a machine is purchased and is expected to be used for four years, then depreciation on the machinery appears as an expense in the income statement for the four years the machine is used. This represents how the cost of machinery is being allocated over the four-year period.

Depreciation also appears on the statement of financial position. On this statement, you subtract the accumulated amount of depreciation from the cost of the non-current asset. The result is the net book value. The accumulated depreciation is the amount of depreciation that is put in expenses added up for each year you have the asset. This means the net book value of the non-current asset will fall over time. If the net book value reaches zero, the full cost of the asset has been allocated.

Key knowledge

Depreciation is used to spread the cost of a non-current asset (in the income statement) over its lifespan. The payment for the non-current asset normally happens when the asset is purchased. However, the charge in the income statement for the non-current asset appears each year the business has the asset available.

Key knowledge

Depreciation may be mistakenly assumed to be money put aside by the business to save up to replace the asset at the end of its life. This is not true. Depreciation is a provision not an expense – it involves no money being paid out.

Factors affecting the useful economic life of assets

Depreciation is charged to reflect the use of a non-current asset over time. The assets that are depreciated have a limited lifespan. The lifespan of a non-current asset is measured in years and is referred to as the asset's **useful economic life** or its **expected lifespan**. Factors determining the useful economic life of a non-current asset include:

- **Wear and tear** – assets gradually become damaged and wear out, especially anything that has moving parts like machinery or motor vehicles, as they are used. For example, a car's condition worsens through years of use. Repair costs may increase as the asset gets older and maintenance costs will also increase. Eventually, the asset may become unusable.

- **Depletion** – assets may be depleted as they are used. This means that the asset is physically exhausted or 'used up'. The rate of depletion determines how long the asset will last. Coal mines, oil fields and other natural resources are subject to depletion. For example, an oil field which has been depleted will have no resources left to depreciate.

- **Obsolescence** – there are two ways that non-current assets become outdated:

  - Advances in technology make an asset less useful to a business. For example, as processing speeds increase, older computers which still function will become outdated on technological grounds.

  - The useful economic life of an asset can be unexpectedly changed if market trends change or are incorrectly forecast. If a product declines in popularity or fails to generate the expected revenue, its lifespan will be shorter than expected. For example, the useful economic life of the fleet of supersonic jets owned by some airlines was probably shorter than expected due to lower than expected global demand for high-speed air travel.

Not all non-current assets have a limited lifespan. There are some assets, such as land, that are not affected by the factors above.

 If assets do not have a limited lifespan, should they be depreciated?

Methods of depreciation

There are a number of different methods of depreciation. These include:

- straight line
- reducing balance
- revaluation.

If assets are depreciated, the most appropriate method must be chosen.

Method 1: Straight line

The straight line method of depreciation is the easiest method to use. The amount of depreciation charged each year remains constant throughout the asset's life.

Key knowledge

Straight line depreciation is calculated as follows:

$$\frac{\text{Depreciation}}{\text{each year (\$)}} = \frac{(\text{Original cost of asset (\$)} - \text{Residual value (\$)})}{\text{Expected lifespan of asset (in years)}}$$

The **residual value** (also known as **scrap value**) is the estimated value of the asset at the end of its useful economic life in the business. This is often estimated to be zero.

Key terms

Straight line method of depreciation: A method of depreciation in which the amount of depreciation charged each year remains constant throughout the asset's life.

Residual value: The estimated value of a non-current asset at the end of its life.

2 Why do you think the residual value is often estimated to be zero?

Worked example 1

A van purchased to be used in a business cost $20 000. The van is expected to last for five years and it is estimated to have no residual value. What is the depreciation charge for each year?

Depreciation charge (per year) = $\dfrac{\$20\,000}{5\ \text{years}}$ = $4000 each year

In worked example 1, a depreciation charge on the van of $4000 appears as an expense in the income statement for each of the five years. Although depreciation is classed as an expense, it is actually a provision. This means there is no cash outflow of $4000. The money left the business when the van was bought – this is the $20 000 purchase price for the van.

With this method, the yearly charge for depreciation on the asset remains the same. The deprecation remains the same and is not affected by how much the asset is actually used.

3 It is decided that the residual value of the van in worked example 1 should be $3000. Calculate the revised yearly depreciation charge.

Method 2: Reducing balance

The reducing balance method of depreciation (also known as the **diminishing balance** method) charges more depreciation in the earlier years of an asset's life and the amount is reduced with every successive year of the asset's life. Using this method, depreciation is calculated as a percentage of the asset's net book value. The net book value of an asset is used on the statement of financial position. It is calculated as the original cost of an asset less all accumulated depreciation to the date of the statement of financial position.

For the reducing balance method, the same percentage is used each year. The net book value will become smaller over time as each successive year's depreciation is subtracted from the previous net book value. As a result, the amount charged each year for depreciation will be smaller than the previous year.

Key knowledge
....

Reducing balance depreciation for the year ($) = percentage rate × net book value of asset ($)

Key knowledge
....

Net book value = original cost of asset less all accumulated depreciation

The net book value of an asset appears on the statement of financial position.

Worked example 2

A machine costing $20000 is depreciated using the reducing balance method. The percentage rate used is 20%.

How much depreciation is charged in the first three years of the asset's life? Calculate the net book value at the end of each year.

	$
Original cost of machine	20000
Year 1 depreciation (20% of $20000)	4000
Net book value after year 1	16000
Year 2 depreciation (20% of $16000)	3200
Net book value after year 2	12800
Year 3 depreciation (20% of $12800)	2560
Net book value after year 3	10240

A comparison of the straight line and reducing balance methods of depreciation

Both straight line and reducing balance methods of depreciation spread the non-current asset's cost over the asset's life. The amount of depreciation charged and the net book value will differ depending on the method used. A comparison of how they do this is shown in the next worked example. Non-current assets that involve technology, and assets that have repair and maintenance costs that increase over time, such as computers, motor vehicles and machinery, are more suited to the reducing balance method.

Worked example 3

A machine costs $50000.

It is expected to last five years with a residual value of $4000. Use the straight line method to calculate:

- the depreciation charged each year
- the net book value of the machine at the end of each year.

Use the reducing balance method with a percentage rate of 40% to also calculate:

- the depreciation charged each year
- the net book value of the machine at the end of each year.

Compare the net book value of the machine after five years.

The first year's depreciation is calculated using the percentage rate given (20%). It is 20% of the net book value of the asset (which is the same as the cost of the asset in the first year).

At the end of the first year, the asset's net book value is $16000 based on the original net book value less the first year's depreciation.

The second year's depreciation is calculated using the same percentage rate (20%) and the new, smaller net book value of $16000, giving depreciation in year 2 of $3200.

The net book value at the end of the second year is smaller as the second year's depreciation has been subtracted from the first year's net book value ($16000 - $3200).

The third year's depreciation is calculated as 20% of the net book value at the end of year 2, that is 20% of $12800 = $2560.

The net book value at the end of the third year is now $10240 after subtracting the third year's depreciation ($2560) from the previous net book value ($12800).

	Straight line ($)	Reducing balance ($)
Cost	50000	50000
Depreciation in year 1	9200	20000
Net book value at end of year 1	40800	30000
Depreciation in year 2	9200	12000
Net book value at end of year 2	31600	18000
Depreciation in year 3	9200	7200
Net book value at end of year 3	22400	10800
Depreciation in year 4	9200	4320
Net book value at end of year 4	13200	6480
Depreciation in year 5	9200	2592
Net book value at end of year 5	4000	3888

The amount of deprecation is the same for each year. This means the net book value falls by the same amount each year.

The depreciation charged each year is always lower than the depreciation charged in the previous year. This means that the asset depreciates at a faster rate earlier in its life.

At the end of its useful life, the net book value of the machine is similar for both methods.

Method 3: Revaluation method

The revaluation method of depreciation involves the business deciding each year on a fair value for the asset. The value of the asset can be increased or decreased based on an estimate of its value. The revaluation method is most likely to be used when a business owns lots of small value items that are held by the business for more than one year, such as loose tools, small electrical appliances or kitchen cutlery and crockery.

Using the revaluation method, the yearly depreciation is based on the change in the estimated value of the asset between the start and the end of the year. Adjustments are also made for any purchases of the non-current asset during the year.

You will see in the next section how depreciation using the straight line and reducing balance methods is recorded in the ledger accounts. There is no ledger account for depreciation using the revaluation method. Any depreciation using this method is credited to the asset account. Crediting the asset account reduces the asset's value.

Key knowledge

The revaluation method of depreciation involves no separate ledger account to record depreciation. All adjustments for deprecation are made in the asset account.

Key terms

Revaluation method of depreciation: A method of depreciation in which the amount of depreciation charged each year is the change in the asset's estimated value between the start and the end of the year.

Worked example 4

A business holds loose tools as an asset.

- Start of year valuation of loose tools: $460
- Purchases of loose tools during year: $95
- End of year valuation of loose tools: $490

Calculate the amount of depreciation on loose tools using the revaluation method. Prepare the loose tools ledger account for the year.

Depreciation to be included:	$
Balance of loose tools at start of year	460
Add: Purchases during year	95
	555
Less: Value of loose tools at end of year	490
Equals: Depreciation for year	65

The depreciation for the year is credited to the loose tools account and debited to the income statement as an expense.

Loose tools			
	$		$
Balance b/d	460	Income statement (the **depreciation**)	65
Bank	95	Balance c/d	490
	555		555
Balance b/d	490		

The opening balance is the valuation of loose tools at the start of the year.

The closing balance represents the revalued amount for loose tools held at the end of the year.

Which method is best?

The advantages of each method of depreciation		
Straight line method	**Reducing balance method**	**Revaluation method**
• It is quick and easy to calculate • The impact on the profit of the business is consistent	• It is quick and relatively easy to calculate • Charging less depreciation in later years compensates for the likelihood of higher repair and maintenance costs as an asset gets older	• No need to make entries in a separate provision for depreciation account • Useful for businesses that own many relatively small-value individual assets

Consistency is essential in the choice and use of depreciation. Once selected, the business will tend to use the same method and policy for all assets of that type.

 4   Why do you think the reducing balance method is more often used for the depreciation of vehicles?

Ledger accounts and journal entries for the provision of depreciation

Depreciation charges are entered first in the general journal before posting to the double entry accounts. The full title for the ledger accounts is the *'provision for depreciation'* of the asset that is being depreciated. There is a separate provision for depreciation account for each type of non-current asset.

The double entry needed to record depreciation is as follows:

Account to be debited	Account to be credited
Income statement	Provision for depreciation of relevant asset

Debiting the income statement means depreciation appears as a provision in expenses. However, accounts of expenses are balanced and transferred (i.e. emptied of the amounts paid) to the income statement each year. For depreciation, the balance on the ledger account is not emptied and the balance remains on the account for as long as the business owns the asset that is being depreciated.

In the account of the asset, the value of the asset is maintained at the original purchase price of the asset. This value is only adjusted if the business buys more assets of the same type or if the asset is sold or scrapped (i.e. disposed of and no longer used).

On the statement of financial position, the original cost value of the asset is shown together with the value of accumulated depreciation on the asset on the date the statement is prepared. This is subtracted from the original cost value to give the net book value of the asset.

Worked example 5

On 1 January 2018, equipment is bought for $10 000 with payment by bank transfer. It is expected to last four years and have no residual value. Depreciation is provided using the straight line method. The financial year ends on 31 December.

Prepare the relevant entries for depreciation in the ledger accounts for each year of the asset's life.

Equipment at cost						
2018		$	2018			$
1 Jan	Bank	10 000	31 Dec	Balance c/d		10 000
2019			2019			
1 Jan	Balance b/d	10 000	31 Dec	Balance c/d		10 000
2020			2020			
1 Jan	Balance b/d	10 000	31 Dec	Balance c/d		10 000
2021			2021			
1 Jan	Balance b/d	10 000	31 Dec	Balance c/d		10 000

Provision for depreciation of equipment						
2018		$	2018			$
31 Dec	Balance c/d	2 500	31 Dec	Income statement		2 500
2019			2019			
31 Dec	Balance c/d	5 000	1 Jan	Balance b/d		2 500
			31 Dec	Income statement		2 500
		5 000				5 000
2020			2020			
31 Dec	Balance c/d	7 500	1 Jan	Balance b/d		5 000
			31 Dec	Income statement		2 500
		7 500				7 500
2021			2021			
31 Dec	Balance c/d	10 000	1 Jan	Balance b/d		7 500
			31 Dec	Income statement		2 500
		10 000				10 000

The term 'at cost' can be added to the title of accounts of non-current assets.

The equipment at cost account maintains the original cost of the asset. The balance remains until the equipment is either sold or scrapped.

Each year the depreciation account is credited with the yearly charge of $2 500. This appears as an expense in the income statement. This means the cost of the asset is spread over the asset's life.

The balance on the depreciation account will accumulate as the next year's depreciation is added on to the previous year's depreciation. This process is repeated over the life of the asset. For example, by the end of 2021, the accumulated depreciation has risen to $10 000 – representing four years of depreciation.

The balance on the depreciation account is used to calculate the net book value of the asset which appears on the statement of financial position.

Entries in the books of prime entry

When a non-current asset is bought, entries are made in the relevant books of prime entry. These are posted to the ledger accounts. A non-current asset paid for on the date of purchase would be credited to the cash book.

 5 In which book of prime entry would the purchase of a non-current asset on credit be recorded?

Depreciation entries are recorded in the general journal. The record contains the details of the transaction along with a narrative explaining what has happened.

Worked example 6

A car for business use is bought on credit from Sem for $18000. It is depreciated using the reducing balance method with a rate of 25%.

Prepare the entries in the relevant book of prime entry for buying the asset, and showing depreciation on the asset for the first year of ownership.

Depreciation on the asset is 25% of $18000 = $4500

The general journal appears as:

General journal	Dr	Cr
	$	$
Car	18000	
Sem		18000
Asset bought on credit for business use		
Income statement	4500	
Provision for depreciation of car		4500
Depreciation for year entered and transferred to income statement		

Purchasing the asset on credit is recorded in the general journal.

Provision for depreciation is credited to the account and debited to the income statement. The following year's depreciation would be smaller: 25% of ($18000 - $4500) = $3375.

The entries in the general journal are transferred to the relevant ledger accounts as outlined in the journal entries.

Sales of non-current assets

A sale of a non-current asset is classified as a **capital receipt** because the money received from the sale does not belong to a particular period of time. However, when a non-current asset is sold, any profit or loss on the sale does appear in the income statement. This is because the profit or loss made on the sale can be linked to a particular period of time (i.e. when the sale happens). A profit or loss is always included in the period when it occurred.

A sale of non-current assets is referred to as an **asset disposal**. Asset disposal also applies to the situation of a business scrapping a non-current asset before the end of its useful life.

The profit or loss on asset disposal is based on how much the asset is sold for compared with the net book value of the asset at the time of sale.

Key terms

Asset disposal: The selling or scrapping of a non-current asset.

Asset disposal account: The ledger account used to record asset disposal and to calculate the profit or loss on the disposal.

When an asset is sold, an asset disposal account is opened to record the transactions connected to the sale. The entries needed in the asset disposal account are:

Entries in asset disposal account	
Debit entries	**Credit entries**
Original cost value of asset being sold/scrapped	Accumulated depreciation of asset sold/scrapped
Profit on disposal*	Proceeds from sale (or trade receivables if on credit)
	Loss on disposal*

* At most one of these will appear in the disposal account. If the asset is sold for the net book value, there is no profit or loss and neither entry will appear.

Once these entries have been made, the account is closed. If the asset is sold for the same amount as its net book value, there will be no profit or loss made on its disposal. The account would balance without any entry to transfer amounts to the income statement.

Key knowledge
....

The money received from the sale of a non-current asset is classed as a **capital receipt** and does not appear in the income statement.

The profit or loss on the sale of a non-current asset does appear in the income statement as either an income (if sold for a profit) or an expense (if sold at a loss).

Worked example 7

Some machinery is bought on 1 January 2018 for $10000. The asset is depreciated using the straight line method. The machinery has an expected life of four years and no residual value. The machinery is sold on 1 January 2021 for $2000 cash.

Prepare the entries in the general journal and the ledger accounts for the machinery disposal account.

General journal	Dr	Cr
	$	$
Machinery disposal	10000	
Machinery		10000
Machinery sold – transfer to disposal account made		
Provision for depreciation of machinery	7500	
Machinery disposal		7500
Depreciation on machinery transferred to disposal account		
Income statement	500	
Machinery disposal		500
Loss on disposal of machinery transferred to income statement		

Explanations of these transactions are developed when the entries are posted to the ledger accounts.

Yearly depreciation is $10000 ÷ 4 = $2500 each year.

Machinery at cost					
2021		$	2021		$
1 Jan	Balance b/d	10000	1 Jan	Machinery disposal	10000

Provision for depreciation of machinery					
2021		$	2021		$
1 Jan	Machinery disposal	7500	1 Jan	Balance b/d	7500

Machinery disposal					
2021		$	2021		$
1 Jan	Machinery	10000	1 Jan	Provision for depreciation of machinery	7500
			1 Jan	Bank	2000
			1 Jan	Income statement	500
		10000			10000

The accumulated depreciation on the machinery (three year's depreciation) is transferred to the credit side of the disposal account.

These first two entries in the disposal account reflect the net book value of the asset at the moment of sale. It is the original cost offset by the accumulated depreciation on the machinery at the moment of sale, i.e. $10000 – $7500 = $2500.

To calculate the profit or loss on the sale, a final entry in the account is made which will ensure there is no outstanding balance remaining on the account. This amount will be transferred to the income statement as either revenue expenditure (if sold for a loss) or revenue receipt (if sold for a profit).

Here, the income statement entry represents a $500 loss made on the asset's sale. You can tell this is a loss as $500 is debited to the income statement. Debits in the income statement represent revenue expenditure.

The following is an example of asset disposal for the reducing balance method of depreciation.

Key knowledge

Although the business can receive cash when it sells a non-current asset, the effect on profit is in the opposite direction if it makes a loss on the sale. This is one way in which profit and cash flow can move in opposite directions to one another.

The credit entry in the machinery account, in effect, cancels out the debit balance for the machinery. The balance on the machinery at cost account is transferred to the machinery disposal account.

If only some of the asset held is sold then only the value of the amount being sold is credited to the asset account (and debited to the asset disposal account).

After three years of ownership, accumulated depreciation on the account is $7500 (3 years × $2500 per year). The debit entry in the depreciation account, in effect, cancels out the accumulated depreciation on the machinery and it is transferred to the machinery disposal account.

The original cost value of the machinery sold is transferred to the disposal account on the debit side.

The credit entry for bank is the receipt from the sale of the machinery ($2000). This is debited to the cash book.

Worked example 8

A vehicle that originally cost $20 000 is sold two years later on credit to Xia for $6000. The vehicle was depreciated using the reducing balance method with a percentage rate of 50%.

Prepare the general journal entries needed to record the vehicle disposal. (Narratives are not required.)

The accumulated depreciation on the vehicle is calculated as follows:

Year 1 depreciation = $20 000 × 50% = $10 000

Year 2 depreciation = $10 000 × 50% = $5000

Accumulated depreciation = $10 000 + $5000 = $15 000

General journal (extract)	Dr	Cr
	$	$
Vehicle disposal	20 000	
Vehicle at cost		20 000
Provision for depreciation of vehicle	15 000	
Vehicle disposal		15 000
Xia	6000	
Vehicle disposal		6000
Vehicle disposal	1000	
Income statement		1000

It is a good idea to do the calculations for depreciation in advance and certainly before producing the ledger accounts. Here, the accumulated depreciation on the vehicle is $15 000.

This pair of entries transfers the original cost value of the vehicle to the disposal account.

This pair of entries transfers the accumulated depreciation on the vehicle to the disposal account.

The vehicle is sold on credit to Xia. His account is debited and the disposal account is credited.

The vehicle is sold for a profit of $1000. Profit on the disposal of an asset is treated as a revenue receipt so you credit the income statement with $1000.

 6 Prepare the vehicle disposal ledger account for Worked example 8.

Mid-year transactions

Most transactions for buying and selling non-current assets take place during the business year rather than at the start or end of the year. When acquiring or disposing of non-current assets the business will have a depreciation policy outlining how depreciation will be charged for mid-year transactions.

If the asset disposal occurs at a convenient point in the accounting year, for example after 3 months (a quarter of a year), 4 months (a third of a year) or 6 months (half a year), the depreciation may be calculated based on it being a proportion of a year. For example, if an asset is purchased after three months (i.e. ¼) of the accounting year and the yearly depreciation is $8000, the amount of depreciation charged for the year may be ¾ × $8000 = $6000. This approach to calculating depreciation is usually only used for the straight line method.

An alternative approach is to allocate a full year's depreciation for an asset even if the asset was bought during the year.

Key knowledge

Although the disposal account is the formal way of calculating profit or loss on disposal, the calculation can be done without using ledger accounts if an estimate is needed. The profit or loss on disposal can be calculated as follows:

Profit or loss on disposal = selling price of asset – net book value of asset

 7 What is the meaning of an asset disposal account that already balances before the entry for income statement is debited or credited to the account?

Applying

Complete this task in pairs.

Task

A business has made the following purchases of machinery:

- 1 January 2018 $40 000
- 1 July 2019 $50 000
- 1 October 2019 $20 000

All machinery is depreciated using the straight line method based on no residual value and an expected life of ten years. It is company policy to depreciate machinery for each proportion of a year an asset is held.

Prepare the provision for depreciation of machinery account for 2018 and 2019.

Knowledge check

1   Equipment is purchased for $20 000 and is depreciated using the reducing balance method at a rate of 20%. What is the depreciation to be provided for in year 2 of its life?

 A $3200
 B $4000
 C $5000
 D $7200

2   A machine is bought for $25 000 and is depreciated using the reducing balance method at a rate of 20%. What is the machine's net book value after three years?

 A $10 000
 B $12 800
 C $15 000
 D $16 000

3 Which of the following is the correct double entry to record a profit on disposal of an asset?

	Debit	Credit
A	Income statement	Bank
B	Bank	Income statement
C	Disposal account	Income statement
D	Income statement	Disposal account

4 A car was bought for $15000. It is sold after three years for $4500. It had been depreciated using the straight line method based on no residual value and an expected life of five years. What is the profit or loss on the sale?

    A Loss of $9500

    B Profit of $4500

    C Profit of $1500

    D Loss of $1500

5 A business buys equipment for $50000. Equipment is depreciated using the straight line method based on no residual value and an expected life of four years.

    (a) Calculate the depreciation and net book values for years 1 to 4.

    (b) Prepare the ledger account for depreciation on the equipment for the first two years.

6 A business buys equipment for $50000. Equipment is depreciated using the reducing balance method at a rate of 50%.

    (a) Calculate the depreciation and net book values for years 1 to 4.

    (b) Prepare the ledger account for depreciation on the equipment for the first two years.

7 A van originally costing $30000 has been depreciated using the straight line method based on an expected life of six years and no residual value. The van is sold for $5000 after it has been in the business for four years.

    (a) Prepare the entries in the general journal relating to the sale of the van. (Narratives are not required.)

    (b) Prepare the disposal account for the van.

Check your progress

Read the unit objectives below and reflect on your progress in each.

	I struggle with this and need more practice.
	I can do this reasonably well.
	I can do this with confidence.

- Define depreciation
- Explain the reasons for accounting for depreciation
- Name and describe the straight line, reducing balance and revaluation methods of depreciation
- Prepare ledger accounts and journal entries for the provision of depreciation
- Prepare ledger accounts and journal entries to record the sale of non-current assets, including the use of disposal accounts.

Other payables and other receivables

Learning objectives

By the end of this unit, you should be able to:

- recognise the importance of matching costs and revenues
- prepare ledger accounts and journal entries to record accrued and prepaid expenses
- prepare ledger accounts and journal entries to record accrued and prepaid incomes.

Starting point

Answer these questions in pairs.

1. Cash is on the debit side of a trial balance. Is profit in the trial balance?

2. Do you think business profit for this year would be higher if a business delayed paying its expenses until next year?

Exploring

Discuss these questions in pairs.

1. A credit sale is made in December 2018 but the amount owing to the business is received in January 2019. Which year's profit would the sale count towards?

2. Insurance is paid on the business premises before the start of the next financial year. How would you treat this expense when calculating profit?

Developing

The matching principle

Key knowledge

The income statement will include all incomes and all expenses for a period even if they have not all been fully paid and received. Applying the matching principle means that all incomes and all expenses must be entered into the accounts of the period in which they are earned or incurred.

Profit is calculated by subtracting total expenses from total income for that year. However, it is important to only include incomes and expenses relating to that year in the calculation.

Key term

Matching principle: This principle ensures that incomes are matched to expenses in a particular accounting period. Incomes and expenses need to be entered into a business's financial statements as they are earned or incurred, not when the money is received or paid.

- Incomes earned for a period of time can include incomes for which the money has not yet been received. For example, a credit sale made on the last day of the financial year is included as an income for that year even though the money from the sale isn't received until the next financial year.
- Expenses incurred for a period of time can include expenses which have not been paid. For example, a utilities bill received in January 2018 for the amount of gas used the preceding year must be included in the accounts of 2017 and not 2018.

The accounting year of a business might be 1 January to 31 December but the expenses due might not match this.

Expense	Date of bill
Insurance for a van	1 June paid in advance, valid for a year
Rent on premises	1 December paid yearly in advance
Heat and lighting	28 February paid quarterly in arrears
Business rates	30 April paid quarterly in advance

When expenses and incomes are paid or received in the period to which they relate, the full amount is transferred from the ledger account to the income statement. This means that at the year end there are no closing balances on ledger accounts of incomes and expenses.

When an expense or income is paid or received that does not relate to the current financial year, an outstanding balance is created on the ledger account.

Adjustments are made in the ledger accounts for expenses paid and incomes received that do not relate to the current financial period. There are four adjustments that are made:

- Accrued expenses: Expenses relating to the current accounting period that remain unpaid at the end of a period
- Prepaid expenses: Expenses that have been paid in advance of the accounting period to which they relate
- Accrued incomes: Incomes that have been earned during the accounting period but not yet received
- Prepaid incomes: Incomes that have been received in advance of the accounting period to which they relate.

Key knowledge

Adjustments for accruals and prepayments appear in the income statement, and the amounts owing or prepaid can be found on the statement of financial position (see Chapter 5).

Recording accrued and prepaid expenses

Accrued expenses

Accrued expenses (also known as other payables, accruals, expenses in arrears, or simply expenses owing) are expenses relating to the current accounting period that have either not been paid in full or

Key term

In arrears: An expense paid in arrears is one which is paid for after having been received, for example electricity is often paid for in arrears – the amount owing is calculated after the electricity has been used.

Key terms

Accrued expenses: Expenses relating to the current accounting period that remain unpaid at the end of the period. Also known as Other payables.

Prepaid expenses: Expenses that have been paid in advance of the accounting period to which they relate. Also known as Other receivables.

have not been paid at all. The amount transferred to the income statement is always the full amount due. This means a ledger account adjustment is made when there are accrued expenses.

Worked example 1

Heating and lighting for the year ended 31 December 2018 is $2400 and is paid in four instalments of $600 every three months. The last payment covering October to December was unpaid at the year end.

Prepare the entries in the ledger account and in the general journal.

Heating and lighting						
2018		$	2018			$
10 Mar	Bank	600	31 Dec	Income statement		2400
13 Jun	Bank	600				
20 Sep	Bank	600				
31 Dec	Balance c/d	600				
		2400				2400
2019			2019			
			1 Jan	Balance b/d		600

The entries in the general journal:

General journal			
		Dr	Cr
2018		$	$
31 Dec	Income statement	2400	
	Heating and lighting		2400
	Transfer of yearly expense to income statement		
31 Dec	Heating and lighting	600	
	Other payables (accrued expenses)		600
	Unpaid heating and lighting for period 1 Oct – 31 Dec 2018		

Prepaid expenses

Prepaid expenses (also known as other receivables or prepayments) are expenses paid in the year before the one to which they relate. Application of the matching principle means expenses that are prepaid expenses are not included with the expenses of the current year. Adjustments are made in the ledger accounts for prepaid expenses.

1. What expenses are usually paid in advance?

The three payments made within 2018 appear on the debit side of the expense account.

The yearly total for heating and lighting of $2400 is transferred to the income statement. This is an application of the matching principle; the income statement includes the full cost of heating and lighting for the financial year.

The amount unpaid is $600. The balancing figure carried down to balance the account is an accrued expense.

The credit balance of $600 on 1 Jan 2019 is the amount still owing for heating and lighting. This balance remains in the account until it is paid.

The full year's expense is transferred to the income statement. It is always the full amount that is transferred even if the business has not paid the full amount.

This entry shows the amount owing on the heating and lighting account. This entry creates the credit balance on the account for the heating and lighting at the start of the next period.

Worked example 2

A business rents property from 1 July 2018. A full year's rent is $6000 and is paid in advance on 1 July 2018. The business year ends on 31 December.

Prepare the entries in the ledger account and in the general journal.

Rent						
2018		$	2018			$
1 Jul	Bank	6000	31 Dec	Income statement		3000
			31 Dec	Balance c/d		3000
		6000				6000
2019			2019			
1 Jan	Balance b/d	3000				

General journal			Dr	Cr
2018			$	$
31 Dec	Income statement		3000	
	Rent			3000
	Transfer of yearly expense to income statement			
31 Dec	Other receivables (prepaid expenses)		3000	
	Rent			3000
	Prepaid rent for period 1 January – 30 June 2019			

Only six months' rent is included as an expense for 2018. Although a full year's rent was paid, half of what was paid relates to the next business year.

The full year's payment of $6000 is debited to the account.

The prepaid expense for 1 Jan 2019 – 30 June 2019 isn't included as an expense for 2018. So, the prepaid rent for 2019 is shown as a debit balance of $3000.

The cost of six months' rent appears in the income statement as an expense.

This entry recognises that a full year's rent was paid but that half of the amount paid relates to the next financial year.

Recording accrued and prepaid incomes

Sales revenue provides most business income. Sales revenue is included as business income in the period when the sale is made. This is true for cash and credit sales. Money received from a credit sale may not be received until the next accounting period. However, the income from sales is always included in the period in which the sale was made. This means that sales revenue is credited to the income statement and contributes to profit even if money has not yet been received from a sale.

This also applies to additional incomes received by businesses. Many businesses have additional sources of income included as revenue receipts in a financial year. Any additional incomes are credited to the income statement and added to profit in the period the income is earned even if the money from the income is still owing to a business.

Key terms

Accrued incomes: Incomes earned but not yet received by the business at the end of the period.

Prepaid incomes: Incomes received in advance of the period in which they were earned by the business.

Accrued incomes

Accrued income (or **revenue owing**) includes income earned but not received by the end of the financial year. Applying the matching principle means any income not received by the end of the year is still included in that year's profit.

Key knowledge

Commission is often received for referrals or when a business promotes or sells products or services on behalf of another company.

Worked example 3

A business receives commission of $350 every three months. Amounts received for the financial year ended 31 December 2018 are as follows:

- 21 March $350
- 17 June $350
- 29 September $350

The commission due in December has been delayed and will not be received until January 2019.

Prepare the entries in the ledger account and in the general journal.

Commission received						
2018		$	2018			$
31 Dec	Income statement	1400	21 Mar	Bank		350
			17 Jun	Bank		350
			29 Sep	Bank		350
			31 Dec	Balance c/d		350
		1400				1400
2019			2019			
1 Jan	Balance b/d	350				

General journal				
			Dr	Cr
2018			$	$
31 Dec	Commission received		1400	
	Income statement			1400
	Transfer of yearly commission received to income statement			
31 Dec	Accrued income		350	
	Commission received			350
	Income owing to business for period October – December 2018			

The payments received are credited to this income account.

The $350 still owed to the business is credited here as accrued income. The debit balance of $350 represents the income still owing to the business.

The total income due in 2018 is four payments of $350 (i.e. $1400) and this is credited to the income statement as income for the year.

Yearly commission received appears in the income statement as an income.

This entry shows that income is still owing to the business. Commission of $350 has been earned but has not been received. This creates a debit balance on the account.

Prepaid incomes

Prepaid incomes are incomes paid in advance of the period in which the income was earned. The business will receive prepaid incomes as receipts but these are not included as income towards profit until the period it relates to.

Worked example 4

A business has a year end of 31 December and generates income by renting out an office for $4000 per year. Rent is received in advance, in equal instalments of $1000 on 1 January, 1 April, 1 July and 1 October. The receipt due for 1 January 2019 was received by the business on 22 December 2018.

Prepare the entries in the ledger account and in the general journal.

Payments received are credited to this account, including the payment received in December for the period covering 1 January – 31 March 2019. These entries would all be debited to the bank (or cash book).

Rent received						
2018		$	2018			$
31 Dec	Income statement	4000	1 Jan	Bank		1000
31 Dec	Balance c/d	1000	1 Apr	Bank		1000
			1 Jul	Bank		1000
			1 Oct	Bank		1000
			22 Dec	Bank		1000
		5000				5000
2019			2019			
			1 Jan	Balance b/d		1000

The rent received earned for 2018 was $4000. According to the matching principle you only include the amount relating to 2018 in the income statement.

The balance brought down on the account is the prepaid income for rent received of $1000.

General journal			Dr	Cr
2018			$	$
31 Dec	Rent received		4000	
	Income statement			4000
	Transfer of yearly rent received to income statement			
31 Dec	Rent received		1000	
	Prepaid income			1000
	Rent received due in 2019 received in December 2018			

Rent received for the year appears in the income statement as an income.

This entry recognises that income has been received in advance of the period it relates to.

2 Why do you think accruals and prepayments are recorded in the general journal?

Recording accrued and prepaid amounts for multiple periods

Both accrued and prepaid amounts result in an outstanding balance remaining on the ledger account. The outstanding balance will be carried to the next accounting period as either a credit or a debit balance. This means that when preparing ledger accounts, any outstanding balances from previous periods must also be added on to the account as an opening balance. This opening balance from a previous outstanding balance is in addition to any outstanding balances that may exist at the end of the current period.

The matching principle applies when there are outstanding balances from previous periods as well as outstanding balances at the end of the current period. The income statement must include only incomes and expenses that relate to the current period. Any amounts outside the current period must not be recorded in the income statement.

Worked example 5

A business has a financial year end of 31 December. The following data relates to the advertising expenses of the business:

		$
1 Jan 2018	Advertising owing for 2017	43
1 Dec 2018	Advertising paid for by cheque	580
31 Dec 2018	Advertising paid in advance for 2019	31

What is the correct amount to be included in the income statement for advertising in 2018?

The correct amount is	$
Amount paid in 2018	580
Less amount belonging to 2017	– 43
Less amount belonging to 2019	– 31
	506

$43 is subtracted from the amount paid in 2018 as it relates to an earlier period (i.e. it is for 2017).

It is best to start with the payment made for advertising in 2018 and then make adjustments for any prepaid or accrued balances.

Although this is paid in 2018, it relates to 2019. This means it must be subtracted from the amount paid in 2018 as it does not relate to the current period.

£506 is the amount to be debited to the income statement as the advertising expense for 2018.

Ledger accounts for outstanding balances covering multiple periods

When there are outstanding balances from earlier, as well as for later periods, these can be incorporated into the ledger account.

Worked example 6

The following data relates to a wages account for the year ended 31 December 2018:

- Wages paid in advance during 2017 for 2018 $311
- Wages paid during 2018 $5980
- Wages owing as at 31 December 2018 $444

Prepare the wages account for 2018.

The opening debit balance is the prepaid expense that was paid in 2017 but relates to the wage expense of 2018.

The amount paid for wages is entered on the debit side of the account and credited to the bank account.

			$				$
					Wages		
2018			$	2018			$
1 Jan	Balance b/d		311	31 Dec	Income statement		6735
31 Dec	Bank		5980				
31 Dec	Balance c/d		444				
			6735				6735
2019				2019			
				1 Jan	Balance b/d		444

The accrued expense for wages is the amount owing at the end of the year. This is brought down as a credit balance at the start of 2019.

The wage expense for 2018 is $6735 – this is the amount that relates to this year. This amount is debited to the income statement as an expense for 2018.

Applying

Complete this task in pairs.

Task

Eastwood Ltd has two different suppliers for gas and electricity but prefers to have one heating and lighting ledger account. Use the following information to prepare the ledger account and balance the account on 31 December 2018, which is also the business's year end.

- Amount for gas owing as at 1 Jan 2018 $34
- Electricity prepaid as at 1 Jan 2018 $64
- Gas paid by direct debit $77 per month
- Electricity paid by cheque on 1 Mar $432
- Electricity paid by cheque on 15 Jun $511
- Amount for gas owing as at 31 Dec 2018 $31
- Electricity unpaid as at 31 Dec 2018 $99

Knowledge check

1 Which one of the following does not mean the same as the other three?
   A Matching   C Accrued
   B Owing   D Arrears

2 Which of the following appears as a balance brought down on the debit side in a ledger account at the start of an accounting period?
   A Expenses owing   C Accrued expenses
   B Prepaid incomes   D Prepaid expenses

3 A business paid $4350 for electricity in 2018. At the year end, there is a balance carried down on the debit side of the account of $210. How much is debited to the income statement for electricity in 2018?
   A $4140   C $4560
   B $4350   D $5000

4 A business receives $9800 in commission during 2018. This includes $400 for services due in 2019. How much should the income statement be credited with for commission received?
   A $9800   C $10 200
   B $9400   D $9200

5 The following transactions took place in the financial year ended 31 December 2018. Prepare a ledger account for each of the following:
   (a) Office expenses paid during 2018 totalled $640 but as at 31 December 2018 there was $82 still owing.
   (b) Insurance paid during 2018 totalled $1190. Out of the total paid, $210 was for January 2019.

6 The following transactions took place during the financial year ended 31 December 2018. Prepare a ledger account for each of the following:
   (a) Administration expenses paid during 2018 were $450 of which $50 was for 2019.
   (b) Cheques received for rent during the year totalled $3400. By the end of the year the business is still owed $550.

7 Prepare the ledger accounts for the following data:
   (a) Rent owing as at 1 January 2018 $91
       Amount paid for rent during 2018 $4355
       Rent owing as at 31 December 2018 $145
   (b) Insurance prepaid at 1 January 2018 $77
       Amount paid for insurance during 2018 $844
       Insurance owing as at 31 December 2018 $19
   (c) Commission received during 2018 $922
       Commission owing to the business as at 1 January 2018 $112
       Commission received for 2019 as at 31 December 2018 $29

Check your progress

Read the unit objectives below and reflect on your progress in each.

- Recognise the importance of matching costs and revenues
- Prepare ledger accounts and journal entries to record accrued and prepaid expenses
- Prepare ledger accounts and journal entries to record accrued and prepaid incomes.

 I struggle with this and need more practice.

I can do this reasonably well.

I can do this with confidence.

Irrecoverable debts and provision for doubtful debts

Learning objectives

By the end of this unit, you should be able to:

- understand the meaning of irrecoverable debts and recovery of debts written off
- prepare ledger accounts and journal entries to record irrecoverable debts
- prepare ledger accounts and journal entries to record recovery of debts written off
- explain the reasons for maintaining a provision for doubtful debts
- prepare ledger accounts and journal entries to record the creation of, and adjustments to, a provision for doubtful debts.

Starting point

Answer these questions in pairs.

1. Why do you think businesses offer credit terms when selling goods?

2. What risks are involved in offering credit terms?

Exploring

Discuss these questions in pairs.

1. How can a business avoid situations where it fails to collect trade receivables?

2. How do you think the failure to collect trade receivables affects profit?

Developing

Irrecoverable debts and recovery of debts written off

Irrecoverable debts

Any business allowing credit to its customers runs the risk of not being able to collect amounts owing to the business. There are several reasons an amount owing may fail to be collected. The main reason is insolvency of the customer that was allowed credit when the sale was originally made. Other reasons include credit customers disputing the amounts owing and refusing to pay and being unable to trace customers which have purchased goods fraudulently.

Key term

Recovery of debts written off: When money is received in payment of a debt that had been previously written off.

Poor credit control by the business could also lead to increased irrecoverable debts. A credit customer will be given a period of time to pay the amount owing. If this is not paid by the date set then telephone calls, letters and even visits to the customer will follow to encourage payment. As a last resort, court action may be taken by the business to recover all or some of the debt owing. However, at some point a business will decide that the amount owing is unlikely to be received and the debt will be classified as an irrecoverable debt (also known as a bad debt).

Once a debt is classed as irrecoverable, entries are made in the books to record this loss of income. This is known as writing off the debt. An irrecoverable debt is treated as an expense in the period in which the business decides the debt is irrecoverable. This involves cancelling the balance on the relevant trade receivables account.

Key term

Credit control: the monitoring of credit sales and the collection of payments from credit customers.

Key knowledge

Irrecoverable debts are treated as an expense.

1. How is the value of irrecoverable debts in a year affected by external factors, such as the state of the national economy?

Worked example 1

During 2018, a business makes these credit sales:

- 25 March, sales of $240 were made to Omri
- 30 June, sales of $385 were made to Fraser

During 2018, the businesses of both Omri and Fraser failed. On 31 December 2018, both of these outstanding trade receivables are written off as irrecoverable debts.

Prepare the entries in the general journal and the ledger accounts to record these irrecoverable debts.

General journal		Dr	Cr
2018		$	$
31 Dec	Irrecoverable debts	240	
	Omri		240
Debts written off as irrecoverable – result of business failure of customer			
31 Dec	Irrecoverable debts	385	
	Fraser		385
Debts written off as irrecoverable – result of business failure of customer			
31 Dec	Income statement	625	
	Irrecoverable debts		625
Total debts written off for year			

The double entry book-keeping needed to write off each debt is recorded in the general journal. The narratives explain why the debts were written off.

Individual accounts appear as follows:

Omri					
2018		$	2018		$
25 Mar	Sales	240	31 Dec	Irrecoverable debts	240

Fraser					
2018		$	2018		$
30 Jun	Sales	385	31 Dec	Irrecoverable debts	385

Irrecoverable debts					
2018		$	2018		$
31 Dec	Omri	240	31 Dec	Income statement	625
31 Dec	Fraser	385			
		625			625

Sometimes, only part of the outstanding amount is written off. A debt may be partially written off and the remaining balance received. For example, it might be that when a business fails, there are some resources available for settling amounts the business owes. The amount received may be expressed as a proportion of the outstanding amount owing (e.g. $0.20 for each $1 owed by the customer).

Recovery of debts written off

An irrecoverable debt written off may be recovered in the future. This means that the business is paid an amount it had already written off as an irrecoverable debt. The recovery of debts written off is also known as 'bad debts recovered'.

There are two approaches to accounting for the recovery of debts written off.

1   Amounts received are debited to the bank and credited to the income statement as a revenue receipt.

2   Amounts received are debited to the bank and credited to the income statement as a revenue receipt *and* the original amount owing is reinstated as a trade receivable. The personal account of the credit customer in the sales ledger is credited with the amount received on recovery of the debt.

2   An irrecoverable debt has been recovered. Why would a business consider allowing credit sales to that customer again?

> Once the decision is taken to write off debts as irrecoverable, the personal account of the customer in the sales ledger is credited with the amount to be written off.

> Crediting the account cancels the amount owing to the business and reduces the overall total for trade receivables.

> The total amount written off will be transferred to the income statement as an expense.

> Trade receivables written off as irrecoverable appear on the debit side of the account.

Worked example 2

A debt written off in 2018 as irrecoverable is recovered when full settlement is received on 11 May 2019. The original debt was owed by Omri and totalled $240.

Prepare the entries needed to record the recovery of a debt written off in the general journal and in the ledger accounts. The debt is to be reinstated to the customer's personal account.

General journal		Dr	Cr
2019		$	$
11 May	Omri	240	
	Recovery of debt written off		240
Debt written off now recovered and reinstated in trade receivables account			
31 Dec	Recovery of debt written off	240	
	Income statement		
Transfer of recovery of debts written off to income statement			

Omri		$	2019		$
2019					
11 May	Recovery of debt written off	240	11 May	Bank	240

Recovery of debts written off		$	2019		$
2019					
31 Dec	Income statement	240	11 May	Omri	240

Provision for doubtful debts

Any business allowing credit sales is likely to experience irrecoverable debts. When a business does not receive payment of amounts owing to it, this makes it more difficult for the business to pay its own debts. However, businesses do not know which credit customers will not pay their debts; if they did, they would not have allowed them credit in the first place. As recognition of the likelihood of irrecoverable debts, businesses can create a provision for doubtful debts.

A provision for doubtful debts is an estimate of the value of likely future irrecoverable debts. If irrecoverable debts are likely to occur, then it is important that a business presents its assets with realistic values. This is an application of the prudence principle (which you will meet in Unit 7.1). The value of trade receivables will be unrealistically high if it is known that some of the trade receivables are likely to be written off as irrecoverable in the future. Therefore, subtracting a provision for doubtful debts from trade receivables shows a more realistic value for trade receivables.

The double entries needed to write off each debt are recorded in the general journal. The narratives explain why the debts were written off.

Debiting the account with the recovery of the debt reinstates the original debt.

At the same time, the account is credited with the amount recovered and this is debited to the bank account.

The account is credited with the amount received from Omri.

Any other debts recovered through the year are also credited here (with the corresponding debit entries reinstating the original amounts owing).

The total amount received from the recovery of debts written off is transferred to the credit side of the income statement as a revenue receipt.

Key term

Provision for doubtful debts: An adjustment made to trade receivables based on an estimate of future irrecoverable debts.

Estimating the size of the provision for doubtful debts

The value of future irrecoverable debts is uncertain. Therefore, the size of the provision for doubtful debts is only an estimate of future irrecoverable debts. This estimate is based on:

- how long debts have been outstanding
- historical trends for irrecoverable debts in the industry of the business
- economic factors – in economic downturns or recessions, business failure is more common and irrecoverable debts are more likely.

3 How does the age of the debt affect the likelihood of it becoming an irrecoverable debt?

Creating a provision for doubtful debts

Accounting entries for the provision for doubtful debts are similar to the provision for depreciation. The provision for doubtful debts is a credit balance in the ledger account. Adjustments to the size of the provision for doubtful debts are made in the ledger accounts. These changes are transferred to the income statement.

4 What is the difference between irrecoverable debts and a provision for doubtful debts?

Worked example 3

A business creates a provision for doubtful debts of 5% of the year-end balance on trade receivables. The year-end value of trade receivables for 2018 is $25000.

Prepare the entries needed in the general journal and in the ledger accounts for the provision for doubtful debts.

Entries for the provision for doubtful debts are entered first into the general journal.

General journal		Dr $	Cr $
2018			
31 Dec	Income statement	1250	
	Provision for doubtful debts		1250
Creation of provision in response to likely irrecoverable debts			

The size of the new provision is 5% of $25000 = $1250.

This is credited to the account and then debited (as an expense) to the income statement.

Provision for doubtful debts					
2018		$	2018		$
31 Dec	Balance c/d	1250	31 Dec	Income statement	1250
			2019		
			1 Jan	Balance b/d	1250

The balance for the provision is carried down to the next year. This amount will be subtracted from trade receivables.

Adjusting the provision for doubtful debts

If the business maintains a provision for doubtful debts then the balance on the ledger account for the provision will need adjusting. If the risk of irrecoverable debts increases, the provision can be increased in size to reflect the increased risk of debts not being recovered. If economic conditions improve it may mean that the provision can be reduced.

Even if the provision is maintained at the same percentage, the value of trade receivables will change over time and therefore the size of the provision for doubtful debts will need adjusting.

Worked example 4

The provision for doubtful debts created in Worked example 3 is carried down to 2019. The following information is available for the value of trade receivables and the size of the provision for doubtful debts.

Year	Trade receivables at 31 December ($)	Size of provision (5%)
2019	30 000	1500
2020	30 000	1500
2021	23 000	1150

Prepare the ledger account for provision for doubtful debts for 2019 to 2021.

Provision for doubtful debts					
2019		$	2019		$
31 Dec	Balance c/d	1500	1 Jan	Balance b/d	1250
			31 Dec	Income statement	250
		1500			1500
2020			2020		
31 Dec	Balance c/d	1500	1 Jan	Balance b/d	1500
2021			2021		
31 Dec	Income statement	350	1 Jan	Balance b/d	1500
31 Dec	Balance c/d	1150			
		1500			1500
2022			2022		
			1 Jan	Balance b/d	1150

The balance created is in 2018 and remains in the account into 2019.

The provision for 2019 is 5% of $30 000 = $1500.

The provision is increased by $250 (the difference between the old provision of $1250 and the new provision of $1500.)

The increase is credited to the account to increase the balance on the provision for doubtful debts account to $1500.

The increase of $250 is debited to the income statement as a revenue expense.

The new balance of $1500 is carried down from 2019 to 2020.

The provision for doubtful debts for 2020 is kept at the same size as in 2019. This means no adjustment is needed in the ledger account or the income statement.

The provision for doubtful debts in 2021 falls to 5% of $23 000 = $1150.

This means the provision for doubtful debts needs reducing by $350.

Reducing the size of the account's credit balance requires a debit entry. The debit entry is credited to the income statement as a revenue receipt.

Adjustments on the statement of financial position

Key knowledge

Changes in the provision for doubtful debts appear in the income statement:

An increase appears as an expense

A decrease appears as an income

An unchanged provision requires no income statement entry.

The full provision (the balance carried down on the provision for doubtful debts account) appears on the statement of financial position and is subtracted from trade receivables.

Changes in the size of the provision for doubtful debts appear in the income statement. The full provision is subtracted from trade receivables on the statement of financial position to show a more realistic value for trade receivables. This net value of trade receivables is the amount the business will probably collect from its credit customers.

Worked example 5

A business has a year end of 31 December. For the end of year accounts for 2018, the current provision for doubtful debts is reduced from $800 to $650. Trade receivables at the year end after irrecoverable debts have been deducted are $12 700.

Prepare the provision for doubtful debts account for the year and an extract of the statement of financial position at the year end showing trade receivables.

Provision for doubtful debts						
2018		$	2018			$
31 Dec	Income statement	150	1 Jan	Balance b/d		800
31 Dec	Balance c/d	650				
		800				800

Statement of financial position (extract) as at 31 December 2018		
	$	$
Current assets:		
Trade receivables	12700	
Less provision for doubtful debts	650	12050

The reduction in the provision for doubtful debts requires a debit entry in the account. This entry is also credited to the income statement as a revenue receipt.

Trade receivables appears with current assets. The full provision is subtracted from trade receivables giving a more realistic estimate of how much will be collected from the credit customers of the business.

Key knowledge

For provision accounts – both for doubtful debts and for depreciation – it is the change in the size of the provision that appears in the income statement. An increase in the size of the provision appears as an expense; a reduction in the size of the provision appears as an income.

The full amount of the provision appears on the statement of financial position. This amount is the same as the closing balance on the provision account. The balance is subtracted from the original value of assets on the statement of financial position.

Applying

Complete this task in pairs.

> ### Task
>
> A firm decides to create a provision for doubtful debts equivalent to 4% of trade receivables at the year end. Trade receivables figures for the years ended 31 December are as follows:
>
> | Year | Trade receivables |
> |------|-------------------|
> | 2018 | $25 000 |
> | 2019 | $19 600 |
> | 2020 | $23 300 |
> | 2021 | $27 980 |
>
> (a) Prepare the provision for doubtful debts account for the years 2018 to 2021.
>
> (b) Prepare an extract of the statement of financial position for 2021 showing trade receivables.

Knowledge check

1 What is the correct double entry needed to record an irrecoverable debt being written off?

	Debit	Credit
A	Trade receivables	Irrecoverable debts
B	Irrecoverable debts	Trade receivables
C	Trade receivables	Income statement
D	Income statement	Trade receivables

2 Which of the following is credited to the income statement?

A Increases in the provision for doubtful debts

B Creation of the provision for doubtful debts

C Irrecoverable debts written off for the year

D Decreases in the provision for doubtful debts

3 Year-end trade receivables are $12000. The opening balance on the provision for doubtful debts account is $600. The provision for doubtful debts remains at 4% of trade receivables. Which of the following is the correct entry in the accounts to record the adjustment to provision for doubtful debts?

	Debit	Credit
A	Income statement $120	Provision for doubtful debts $120
B	Provision for doubtful debts $480	Income statement $480
C	Provision for doubtful debts $120	Income statement $120
D	Income statement $480	Provision for doubtful debts $480

4 A new business started trading on 1 January 2018 and the following debts are written off as irrecoverable during the year.

15 April	Rani	$65
8 May	Jana	$56
10 November	Fahad	$141

Prepare the irrecoverable debts account for 2018.

5 Riko decides to increase the current provision for doubtful debts from $250 to $340 for the financial year ended 31 December 2018. Prepare the provision for doubtful debts account for the full year.

6 As at 31 December 2018 it is decided to reduce the provision from 5% of trade receivables, which was used for 2017, to 3% of trade receivables at the year end. Trade receivables as at 31 December 2018 are $50000 and are exactly 30% lower as at 31 December 2019. The balance on the provision for doubtful debts as at 31 December 2017 was $980.

Prepare the provision for doubtful debts account for the years ended 31 December 2018 and 2019.

7 A debt owing to the business from Jow for $490 was written off as irrecoverable in 2017. On 3 November 2018, Jow unexpectedly paid the business the full amount owing.

Using the method of reinstating the amount owing in Jow's account, prepare the ledger accounts recording the recovery of this debt.

Check your progress

Read the unit objectives below and reflect on your progress in each.

▲	I struggle with this and need more practice.
▲▲	I can do this reasonably well.
▲▲▲	I can do this with confidence.

• Understand the meaning of irrecoverable debts and recovery of debts written off

• Prepare ledger accounts and journal entries to record irrecoverable debts

• Prepare ledger accounts and journal entries to record recovery of debts written off

• Explain the reasons for maintaining a provision for doubtful debts

• Prepare ledger accounts and journal entries to record the creation of, and adjustments to, a provision for doubtful debts.

Valuation of inventory

Learning objectives
By the end of this unit, you should be able to:
- understand the basis of the valuation of inventory at the lower of cost and net realisable value
- prepare simple inventory valuation statements
- recognise the importance of the valuation of inventory and the effect of an incorrect valuation of inventory on gross profit, profit for the year, equity, and asset valuation.

Starting point

Answer these questions in pairs.

1 Why do businesses keep records of the amount of inventory they hold?

2 What are benefits of holding large quantities of inventory?

Exploring

Discuss these questions in pairs.

1 Many businesses have moved away from holding large quantities of inventory. Why did they make this move?

2 What problems do businesses face if they hold small quantities of inventory?

Developing

How inventory is valued

Trading businesses generate profits by buying goods and selling them for a profit. Most trading businesses hold inventory of goods available for sale. Manufacturing businesses transform raw materials into finished goods for sale. Most manufacturing businesses hold inventory as finished goods, partly finished goods and raw materials. Service businesses, such as those providing financial advice, do not hold inventory.

Inventory is a **current asset**. It appears in the income statement and on the statement of financial position.

Key knowledge

For businesses that are traders, inventory is bought and then sold for a price higher than the original cost. For manufacturing businesses, inventory may be held as raw materials, part-finished goods or finished goods.

Key term

Net realisable value (of inventory): The selling price less any costs incurred getting the inventory into saleable condition.

Inventory is valued at original cost or its net realisable value, whichever is lower. The original cost is how much the business paid for the inventory when purchased. The net realisable value is the expected selling price less any costs incurred getting the inventory ready for sale. For example, inventory may be damaged and need repairing before it can be sold. Normally, the original cost is lower than the net realisable value as it is expected a business will sell inventory for more than its original cost.

Key knowledge

Inventory is valued at original cost or its net realisable value, whichever is lower.

Worked example 1

A business purchased inventory for $420. The inventory is damaged and can now be sold for $450 only after spending $80 on repairs.

What is the correct value of the inventory?

Original cost of the inventory:	$420
Net realisable value of the inventory:	$450 − $80 = $370.
Correct value of the inventory:	$370

To calculate the net realisable value the cost of the repairs must be subtracted from the selling price.

The net realisable value is lower than the original cost so the inventory should be valued at $370.

 Is inventory ever valued at its selling price?

Key knowledge

The replacement cost, that is, the cost of replacing the inventory, should not be used for valuing inventory even if lower than both the net realisable value and the original cost.

Inventory valuation statements

A business selling different products will hold different kinds of inventory. Rules for valuing inventory apply to all kinds of inventory. Therefore, inventory can be valued at a combination of original costs and net realisable values depending on the inventory. An inventory valuation statement allows different valuing methods to be used for different types of inventory. The statement shows the total inventory value based on each type of inventory held.

Key term

Inventory valuation statement: A report including the different valuations for each type of inventory held by a business.

Worked example 2

The following is an inventory valuation statement of Antliff Ltd.

Calculate the total value of inventory as at 31 December 2018.

Antliff Ltd Inventory valuation statement as at 31 December 2018				
	Number of items held	Original cost per unit ($)	Net realis- able value ($)	Total value
Product A2	12	4	6	?
Product F4	8	8	7	?
Product G8	10	12	9	?
Total value of inventory held				?

Product A2 is valued at original cost as it is lower than net realisable value (12 × $4 = $48).

Product F4 is valued at net realisable value as it is lower than original cost (8 × $7 = $56).

	$
Product A2	48
Product F4	56
Product G8	90
Total inventory value	194

Product G8 is valued at net realisable value as it lower than original cost (10 × $9 = $90).

This total is used in the financial statements – the income statement and statement of financial position.

The effect of an incorrect valuation of inventory

Effect on gross profit and profit for the year

Gross profit and profit for the year are covered in more detail in Chapters 5 and 6. However, if inventory is incorrectly valued, both gross profit and profit for the year will be incorrect. Applying the matching principle when calculating gross profit involves subtracting any inventory held at the end of the period from the purchases made for that period when calculating the expenses for that period. Inventory held at the end of the period is known as closing inventory.

Key term

Closing inventory: Value of inventory held by the business at the end of the accounting period.

Gross profit: Sales revenue less cost of sales.

Profit for the year: Gross profit less expenses.

2 Why do you think inventory held at the end of the period is subtracted from purchases when calculating gross profit?

Worked example 3

At the end of its first year of trading, a business has sales revenue for the year of $80000 and purchases of $65000.

Closing inventory cost $10000 and has a net realisable value of $13000.

where

Gross profit = sales – cost of sales

Cost of sales = opening inventory + purchases – closing inventory.

The inventory is incorrectly valued at the net realisable value. What is the effect on gross profit?

Gross profit calculated using net realisable value is
$80000 – ($0 + $65000 – $13000) = $28000

Gross profit calculated using cost value is
$80000 – ($0 + $65000 – $10000) = $25000

If inventory is incorrectly valued at net realisable value, gross profit is overstated.

> Subtracting the larger amount from purchases means that the amount subtracted from sales is lower than the correct amount. As a result, gross profit is higher than the correct value.

Key knowledge

The effects of incorrect valuation of closing inventory will also affect profit for the year.

If closing inventory is overstated, gross profit and profit for the year will be overstated.

If closing inventory is understated, gross profit and profit for the year will be understated.

Effect on asset valuation and equity

If closing inventory is overstated, assets on the statement of financial position are also overstated. However, the statement of financial position still balances.

If closing inventory is overstated, profit for the year is also overstated. On the statement of financial position, profit for the year is added to owner's equity. If profit for the year is overstated, then equity is also overstated. This means that the assets side and the liabilities and equity side of the statement of financial position are both incorrect and are both higher than the correct value.

Understating closing inventory results in lower profit for the year and lower values for both assets and equity.

Overstating closing inventory results in higher profit for the year and higher values for both assets and equity.

Key knowledge

If closing inventory is overstated, assets *and* equity on the statement of financial position will be overstated.

If closing inventory is understated, assets *and* equity on the statement of financial position will be understated.

Applying

Discuss these questions in pairs.

1 Closing inventory is overvalued. What effect will this have on the following year's gross profit for the year?

2 Why does it matter that assets and equity are incorrectly valued because of incorrect inventory valuation?

Knowledge check

1 Which of the following is included as inventory for a trading business selling computer printers?

   A Purchases of office furniture

   B Purchases of computers

   C Purchases of computer printers

   D Purchases of vehicles used to deliver printers

2 Which one of the following is used to value inventory?

   A Selling price   **C** Net resalable value

   B Net realisable value   **D** Cost plus profit

3 What is the correct value for the following inventory:

   Cost $56; replacement cost $43; selling price $62 (only after spending $11 getting the inventory into saleable condition)

   A $43   **C** $51

   B $56   **D** $62

4 A business has 15 units of inventory costing $12 each. These could be sold for a total of $200 after spending a total of $25 to update the products. In the end-of-year accounts this inventory is valued at original cost as $180.

   (a) How much should this inventory be valued at in the accounts?

   (b) How will the correction to the inventory valuation affect the assets and the profit for the year of the business?

5   Krste valued his inventory in the end-of-year accounts at original cost as $566.

	Number of items held	Original cost per unit ($)	Net realisable value ($)
Product B12	25	7	6
Product ZX8	35	5	8
Product S7	18	12	15
Total value of inventory held			

(a) Calculate the correct value for closing inventory to be included in the accounts.

(b) Krste calculated his profit for the year as $3780. Calculate the profit for the year adjusted for the correction to the valuation of inventory.

Check your progress

Read the unit objectives below and reflect on your progress in each.

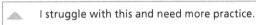 I struggle with this and need more practice.

• Understand the basis of the valuation of inventory at the lower of cost and net realisable value

 I can do this reasonably well.

• Prepare simple inventory valuation statements

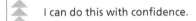 I can do this with confidence.

• Recognise the importance of valuation of inventory and the effect of an incorrect valuation of inventory on gross profit, profit for the year, equity, and asset valuation.

Chapter review

1 Which of the following are classed as revenue expenditure?

(a) Installation costs of computer network for office

(b) Petrol for motor van

(c) Painting of new office

(d) Replacement headlights for car

    A (a), (b) and (d)   **C** (b) and (d)

    B (b), (c) and (d)   **D** (a) and (c)

2 Which of the following is not an example of capital expenditure?

    A Delivery costs of car used within business

    B Legal costs of buying premises

    C Installation cost of photocopier in office

    D Delivery costs of replacement parts for photocopier

3 Which of the following does not explain why non-current assets are depreciated?

    A Land does not have a limited useful economic life

    B Machinery wears out over time

    C A computer becomes outdated as faster models are introduced

    D A coal mine becomes depleted of its natural resources over time

4 Which of the following is not a recognised method of depreciation?

    A Revaluation   **C** Net realisable value

    B Straight line   **D** Reducing balance

5 A machine was purchased for $11 000 and is depreciated at 20% using the reducing balance method. What is the net book value of the asset exactly two years later?

    A $6600   **C** $5632

    B $7040   **D** $8800

6 A machine is bought for $50 000 that is expected to last for five years and have no residual value. It is depreciated using the straight line method and fractions of years of ownership are included in depreciation calculations. The machine is sold for $8000 exactly three and a half years later. What is the profit or loss on disposal

    A Profit of $7000   **C** Profit of $2000

    B Loss of $2000   **D** Loss of $7000

7 The correct treatment of writing off an irrecoverable debt is:

	Debit	Credit
A	Irrecoverable debts	Trade receivable
B	Trade receivable	Income statement
C	Irrecoverable debts	Income statement
D	Irrecoverable debts	Provision for doubtful debts

8   The provision for doubtful debts is currently $210. The business increases the provision to $300. Which is the correct double entry to record this?

	Debit	Credit
A	Provision for doubtful debts $300	Income statement $300
B	Provision for doubtful debts $90	Income statement $90
C	Income statement $90	Provision for doubtful debts $90
D	Income statement $300	Provision for doubtful debts $300

9   Inventory bought for $91 can be replaced at a cost of $86. The inventory could be sold for $101 if $9 was spent repairing the inventory. How should the inventory be valued in the accounts?

A	$91	**C**	$86
B	$101	**D**	$92

10   Closing inventory is undervalued. Which of the following will happen?

A	Profit will be understated	**C**	Assets will be overstated
B	Sales will be understated	**D**	Equity will be overstated

11   The draft profit of a business for the year ended 31 December 2018 was calculated as $4501. However, the following information was discovered immediately after the calculation of profit.

  (i)   A debt owing from Kasi of $89 is unlikely to be received as the business has failed and all the debts are assumed to be irrecoverable.

  (ii)   A provision for doubtful debts should have been created equivalent to 4% of trade receivables. (Trade receivables totalled $4500 after the deduction of Kasi's debt).

  (iii)   Wages of $22000 were paid during the year. However, this included wages of $380 for the next year.

  (iv)   Heating costs of $980 charged to the income statement for the year did not include a bill owing of $213.

  (v)   Depreciation on equipment had been undercast by $200.

  (a) Prepare the journal entries needed to record (i)–(v) (narratives are not required). **[10]**

  (b) Calculate the corrected yearly profit. **[6]**

  (c) Prepare an extract from the statement of financial position showing trade receivables as at 31 December 2018. **[3]**

  (d) State the effect on profit if capital expenditure is debited to the income statement. **[1]**

  [Total 20]

12   Pummell Ltd purchases these non-current assets during 2018:

		$
1 Jan	Machinery	12000
31 Mar	Equipment	8000
30 Jun	Equipment	7000
31 Aug	Machinery	9000
30 Sep	Machinery	5000

Machinery is depreciated using the straight line method with an expected life of 10 years and no residual value. Machinery purchased during the year should be depreciated based on the fraction of the year for which it is owned.

Equipment is depreciated at 20% using the reducing balance. A full year's depreciation is provided in the year of purchase.

The balance on the machinery account as at 1 January 2018 was $18000, and the balance on the provision for depreciation of machinery was $8000. On 31 December 2018, the machinery purchased on 1 January 2018 was sold for $9000.

(a) State two factors that affect the useful economic life of non-current assets. **[2]**

(b) State the most appropriate method of depreciation for a motor vehicle. **[1]**

(c) Construct the following:

   (i)   Machinery account for 2018 **[5]**

   (ii) Provision for depreciation of machinery for 2018 **[4]**

   (iii) Machinery disposal account for 2018 **[4]**

   (iv) Equipment at cost account for 2018 **[2]**

   (v)   Provision for depreciation of equipment for 2018 **[2]**

[Total 20]

13   A trial balance is extracted on 31 December 2018. There are several errors within the trial balance and a suspense account is opened.

	Dr	Cr
	$	$
Revenue	41341	
Purchases		21313
Irrecoverable debts		531
Provision for doubtful debts		560
Machinery		36500
Provision for depreciation on machinery	12500	
General expenses		14500
Inventory at 1 January 2018	8870	
Inventory at 31 December 2018	11314	
Trade payables		5211
Trade receivables	6700	
Bank	2121	
Office salaries		18677
Owner's equity	65000	
Drawings	15400	
Suspense		65954
	163246	163246

(a) Prepare a corrected trial balance. **[10]**

(b) Distinguish between irrecoverable debts and a provision for doubtful debts. **[2]**

(c) Explain how the sale of a non-current asset can appear as an expense in the income statement. **[3]**

(d) Explain two reasons why a business would increase its provision for doubtful debts. **[4]**

(e) State how the recovery of debts written off would appear in the income statement. **[1]**

[Total 20]

14 Until 2015, Zhao did not offer his customers credit and he always paid his suppliers in cash. He now offers credit terms to his customers in an attempt to increase sales and has begun to use the credit offered by his suppliers. As the level of irrecoverable debts rose he decided in 2017 to maintain a provision for doubtful debts of 5% of trade receivables at the year end.

Additional information

1 The following data is from Zhao's accounts:

(a) Trade receivables as at 31 December 2017	$4900
(b) Trade receivables as at 31 December 2018 after adjustments for (iii) and (iv)	$5600
(c) Irrecoverable debts for year ended 31 December 2018	$235
(d) Recovery of debts written off for year ended 31 December 2018	$54

No adjustments have been made for the provision for doubtful debts, the irrecoverable debts or the recovery of debts written off in the income statement for 2018.

2 During 2018, Zhao purchased a computer for business use costing $1100. Additional costs associated with the computer included $100 for its installation. Zhao included $1100 as a business expense on his income statement.

3 Zhao has included within his closing inventory, items which cost $45 but which have been damaged and can now only be sold for $35 once they are repaired. Repair costs are estimated to be $8. Zhao included these items at their cost value of $45.

4 Zhao calculated his profit for the year as $1780.

(a) Explain the difference between irrecoverable debts and provision for doubtful debts. [2]

(b) Prepare a ledger account for provision for doubtful debts for the year ended 31 December 2018. [3]

(c) Zhao has been advised to depreciate his computer using the reducing balance method at a rate of 20%. Calculate the depreciation on the computer in 2018. [2]

(d) Calculate the profit for the year after adjusting for the additional information 1–4 given above. [8]

(e) Prepare an extract from the balance sheet for trade receivables as at 31 December 2018. [3]

(f) How should inventory be valued in the accounts of a business? [2]

[Total 20]

Preparation of financial statements

5

5.1 Sole traders

5.2 Partnerships

5.3 Limited companies

5.4 Clubs and societies

5.5 Manufacturing accounts

5.6 Incomplete records

This chapter explores the preparation of financial statements for a range of business organisations. It considers the range of financial statements that are prepared for both profit-making and non-profit-making organisations. The differing requirements for trading and services businesses are considered throughout.

The chapter develops further the adjustments considered in previous chapters, applying the various principles to the financial statements of business organisations.

Sole traders

Learning objectives

By the end of this unit, you should be able to:

- explain the advantages and disadvantages of operating as a sole trader
- explain the importance of preparing income statements and statements of financial position
- explain the difference between a trading business and a service business
- prepare income statements for trading businesses and for services businesses
- understand that statements of financial position record assets and liabilities on a specified date
- recognise and define the content of a statement of financial position: non-current assets, intangible assets, current assets, current liabilities, non-current liabilities and capital
- understand the interrelationship of items in a statement of financial position
- prepare statements of financial position for trading businesses and services businesses
- make adjustments for provision for depreciation using the straight line, reducing balance and revaluation methods
- make adjustments for accrued and prepaid expenses and accrued and prepaid income
- make adjustments for irrecoverable debts and provisions for doubtful debts
- make adjustments for goods taken by the owner for own use.

· ·

Starting point

Answer these questions in pairs.

1 Define the term depreciation.

2 Explain the difference between prepaid and accrued expenses.

3 Describe how to account for capital and revenue items of expenditure.

Exploring

Discuss these questions in pairs.

1 Djamel runs a small retail store operating as a sole trader. Discuss the benefits to Djamel of operating the retail store on his own.

2 Identify **three** non-current assets that a supermarket would own that would need to be depreciated when preparing their financial statements.

3 Make a list of expenses that a small hotel may need to pay and include in their financial statements.

Developing

Advantages and disadvantages of operating as a sole trader

Sole trader describes any business that is owned and controlled by one person.

The owner, however, may decide to employ other people to work alongside them within the business. Examples include plumbers, newsagents and gardeners.

Key knowledge

Sole traders do not have a separate legal existence from their owner. This means that the owner is personally liable for the debts of the business. This is known as **unlimited liability.**

Key terms

Sole trader: A business that is owned and controlled by one individual.

Unlimited liability: The owner(s) of a business are personally liable for the debts of the business if the business is unable to repay them.

Advantages	Disadvantages
Small businesses are easy to set up.	
Low initial start-up costs. The owner is only required to find a small amount of capital.	Business growth is limited by the amount of capital available from the sole trader.
The sole trader is responsible for all business decisions.	The sole trader has no one to share the responsibility of running the business with.
The sole trader can choose their own working conditions, hours and holidays to be taken.	The sole trader often has to work long hours and may find it difficult to take holidays or find cover when they are unwell.
The sole trader does not need to share their profit with any other owner.	The sole trader will be liable for any debts that the business cannot pay; there is unlimited liability.
A sole trader has limited legal requirements for the preparation of financial records. Sole traders do need to register to pay tax. Also, if they employ workers, they are responsible for complying with tax, employee and health and safety legislation.	

Sole traders use their income statements and statements of financial position to assess the business's financial performance. This may include a review of their gross profit and profit for the year. They may use the details to support an application for finance or to assess how much they can take as drawings.

It is often useful for the sole trader to compare income statements over a period of several years. Businesses will analyse changes in revenue, cost of sales and expenses and make adjustments to their business practices as required.

Key knowledge

A trading business buys goods with the intention of selling them to consumers and other businesses. Examples include supermarkets, clothes stores and other retail outlets.

A service business sells services to their customers rather than goods. Examples include hairdressers, travel agents and garden designers.

 Explain the difference between an income statement and a statement of financial position.

Income statement

A business prepares an income statement for a specific period of time. This is usually one year (12 months). The income statement is prepared at the end of the business's financial year.

An income statement includes:

- A trading account which calculates the gross profit that a business has made by buying and selling its goods during a particular period of time.

Key knowledge

Services organisations do not have a trading account.

- Revenue – this is sales revenue that is earned when goods have been sold to customers. These are goods in which the business normally deals and that were bought with the primary intention of resale.
- Sales returns (returns inwards) – the cost of the goods that have been returned by customers to the business.

Key knowledge

Revenue included in the trading account does not include income received from the disposal of non-current assets or other capital receipts.

- Purchases – the cost of the goods bought for resale.
- Purchases returns (returns outwards) – the cost of the goods that the business has sent back to suppliers.

Key knowledge

The purchase of shop fixtures and other capital expenditure are not classified as purchases in the trading account.

- Opening and closing inventory – the value of the inventory that the business is holding at the start and end of the financial year.
- Carriage inwards – the delivery costs of transporting the goods purchased to the business.

Key term

Income statement:
A financial statement showing a business's income and expenses for an accounting period and the resulting profit or loss.

- Cost of sales – the total purchases made during a financial year adjusted for inventory held.
- Gross profit – calculated as sales revenue less the cost of those same sales.

- Additional income – any income the business has earned from sources other than their normal trading activities. Examples include: rent received and commission received.

- Expenses – the operating costs of a business. Examples include: wages, heat and light, telephone costs, carriage outwards and depreciation.

Key terms

Gross profit: Sales revenue less cost of sales.

Profit for the year: Gross profit less expenses.

	Name of the sole trader			
	Income statement for the year ended....			
		$	$	$
Revenue			X	
Less	Sales returns		(X)	
				X
	Opening inventory	X		
Add	Purchases	X		
Add	Carriage inwards	X		
Less	Purchases returns	(X)		
			X	
Less	Closing inventory		(X)	
Cost of sales				(X)
Gross profit (or loss)				X
Additional income (examples include):				
Decrease in provision for doubtful debts			X	
Rent received			X	
				X
Expenses (examples include):				
Rent and rates			X	
Wages and salaries			X	
Carriage outwards			X	
Heat and light			X	
Insurance			X	
Advertising			X	
Increase in provision for doubtful debts			X	
Repairs and maintenance			X	
Irrecoverable debts			X	
Depreciation			X	
				(X)
Profit (or loss) for the year				X

The revenue a business has earned from selling its goods.

The first two numerical columns in the income statement are used as workings columns. The final column gives the totals for the different sections.

These are not included in the income statement but are here to show you how the different figures are dealt with.

Numbers in brackets are subtracted.

All costs directly related to the purchase of the goods for resale.

Revenue less cost of sales.

Businesses account for their selling and administrative expenses by deducting these from gross profit to calculate their profit for the year.

Key knowledge

Other receivables (prepaid expenses) at the end of the current financial year are SUBTRACTED from the associated expense.

Other payables (accrued expenses) at the end of the current financial year are ADDED to the associated expense.

2 Identify **three** expenses that would be included in the income statement of a local café.

Worked example 1

Zeesham runs a hardware store operating as a sole trader. He has provided the following information on 31 March 2018.

	$
Revenue	15221
Purchases	9787
Inventory as at 1 April 2017	5241
Inventory as at 31 March 2018	1359
Sales returns	774
Purchases returns	363
Carriage inwards	521

Prepare Zeesham's trading account for the year ended 31 March 2018.

Zeesham Trading account for the year ended 31 March 2018				
		$	$	$
Revenue			15221	
	Sales returns		(774)	
				14447
	Opening inventory	5241		
	Purchases	9787		
	Carriage inwards	521		
	Purchases returns	(363)		
			15186	
	Closing inventory		(1359)	
Cost of sales				(13827)
Gross profit (or loss)				620

3 Explain the difference between gross profit and profit for the year.

Worked example 2

Amina is a sole trader. She runs a clothing store.

She has extracted the following information from her books of account on 30 April 2018.

	$
Revenue	18462
Purchases	14629
Salaries	3150
Motor expenses	720
Rent	970
Insurance	111
General expenses	250
Inventory as at 1 May 2017	3750
Inventory as at 30 April 2018	2150

Prepare Amina's income statement for the year ended 30 April 2018.

Amina		
Income statement for the year ended 30 April 2018		
	$	$
Revenue		18462
Less cost of sales:		
Opening inventory	3750	
Purchases	14629	
	18379	
Closing inventory	–2150	
Cost of sales		16229
Gross profit		2233
Less expenses:		
Salaries	3150	
Motor expenses	720	
Rent	970	
Insurance	111	
General expenses	–250	
		5201
Loss for the year		(2968)

Worked example 3

Setka is a sole trader. He works as a painter and decorator.

He has provided the following extract from his books of account on 30 September 2018.

	$
Revenue received from customers	19750
Assistant decorator wage	5350
Commission received	3757
Motor van cost	15000
Motor van running costs	1970
Insurance	950
General expenses	1950
Motor van depreciation	3000

Additional information

On 30 September 2018:

- insurance has been prepaid: $150
- motor van running costs incurred but unpaid: $750
- commission received earned but unpaid: $255
- depreciation is to be charged on the motor van at 20% on a reducing balance basis.

Prepare Setka's income statement for the year ended 30 September 2018.

These adjustments are known as 'post trial balance adjustments'. They need to be accounted for when preparing any financial statements.

Setka		
Income statement for the year ended 30 September 2018		
	$	$
Revenue received from customers		19750
Additional income:		
Commission received		4012
		23762
Less expenses:		
Motor van depreciation	2400	
Assistant decorator wage	5350	
Insurance	800	
Motor van running costs	2720	
General expenses	1950	
		13220
Loss for the year		10542

$3757 + $255 = $4012

20% of ($15000 – $3000) = $2400

New balance of the depreciation account = $3000 + $2400 = $5400

$950 – $150 = $800

$1970 + $750 = $2720

 Describe the difference in the income statements of a sole trader operating in the trading sector and one operating in the services sector.

Statement of financial position

You met the accounting equation in Chapter 1. It states that assets owned by a business always equal the owner's equity and liabilities of the business. Owner's equity is also known as capital.

Key knowledge

Assets = capital + liabilities

A statement of financial position is a formal way of representing the accounting equation.

A business's **statement of financial position** lists all of the **assets** that are **owned** by a business and all of the **liabilities** that are **owed** by the business.

 Identify the key assets and liabilities that would be included in the statement of financial position of a retail store.

A statement of financial position includes:

Key terms

Capital: Resources invested into a business. It is calculated as capital = assets – liabilities. Also known as **owner's equity**.

Statement of financial position: A financial statement showing the assets of the business and the financing for these assets, either from owner's equity or liabilities.

Term	Definition	Examples
Non-current assets	Resources that are acquired by a business and are likely to be used for a considerable amount of time (more than one year).	Premises Fixtures and fittings Machinery Motor vehicles Office equipment
Intangible assets	Assets of a business that do not have a physical existence. Any valuation is subjective.	Patents Copyright Goodwill
Current assets	Resources of a business that are likely to be converted into cash within one year.	**Trade receivables** Inventory Cash at bank Cash in hand Other receivables (prepaid expenses) Accrued income
Current liabilities	Liabilities that occur through day-to-day business activities. These debts are likely to be repaid within one year.	**Trade payables** Bank overdraft Prepaid income Other payables (accrued expenses)
Non-current liabilities	Long-term borrowing that is not likely to be repaid within the next year. These liabilities will appear in a number of consecutive statements of financial position.	Mortgages on business property Long-term bank loans
Capital	Describes how much a business is worth. The capital of a business represents how much the owner(s) of the business have invested.	Capital = assets – liabilities

6. Categorise the following items as assets or liabilities: premises, bank loan, motor vehicles, trade payables, trade receivables, inventory, cash in hand, bank overdraft, fixtures and fittings, mortgage on business property, office equipment.

The statement of financial position lists all of the assets, liabilities and capital of a business. For a sole trader, the following format can be used.

Name of the sole trader Statement of financial position as at			
	$	$	$
	Cost	Depreciation	Net book value
Non-current assets			
Premises	X	X	X
Fixtures and fittings	X	X	X
Equipment	X	X	X
Motor van	<u>X</u>	<u>X</u>	<u>X</u>
	X	X	X
Current assets			
Inventory		X	
Trade receivables	X		
Less provision for doubtful debts	<u>X</u>	X	
Bank		X	
Cash		X	
Accrued income		X	
Other receivables (prepaid expenses)		<u>X</u>	
			<u>X</u>
Total assets			X
Capital and liabilities			
Capital			X
Add profit for the year			<u>X</u>
			X
Less drawings			<u>(X)</u>
			<u>X</u>
Non-current liabilities			
Mortgage			<u>X</u>
			<u>X</u>

Current liabilities			
Trade payables			X
Bank overdraft			X
Other payables (accrued expenses)			X
Prepaid income			X̲
			X̲
Total liabilities			X̲

Worked example 4

Use the following information to prepare a statement of financial position for Maherpa as at 31 December 2018.

	$
Capital	21 750
Trade receivables	3 950
Motor vehicles	6 700
Trade payables	2 450
Fixtures and fittings	5 500
Bank balance	250
Closing inventory	7 800

Maherpa
Statement of financial position as at 31 December 2018

	$	$	$
	Cost	Depreciation	Net book value
Non-current assets			
Motor vehicles	6700	0	6700
Fixtures and fittings	5500	0	5500
	12200	0	12200
Current assets			
Inventory		7800	
Trade receivables		3950	
Bank		250	
			12000
Total assets			24200
Capital and liabilities			21750
Current liabilities			
Trade payables			2450
Total liabilities			24200

Worked example 5

Mahu is a self-employed builder. His financial year ends on 30 September 2018.

Mahu has prepared the following trial balance from his books of account.

Mahu builders
Trial balance as at 30 September 2018

	Dr	Cr
	$	$
Revenue		28794
Purchases	23803	
Rent	854	
Lighting and heating expenses	422	
Salaries and wages	3164	
Insurance	105	
Buildings	51506	
Trade receivables	3166	

Trade payables		1206
Bank	2347	
Inventory: 1 October 2017	1500	
Drawings	2400	
Motor vehicles	5500	
Provision for depreciation: motor vehicles		900
Motor vehicle expenses	1133	
Capital		65000
	95900	95900

Additional information

On 30 September 2018:

- lighting and heating expenses were prepaid: $250
- motor vehicle expenses incurred but unpaid: $500
- inventory on 30 September 2018: $9000
- depreciation is to be charged on the motor vehicle at 20% on cost.

Prepare the income statement for Mahu builders for the year ended 30 September 2018 and the statement of financial position as at 30 September 2018.

Mahu builders Income statement for the year ended 30 September 2018		
	$	$
Revenue		28794
Less cost of sales		
Opening inventory	1500	
Purchases	23803	
	25303	
Closing inventory	9000	
Cost of Sales		16303
Gross Profit		12491
Less expenses		
Lighting and heating	172	
Motor vehicle expenses	1633	
Salaries and wages	3164	
Insurance	105	
Motor vehicle depreciation	1100	
Rent	854	
		7028
Profit for the year		5463

$422 – $250 = $172

$1133 + $500 = $1633

20% of $5500 = $1100

Mahu builders			
Statement of financial position as at 30 September 2018			
	$	$	$
	Cost	Depreciation	Net book value
Non-current assets			
Premises	51 506	0	51 506
Motor vehicles	5 500	2 000	3 500
	57 006	2 000	55 006
Current assets			
Inventory		9 000	
Trade receivables	3 166		
Less provision for doubtful debts	0	3 166	
Bank		2 347	
Other receivables (prepaid expenses)		250	
			14 763
Total assets			69 769
Capital and liabilities			
Capital			65 000
Add profit for the year			5 463
			70 463
Less drawings			(2 400)
			68 063
Current liabilities			
Trade payables			1 206
Other payables (accrued expenses)			500
			1 706
Total liabilities			69 769

Provision for depreciation of $900 + depreciation for this year $1100 = $2000.

Figure from the income statement.

Worked example 6

Use the following information to prepare a statement of financial position for Qi as at 31 March 2018.

	$
Capital	54 000
Trade receivables	15 000
Provision for doubtful debts	3 000
Motor vehicles	35 000
Trade payables	19 000
Fixtures and fittings	25 000
Profit for the year	21 000
Drawings	11 000

Bank overdraft	7500
Closing inventory	17000
Other receivables (accrued income)	3500
Other payables (prepaid income)	2000

<table>
<tr><td colspan="4" style="text-align:center">Qi
Statement of financial position as at 31 March 2018</td></tr>
<tr><td></td><td>$</td><td>$</td><td>$</td></tr>
<tr><td></td><td>Cost</td><td>Depreciation</td><td>Net book value</td></tr>
<tr><td>Non-current assets</td><td></td><td></td><td></td></tr>
<tr><td>Motor vehicles</td><td>35000</td><td>0</td><td>35000</td></tr>
<tr><td>Fixtures and fittings</td><td>25000</td><td>0</td><td>25000</td></tr>
<tr><td></td><td>60000</td><td>0</td><td>60000</td></tr>
<tr><td>Current assets</td><td></td><td></td><td></td></tr>
<tr><td>Inventory</td><td></td><td>17000</td><td></td></tr>
<tr><td>Trade receivables</td><td>15000</td><td></td><td></td></tr>
<tr><td>Less provision for doubtful debts</td><td>3000</td><td>12000</td><td></td></tr>
<tr><td>Other receivables (accrued income)</td><td></td><td>3500</td><td></td></tr>
<tr><td></td><td></td><td></td><td>32500</td></tr>
<tr><td>Total assets</td><td></td><td></td><td>92500</td></tr>
<tr><td></td><td></td><td></td><td></td></tr>
<tr><td>Capital and liabilities</td><td></td><td></td><td></td></tr>
<tr><td>Capital</td><td></td><td>54000</td><td></td></tr>
<tr><td>Add Profit for the year</td><td></td><td>21000</td><td></td></tr>
<tr><td></td><td></td><td></td><td>75000</td></tr>
<tr><td>Less drawings</td><td></td><td></td><td>(11000)</td></tr>
<tr><td></td><td></td><td></td><td>64000</td></tr>
<tr><td>Current liabilities</td><td></td><td></td><td></td></tr>
<tr><td>Trade payables</td><td></td><td>19000</td><td></td></tr>
<tr><td>Bank overdraft</td><td></td><td>7500</td><td></td></tr>
<tr><td>Other payables (prepaid income)</td><td></td><td>2000</td><td></td></tr>
<tr><td></td><td></td><td></td><td>28500</td></tr>
<tr><td>Total liabilities</td><td></td><td></td><td>92500</td></tr>
</table>

Worked example 7

Parwaiz is a sole trader and works as an educational adviser. He has provided the following extract from his books of account on 30 April 2018.

	$
Revenue received from clients	39750
Stationery and educational resources	5350

Commission received		3757
Motor car cost		30000
Motor car running costs		5370
Insurance		1950
General expenses		2750
Motor car depreciation		6000

Additional information

On 30 April 2018:

- general expenses incurred but unpaid: $150
- motor car running costs have been prepaid: $950
- commission received has been prepaid: $357
- depreciation is to be charged on the motor car at 20% on a reducing balance basis.

Prepare Parwaiz's income statement for the year ended 30 April 2018.

Parwaiz Income statement for the year ended 30 April 2018		
	$	$
Revenue received from clients		39750
Additional income		
Commission received		3400
		43150
Less expenses		
Motor car depreciation	4800	
Stationery and educational resources	5350	
Insurance	1950	
Motor car running costs	4420	
General expenses	2900	
		19420
Profit for the year		23730

$3757 − $357 = $3400

20% of ($30000 − $6000) = $4800

New balance of the depreciation account = $6000 + $4800 = $10800

$5370 − $950 = $4420

$2750 + $150 = $2900

Worked example 8

Theodore, the owner of the Teddy Bear toy store, has prepared his trial balance as at 30 April 2018.

Teddy Bear toy store Trial balance as at 30 April 2018		
	Dr	Cr
	$	$
Revenue		179800
Sales returns	605	
Purchases	43100	

Rent	12100	
Lighting and heating expenses	4300	
Discounts received		925
Salaries and wages	28465	
Insurance	3600	
Trade receivables	2250	
Trade payables		1200
Bank		560
Inventory: 1 May 2017	4650	
Irrecoverable debts	210	
Drawings	104255	
Discounts allowed	900	
Provision for doubtful debts		250
Motor vehicles	12000	
Provision for depreciation: motor vehicles		10500
Fixtures and fittings	8000	
Provision for depreciation: fixtures and fittings		6000
Motor vehicle expenses	800	
Capital		26000
	225235	225235

The following information is also available.

- Closing inventory as at 30 April 2018 was $5300

- A general provision for doubtful debts is to be maintained at 10% of closing trade receivables

- During the year, Theodore withdrew goods costing $250 for his own use. This has not been recorded in the books of account.

- Lighting and heating expenses were prepaid: $150

- Motor vehicle expenses due but unpaid: $250

- Depreciation is to be provided as follows:

  – Motor vehicles   50% per annum using the reducing balance method

  – Fixtures and fittings   12.5% per annum using the straight line method

Prepare Teddy Bear toy store income statement for the year ended 30 April 2018 and statement of financial position as at 30 April 2018.

Teddy Bear toy store
Income statement for the year ended 30 April 2018

	$	$
Revenue	179 800	
Sales returns	605	
		179 195
Less cost of sales		
Opening inventory	4 650	
Purchases	42 850	
	47 500	
Closing inventory	5 300	
Cost of sales		42 200
Gross profit		136 995
Additional income		
Discounts received	925	
Provision for doubtful debts	25	950
		137 945
Less expenses		
Rent	12 100	
Lighting and heating expenses	4 150	
Salaries and wages	28 465	
Insurance	3 600	
Irrecoverable debts	210	
Discounts allowed	900	
Motor vehicle expenses	1 050	
Depreciation: motor vehicles	750	
Depreciation: fixtures and fittings	1 000	
		52 225
Profit for the year		85 720

The first column is a working column and the second column shows the final totals.

Theodore withdrew goods for his own use = 43 100 – 250 = $42 850.

10% of 2250 = $225

4300 – 150 = $4150

800 + 250 = $1050

50% of ($12 000 – $10 500) = $750

12.5% of 8000 = $1000

Original provision for doubtful debts = 250

New provision for doubtful debts = 225

Decrease in provision for doubtful debts = $25

Teddy Bear toy store
Statement of financial position as at 30 April 2018

	$ Cost	$ Depreciation	$ Net book value
Non-current assets			
Motor vehicles	12000	11 250	750

Provision for depreciation of $10 500 + depreciation for this year $750 = $11 250

Fixtures and fittings	8 000	7 000	1 000
	20 000	18 250	1 750
Current assets			
Inventory		5 300	
Trade receivables	2 250		
Less provision for doubtful debts	225	2 025	
Other receivables (prepaid expenses)		150	
		7 475	
Total assets		9 225	
Capital and liabilities			
Capital		26 000	
Add profit for the year		85 720	
		111 720	
Less drawings		(104 505)	
		7 215	
Current liabilities			
Trade payables		1 200	
Bank overdraft		560	
Other payables (accrued expenses)		250	
		2 010	
Total liabilities		9 225	

Provision for depreciation of $6000 + depreciation for this year $1000 = $7000

Closing inventory

Lighting and heating expenses, $150

Figure from the income statement

Theodore withdrew goods for his own use of $104 255 + $250 = $104 505

Motor vehicle expenses, $250

Applying

Complete this task in pairs.

Task

Cutz 4 U, hairdressers and barbers is owned and operated by Tamara.

She has provided the following information from her books of account as at 31 March 2018.

Cutz 4 U Trial balance as at 31 March 2018	Dr $	Cr $
Revenue received		75 000
Lighting and heating expenses	32 000	
Rent	10 000	
General expenses	5 000	

Cutz 4 U		
Trial balance as at 31 March 2018		
	Dr	Cr
	$	$
Salaries and wages	10000	
Insurance	2150	
Trade receivables	500	
Trade payables		350
Bank	3000	
Drawings	10000	
Provision for doubtful debts		100
Fixtures and fittings	35000	
Provision for depreciation: fixtures and fittings		7000
Capital		25200
	107650	107650

The following information is also available:

- A general provision for doubtful debts is to be maintained at 10% of closing trade receivables
- General expenses were prepaid: $550
- Lighting and heating expenses due but unpaid: $300
- Depreciation is to be provided as follows:
    - Fixtures and fittings   10% per annum using the straight line method.

Prepare Cutz 4 U's income statement for the year ended 31 March 2018 **and** statement of financial position as at 31 March 2018.

Knowledge check

1   Which of the following are classified as current assets in a business?

(a)   Cash at bank
(b)   Money owed by a customer
(c)   Prepaid amount for water rates
(d)   Unpaid invoice from a local supplier

A   (a), (b) and (c)   C   (a), (b) and (d)
B   (a), (c) and (d)   D   (b), (c) and (d)

2   Which of the following is a non-current asset in the statement of financial position?

A   Cash at bank   C   Motor vehicle
B   Inventory   D   Trade receivables

3   What does a sole trader discover from the contents of their income statement?

A   Amount spent on non-current assets   C   Bank account balance
B   Annual drawings   D   Profit for the year

4   Explain the advantages **and** disadvantages of operating as a sole trader.

5   Explain why it is important for a sole trader to prepare an income statement and statement of financial position.

6   Explain the difference between a trading business and a service business.

7   Rudd Antiques has provided the following information from its books of account for the year ended 31 December 2018.

Prepare the trading account for Rudd Antiques for the year ended 31 December 2018.

	$
Carriage inwards	650
Sales returns	595
Purchases returns	980
Revenue	37950
Purchases	29570
Inventory on 1 January 2018	3950
Inventory on 31 December 2018	5990

8   Hedges and Edges is a garden design company owned and operated by Ulvestad. He has provided the following information from his books of account as at 31 March 2018.

Hedges and Edges Trial balance as at 31 March 2018	Dr $	Cr $
Revenue received		150000
Lighting and heating expenses	14000	
Rent	20000	
General expenses	20000	
Salaries and wages	50000	
Insurance	14300	
Trade receivables	1000	
Trade payables		700
Bank	6000	
Drawings	20000	
Provision for doubtful debts		200
Equipment	35000	
Provision for depreciation: Equipment		7000
Capital		22400
	180300	180300

The following information is also available.

*   A general provision for doubtful debts is to be maintained at 10% of closing trade receivables
*   Rent was prepaid: $550
*   Lighting and heating expenses due but unpaid: $300
*   Depreciation is to be provided on equipment at 10% per annum using the straight line method

Prepare Hedges and Edges' income statement for the year ended 31 March 2018 and statement of financial position as at 31 March 2018.

9   James, the owner of the Bee music store has prepared his trial balance as at 31 August 2018.

Bee music store Trial balance as at 31 August 2018	Dr $	Cr $
Revenue		89900
Sales returns	900	
Purchases	35200	
Rent	12000	
Lighting and heating expenses	8600	
Commission received		175
Salaries and wages	17853	
Insurance	7500	
Trade receivables	3525	
Trade payables		1550
Bank	1500	
Inventory: 1 September 2017	3500	
Irrecoverable debts	175	
Drawings	55550	
Discounts allowed	750	
Provision for doubtful debts		150
Motor vehicles	25000	
Provision for depreciation: motor vehicles		7500
Fixtures and fittings	11000	
Provision for depreciation: fixtures and fittings		5000
Motor vehicle expenses	750	
Capital		79528
	183803	183803

The following information is also available:

- Closing inventory as at 31 August 2018 was $15300
- A general provision for doubtful debts is to be maintained at 20% of closing trade receivables
- During the year, James withdrew goods costing $755 for his own use. This has not been recorded in the books of account
- Motor vehicle expenses were prepaid: $575
- Salaries and wages due but unpaid: $555
- Depreciation is to be provided as follows:
  - Motor vehicles   25% per annum using the reducing balance method
  - Fixtures and fittings   10% per annum using the straight line method.

Prepare Bee Music Store income statement for the year ended 31 August 2018 and statement of financial position as at 31 August 2018.

Check your progress

Read the unit objectives below and reflect on your progress in each.

- Explain the advantages and disadvantages of operating as a sole trader
- Explain the importance of preparing income statements and statements of financial position
- Explain the difference between a trading business and a service business
- Prepare income statements for trading businesses and for services businesses
- Understand that statements of financial position record assets and liabilities on a specified date
- Recognise and define the content of a statement of financial position: non-current assets, intangible assets, current assets, current liabilities, non-current liabilities and capital
- Understand the interrelationship of items in a statement of financial position
- Prepare statements of financial position for trading businesses and services businesses
- Make adjustments for provision for depreciation using the straight line, diminishing balance and revaluation methods
- Make adjustments for accrued and prepaid expenses and accrued and prepaid income
- Make adjustments for irrecoverable debts and provisions for doubtful debts
- Make adjustments for goods taken by the owner for own use.

Partnerships

Learning objectives

By the end of this unit, you should be able to:
* explain the advantages and disadvantages of forming a partnership
* outline the importance and contents of a partnership agreement
* explain the purpose of an appropriation account
* prepare income statements, appropriation accounts and statements of financial position
* record interest on partners' loans, interest on capital, interest on drawings, partners' salaries and the division of the balance of profit or loss
* make adjustments to financial statements as detailed in 5.1 (sole traders)
* explain the uses of, and differences between, capital and current accounts
* draw up partners' capital and current accounts in ledger account form and as part of a statement of financial position.

Starting point

Answer these questions in pairs.

1. Explain the advantages of operating as a sole trader.

2. Review the problems of operating as a sole trader.

3. Describe the difference between a sole trader's income statement and statement of financial position.

Exploring

Discuss these questions in pairs.

1. What are the possible benefits to a sole trader of starting to work alongside another person as part of a partnership?

2. What are the potential problems of working with another person or persons as part of a partnership?

3. How may two or more partners agree to share the business profits?

Developing

Advantages and disadvantages of operating as a partnership

A **partnership** is a business that is owned and controlled by at least two owners.

The minimum number of partners that is required is two and the maximum number allowed in this type of organisation is usually twenty.

However, in professional partnerships, for example solicitors, accountants and estate agents, this number can be exceeded.

Key term

Partnership: A business that is owned and controlled by a minimum of two owners.

Key knowledge

Like a sole trader, a partnership has unlimited liability.

Advantages	Disadvantages
Greater capital and resources can be raised from the partners.	Profits will need to be shared between the partners.
Spreads personal risk across all of the partners, meaning that, in the case of financial difficulty, there are more people able to share the debt burden.	All partners are responsible for the debts of the business.
Partners may bring additional skills and ideas to the business.	There are potential problems if partners disagree over the direction of the business.
Business responsibilities are shared among the partners.	The actions of one partner are binding on all of the other partners.
Partners can discuss issues before final decisions have to be taken.	Decision-making can be time-consuming.
Partnerships may have increased public image and credibility with customers and suppliers when compared with a sole trader.	There is the potential for disputes over workloads.

CASE STUDY

Minnakht has worked as a self-employed builder for the last 10 years.

To improve the efficiency of his business, he has decided to form a partnership with Merkha and Mitry.

Merkha is currently a self-employed plumber and Mitry is a self-employed architect.

Merkha and Mitry will bring added expertise, capital and a number of professional contacts to the business.

This will greatly increase the efficiency and effectiveness of the building business.

Partnership agreements

A deed of partnership may contain:

- the amount of capital invested by each partner
- details of how profits and losses will be divided between the partners
- the amount of interest payable on capital (paid before profits are shared)
- the amount of interest payable on drawings
- the value of partners' salaries
- information on how many votes each partner has when decisions are to be made
- rules on the admission of new partners
- procedures for ending the partnership.

Partnerships are usually set up with a **deed of partnership**.

Partnership Act 1890

If no deed of partnership exists, the details contained in the Partnership Act 1890 apply.

This states that:

- profits and losses are shared equally
- interest on capital is not allowed
- interest on drawings will not be levied on drawings
- partnership salaries are not allowed
- any loans made by partners to the partnership should entitle partners to 5% interest on the loan.

1 Explain why it is important for partners to have a deed of partnership when setting up a new partnership.

There are five main reasons why it is important to have a partnership agreement in place.

- Without an agreement, the Partnership Act 1890 applies to all partnerships. Due to the age of the legislation, its provisions are almost always incompatible with how businesses are run in the twenty-first century.

- If partners are to receive different profit shares, a partnership agreement will be required. Even if a verbal agreement has been made that the profits of the business will be split differently, without a written agreement in place, each partner can claim an equal share.

Key term

Deed of partnership: An agreement that outlines the conditions that partners have consented to. It may also be referred to as a partnership agreement.

- Any buildings used in a partnership will automatically be owned by the partnership. Under the terms of the Partnership Act 1890 they will be shared equally between the partners unless specified in a partnership agreement. It is therefore essential to have a partnership agreement if a building is to be used but not owned by the partnership or not shared equally by the partners.

- The Partnership Act 1890 does not restrict any outgoing partners. Therefore, without a partnership agreement, there would be nothing to stop a partner that has been removed from the business from taking clients from the partnership.

- Under the Partnership Act 1890 no person can be introduced as a partner unless every existing partner agrees. In the same way, a partnership cannot remove a partner for inappropriate behaviour unless all of the partners have agreed on a process with the allocation of powers to do this. Therefore, with no written partnership agreement, partners may not be able to be removed unless the partnership is dissolved.

Features of partnership accounts

Partnership accounts include:

Interest on capital

Partners often contribute different amounts of capital to a partnership. As a reward for contributing capital, partners are credited with interest on this capital.

Interest on drawings

Drawings reduce the resources available within a business. In a partnership, the amount of drawings taken by one partner will impact on the amount of money that is available to the business and for the other partners to take. To deter partners from taking excessive drawings, interest on drawings is charged. This is usually expressed as a set percentage of the drawings taken.

Partnership salaries

Wages and salaries that are paid to a business's employees are classified as an expense in the business's income statement. However, partners are not business employees. Therefore, partners' salaries are not included as expenses in the income statement. Any salary taken by a partner is recorded in the appropriation account.

Key term

Appropriation account: An account that shows how a partnership's profit or loss for the year is shared out between the partners.

Appropriation account

A partnership's profit for the year is calculated in the same way as for a sole trader. An income statement is used. For a sole trader, all of the profit for the year belongs to the sole trader. Partnerships need to share out the profit or loss they have made between the partners. This is completed via an appropriation account.

Profit sharing ratio

The profit for the year of a partnership is allocated in the appropriation account prepared by the partnership. Adjustments are made for partners' salaries, interest on capital and interest on drawings. The balance that remains is shared between the partners in the agreed profit or loss sharing ratio.

Key term

Residual profit: The profit for the year for a partnership + interest on drawings – salaries and interest on capital; residual profit is shared between the partners in the agreed profit sharing ratio.

Key knowledge

Once the profit for the year has been calculated in the income statement, the figure is transferred to the appropriation account.

Any interest on drawings are added to the profit for the year. Salaries and interest on capital are deducted.

The revised total, known as **residual profit**, is shared between the partners in the agreed profit sharing ratio.

Goodwill

Goodwill is classified as an intangible non-current asset. When goodwill exists in a partnership, it is usual that goodwill is written off in the year of creation.

Once a partnership has prepared their income statement, an appropriation account is completed. The following is an example format.

Key term

Goodwill: An intangible non-current asset that represents the value of a business in excess of the assets that physically exist.

Name of business			
Appropriation account for the year ended			
	$	$	$
Profit or loss for the year			X
Add interest on drawings:			
Partner 1		X	
Partner 2		X	
			X
			X
Less salaries:			
Partner 1	X		
Partner 2	X		
		X	
			(X)
Less interest on capital:			
Partner 1	X		
Partner 2	X		
		X	
			(X)

		X
Balance of profits / losses shared:		
Partner 1	X	
Partner 2	X	
		X

Worked example 1

Abu, Bilal and Charlie are in partnership. Their partnership agreement states:

- profits and losses will be shared in the ratio of 3 : 2 : 1
- interest on capital is allowed at 10% per annum
- Abu will receive a partnership salary of $5000 per annum
- interest on drawings is charged at 5% on balances at the end of the year.

At 30 November 2018, the following balances were extracted from the books of account:

	$
Profit for the year	31 500
Capital account balances:	
Abu	16 000
Bilal	12 000
Charlie	12 000
Drawings:	
Abu	9 000
Bilal	6 000
Charlie	6 000

Prepare the appropriation account for Abu, Bilal and Charlie for the year ended 30 November 2018.

Abu, Bilal and Charlie			
Appropriation account for the year ended 30 November 2018			
	$	$	$
Profit or loss for the year			31 500
Add interest on drawings:			
Abu		450	
Bilal		300	
Charlie		300	
			1 050
			32 550

5% of $9000 = $450

5% of $6000 = $300

5% of $6000 = $300

Less salary: Abu		5000	
Less interest on capital:			
Abu	1600		
Bilal	1200		
Charlie	1200		
		4000	
			(9000)
			23550
Balance of profits/losses shared:			
Abu		11775	
Bilal		7850	
Charlie		3925	
			23550

10% of $16000 = $1600

10% of $12000 = $1200

10% of $12000 = $1200

Profit for the year available to be shared between the partners = $23550

Profit sharing ratio = 3 : 2 : 1

Abu $\rightarrow \frac{3}{6} \times 23550 = \$11775$

Bilal $\rightarrow \frac{2}{6} \times 23550 = \$7850$

Charlie $\rightarrow \frac{1}{6} \times 23550 = \$3925$

Capital and current accounts

A partner's claim to the assets and liabilities of a partnership are recorded in partners' capital and current accounts.

Capital accounts

The capital of a sole trader is recorded in a capital account. This obeys the double entry accounting rules. The same principle applies to partners. Each partner will have a separate capital account. It is usual for all partners to keep current accounts in addition to their capital accounts.

Key knowledge

Adjustments are required to a partner's capital account when:

- additional capital is contributed to the partnership
- non-current assets are revalued
- goodwill is introduced
- a partnership is dissolved (ended).

All other adjustments made to the partners' capital are entered in the current accounts.

Each partner prepares a capital account. For convenience and to save space, up to three or four partners can be accommodated in a single account with multiple columns. However, each partner can have their own capital account.

The following is an example format for a columnar capital account for three partners.

Capital account					Partner 1	Partner 2	Partner 3
	Partner 1	Partner 2	Partner 3				
	$	$	$		$	$	$
Goodwill (to be written off)	X	X	X	Balance b/d	X	X	X
Revaluation decrease	X	X	X	Bank/cash introduced	X	X	X
				Assets introduced	X	X	X
				Goodwill (created)	X	X	X
Balance c/d	X	X	X	Revaluation increase	X	X	X
	X̲	X̲	X̲		X̲	X̲	X̲
				Balance b/d	X	X	X

The capital account of each partner includes their original contribution to the partnership and is adjusted when changes take place that involve structural adjustments to the business. These capital accounts are known as **fixed capital accounts**. When maintaining a fixed capital account, partners are also required to prepare a current account. The current account records all entries relating to drawings, interest on capital, interest on drawings and profit or loss share.

Current accounts

A type of account that obeys the same double entry rules as a capital account. A current account includes adjustments to a partner's capital that arise from day-to-day trading operations. This is in contrast to the capital account that only adjusts for one-off structural changes to the partnership.

Key knowledge

The balance on a partner's current account usually has a credit balance. It is possible, however, for the partner to have a debit balance on their current account. This would mean that the partner has withdrawn more money from the partnership than they have 'earned'. If this persisted, the partner would need to transfer capital from their fixed capital account to the current account.

Each partner prepares a separate current account. The following is an example format for a columnar current account for three partners.

Current account as at [date]					Partner 1	Partner 2	Partner 3
	Partner 1	Partner 2	Partner 3				
	$	$	$		$	$	$
Balance b/d	X	X	X	Balance b/d	X	X	X
Share of loss	X	X	X	Interest on capital	X	X	X
Drawings	X	X	X	Salaries	X	X	X
Interest on drawings	X	X	X	Share of profit	X	X	X
Balance c/d	X	X	X	Balance c/d	X	X	X
	X̲	X̲	X̲		X̲	X̲	X̲
Balance b/d	X	X	X	Balance b/d	X	X	X

An alternative to a fixed capital account is a **fluctuating capital account**. When using this method, the capital accounts of partners do not remain fixed. The balances fluctuate from time to time. All entries relating to drawings, interest on capital, interest on drawings and profit or loss share are recorded in the partners' capital accounts. This means there is no need for a current account.

Worked example 2

Sabbir, Ahnaf and Rubel are in partnership. Their financial year ends on 31 October 2018.

They have provided the following information from their books of account:

	Sabbir $	Ahnaf $	Rubel $
On 1 November 2017:			
Capital account	50000	70000	90000
Current account	195 Cr	930 Dr	770 Cr
On 31 October 2018:			
Drawings	15000	11000	17000
Interest on drawings	450	330	510
Interest on capital	5000	7000	9000
Partner's salaries		9500	
Profit share	33000	63000	93000

Prepare the capital accounts and current accounts for all three partners.

Capital account as at 31 October 2018							
	Sabbir $	Ahnaf $	Rubel $		Sabbir $	Ahnaf $	Rubel $
Balance c/d	50000	70000	90000	Balance b/d	50000	70000	90000
	50000	70000	90000		50000	70000	90000
				Balance b/d	50000	70000	90000

Current account as at 31 October 2018							
	Sabbir $	Ahnaf $	Rubel $		Sabbir $	Ahnaf $	Rubel $
Balance b/d		930		Balance b/d	195		770
Drawings	15000	11000	17000	Interest on capital	5000	7000	9000
Interest on drawings	450	330	510	Salaries		9500	
Balance c/d	22745	67240	85260	Share of profit	33000	63000	93000
	38195	79500	102770		38195	79500	102770
				Balance b/d	22745	67240	85260

2 Prepare the current account for Sabbir, Ahnaf and Rubel to illustrate what would happen if they did not have a partnership agreement.

Worked example 3

Zarat and Rihaa are in partnership as estate agents. Their partnership agreement states:

- Profits and losses will be shared in the ratio of 5 : 3 respectively
- Interest on capital is allowed at 7% per annum
- Rihaa will receive a partnership salary of $19000 per annum
- Interest on drawings is charged at 3% on balances at the end of the year.

The partners have prepared their appropriation account to calculate their profit shares for the year ended 30 April 2018:

Zarat $56250

Rihaa $33750

On 30 April 2018, the following balances were extracted from the books of account:

	$
Capital account balances:	
Zarat	19000
Rihaa	9000
Current account balances:	
Zarat	5200 Cr
Rihaa	1900 Dr
Drawings:	
Zarat	9600
Rihaa	7600

Prepare for the year ended 30 April 2018:

- the capital accounts for Zarat and Rihaa
- the current accounts for Zarat and Rihaa

Capital account as at 30 April 2018					
	Zarat	Rihaa		Zarat	Rihaa
	$	$		$	$
Balance c/d	19000	9000	Balance b/d	19000	9000
	19000	9000		19000	9000
			Balance b/d	19000	9000

Current account as at 30 April 2018					
	Zarat	Rihaa		Zarat	Rihaa
	$	$		$	$
Balance b/d		1900	Balance b/d	5200	
Drawings	9600	7600	Interest on capital	1330	630

Interest on drawings	288	228	Salaries	0	19000
Balance c/d	52892	43652	Share of profit	56250	33750
	62780	53380		62780	53380
			Balance b/d	52892	43652

Partnership loans

A partnership may borrow funds from one of the partners if extra finance is required within the business.

Loans from the partners do **not** form part of the capital of the business. They are treated as any other business loan in the double entry accounts.

Rules of double entry book-keeping for partnership loans

Partnership loan obtained from a partner	
Account to be debited	*Account to be credited*
Bank account	Loan from partner account

Partnership loan repaid to a partner	
Account to be debited	*Account to be credited*
Loan from partner account	Bank account

Key knowledge

If the loan is to be repaid within 12 months, it appears as a current liability in the statement of financial position.

If the loan is to be repaid in over 12 months, it appears as a non-current liability in the statement of financial position.

The interest on the loan is included as an expense in the income statement and the loan recorded in the statement of financial position.

Interest on partnership loan PAID	
Account to be debited	*Account to be credited*
Interest on loan account	Bank account

Interest on partnership loan DUE but not PAID	
Account to be debited	*Account to be credited*
Bank account	Interest on loan account

Key knowledge

Interest on a partnership loan is transferred to the income statement for the financial year.

Worked example 4

Orpa and Rafsan are business partners running a local retail store.

Their partnership agreement states:

- Profits and losses will be shared in the ratio of 3 : 2 respectively
- Interest on capital is allowed at 6% per annum
- Rafsan will receive a partnership salary of $9 000 per annum
- No interest is charged on drawings.

On 30 June 2018, the following balances were extracted from the books of account:

	$
Profit for the year	31 500
Capital account balances:	
Orpa	10 000
Rafsan	8 000
Current account balances:	
Orpa	2 200 Cr
Rafsan	3 900 Dr
Drawings:	
Orpa	3 500
Rafsan	6 350

1 Prepare the appropriation account for Orpa and Rafsan for the year ended 30 June 2018.

2 Prepare for the year ended 30 June 2018:
- the capital accounts for Orpa and Rafsan
- the current accounts for Orpa and Rafsan

Orpa and Rafsan			
Appropriation account for the year ended 30 June 2018			
	$	$	$
Profit or loss for the year			31 500
Add interest on drawings:			
Orpa		0	
Rafsan		0	
			0
			31 500
Less salary: Rafsan		9 000	

Less interest on capital:				
Orpa		600		
Rafsan		480		
		1080		
			10080	
			21420	
Balance of profits/losses shared:				
Orpa		12852		
Rafsan		8568		
			21420	

6% of $10000 = $600

6% of $8000 = $480

Profit for the year available to be shared between the partners = $21420

Profit sharing ratio = 3 : 2

Orpa: $\frac{3}{5}$ × $21420 = $12 852

Rafsan: $\frac{2}{5}$ × $21420 = $8 568

Capital account as at 30 June 2018

	Orpa $	Rafsan $		Orpa $	Rafsan $
Balance c/d	10000	8000	Balance b/d	10000	8000
	10000	8000		10000	8000
			Balance b/d	10000	8000

Current account as at 30 June 2018

	Orpa $	Rafsan $		Orpa $	Rafsan $
Balance b/d		3900	Balance b/d	2200	
Drawings	3500	6350	Interest on capital	600	480
Interest on drawings	0	0	Salaries	0	9000
Balance c/d	12152	7798	Share of profit	12852	8568
	15652	18048		15652	18048
			Balance b/d	12152	7798

Statement of financial position

A statement of financial position for a partnership is the same as that for a sole trader, with the exception of the **capital section.**

The capital section of the statement of financial position for a partnership must show the capital account and current account balances for each partner separately.

Worked example 5

Stefan, Ren and Camila are business partners running a local delicatessen.

They have prepared their year-end capital accounts and current accounts as at 30 April 2018.

Prepare an extract from the statement of financial position as at 30 April 2018.

Capital account as at 30 April 2018							
	Stefan	Ren	Camila		Stefan	Ren	Camila
	$	$	$		$	$	$
Balance c/d	15000	17000	19000	Balance b/d	15000	17000	19000
	15000	17000	19000		15000	17000	19000
				Balance b/d	15000	17000	19000

Current account as at 30 April 2018							
	Stefan	Ren	Camila		Stefan	Ren	Camila
	$	$	$		$	$	$
Balance b/d		1200		Balance b/d	1500		1900
Drawings	15000	11000	17000	Interest on capital	15000	17000	19000
Interest on drawings	550	530	710	Salaries		9500	
Balance c/d	20950	53770	63190	Share of profit	20000	40000	60000
	36500	66500	80900		36500	66500	80900
				Balance b/d	20950	53770	63190

Stefan, Ren and Camila Statement of financial position (extract) as at 30 April 2018				
	Stefan	Ren	Camila	Total
	$	$	$	$
Capital accounts	15000	17000	19000	51000
Current accounts	20950	53770	63190	137910
	35950	70770	82190	188910

Worked example 6

Yaka, Niloy and Shourav are professional photographers working in partnership.

Their partnership agreement states:

- Profits and losses will be shared in the ratio of 2 : 2 : 1 respectively
- Interest on capital is allowed at 4% per annum
- Yaka will receive a partnership salary of $15000 per annum. Niloy and Shourav will receive a partnership salary of $10000 each
- No interest is charged on drawings.

The following balances were extracted from the partnership's books of account on 30 September 2018.

	Dr	Cr
	$	$
Capital accounts:		
Yaka		30000
Niloy		30000
Shourav		20000
Current accounts:		
Yaka		1200
Niloy		850
Shourav	400	
Drawings:		
Yaka	20000	
Niloy	20000	
Shourav	14000	
Fees charged to customers		132000
Studio rent	4900	
Staff salaries	37000	
Administration expenses	24700	
Light and heat	14600	
Photography equipment	24000	
Provision for depreciation:		
Photography equipment		12000
Trade receivables	46500	
Trade payables		19300
Cash at bank	39250	
	245350	245350

The following information is available on 30 September 2018.

- Studio rent includes a prepayment of $300

- Administration expenses due and unpaid amount to $400

- Depreciation is provided on photography equipment at 25% per annum using the reducing balance method

- One debt of $1500 is to be treated as an irrecoverable debt due to bankruptcy

- A provision for doubtful debts is be created at 4% of the remaining trade receivables.

Prepare for Yaka, Niloy and Shourav an income statement for the year ended 30 September 2018 **and** a statement of financial position as at 30 September 2018.

Yaka, Niloy and Shourav Income statement and appropriation account for the year ended 30 September 2018			
	$	$	$
Fees charged to customers		132000	
			132000
Less expenses:			
Studio rent		4600	
Staff salaries		37000	
Administrative expenses		25100	

$4900 – $300 = $4600

$24700 + $400 = $25100

Light and heat				14 600		
Depreciation on photography equipment				3 000		
Irrecoverable debts				1 500		
Provision for doubtful debts				1 800		
					87 600	
Net profit					44 400	
Add interest charged on drawings:						
Yaka				0		
Niloy				0		
Shourav				0		
					0	
					44 400	
Less salaries:						
Yaka				15 000		
Niloy				10 000		
Shourav				10 000		
				35 000		
Less interest on capital:						
Yaka			1 200			
Niloy			1 200			
Shourav			800			
				3 200		
					38 200	
					6 200	
Balance of profits shared:						
Yaka (2/5)				2 480		
Niloy (2/5)				2 480		
Shourav (1/5)				1 240		
					6 200	

Current account							
	Yaka	Niloy	Shourav		Yaka	Niloy	Shourav
	$	$	$		$	$	$
Balance b/d			400	Balance b/d	1 200	850	
Drawings	20 000	20 000	14 000	Interest on capital	1 200	1 200	800
				Salaries	15 000	10 000	10 000
				Share of profit	2 480	2 480	1 240
				Balance c/d	120	5 470	2 360
	20 000	20 000	14 400		20 000	20 000	14 400
Balance b/d	120	5 470	2 360				

> Debit balances in the current account will become negative figures in the balance sheet as the partners owe money to the business.

Yaka, Niloy and Shourav			
Statement of financial position as at 30 September 2018			
	Cost	Depreciation	Net book value
	$	$	$
Non-current assets:			
Photography equipment	24000	15000	9000
	24000	15000	9000
Current assets:			
Trade receivables		45000	
Less provision for doubtful debts		1800	
		43200	
Other receivables (prepaid expenses)		300	
Bank		39250	
			82750
Total assets			91750
Capital:			
Capital account : Yaka		30000	
Capital account : Niloy		30000	
Capital account : Shourav		20000	80000
Current account : Yaka		(120)	
Current account : Niloy		(5470)	
Current account : Shourav		(2360)	(7950)
			72050
Current liabilities:			
Trade payables		19300	
Other payables (accrued expenses)		400	
			19700
Total liabilities			91750

Applying

Complete this task in pairs.

> **Project work**
>
> Hana and Anis are partners in a business that provides maintenance services to other businesses.
>
> The partners did not prepare a deed of partnership when the business was set up.
>
> Hana put in $40000 of capital and Anis provided $50000.

In the year ended 31 December 2017 the business made a net loss of $49 200.

During the year Hana withdrew $28 000 from the business and Anis took $23 000. The credit balances on their current accounts at the start of the year had been $24 600 for Hana and $28 600 for Anis.

1 Prepare an appropriation account for Hana and Anis.

2 Prepare the capital accounts for Hana and Anis.

3 Prepare the current accounts for Hana and Anis.

Knowledge check

1 Which of the following appear in the appropriation account of a partnership?

   A Drawings   **C** Interest on loans

   B Interest on drawings   **D** Purchases

2 Which item will appear in both a partnership appropriation account and a partners' current account?

   A Capital   **C** Drawings

   B Current account balances   **D** Interest on drawings

3 In a set of partnership accounts, no adjustment has been made for a prepayment of electricity. What is the effect of this omission?

   A Current liabilities overstated   **C** Profit for the year overstated

   B Current liabilities understated   **D** Profit for the year understated

4 Explain **three** advantages and **three** disadvantages of forming a partnership.

5 Identify **five** items that would appear in a partnership agreement.

6 Explain why it is important for partners to prepare a partnership agreement.

7 Explain the purpose of an appropriation account.

8 Discuss why partners may charge interest on the drawings that they take.

9 Define the term residual profit.

10 Explain why interest on capital is allowed in a partnership.

11 Explain what may have caused a debit balance on a partner's current account.

12 Anton, Basil and Emir are in partnership. Their financial year ends on 31 March 2018.

They have provided the following information from their books of account:

	Anton	Basil	Emir
	$	$	$
On 1 April 2017:			
Capital account	150000	170000	190000
Current account	1195 Cr	1930 Dr	1770 Cr
On 1 May 2018:			
Drawings	25000	21000	27000
Interest on drawings	450	330	510
Interest on capital	5000	7000	9000
Partners' salaries		19500	9550
Profit share	23000	33000	53000

Prepare the capital accounts and current accounts for all three partners.

13 Kwan and Samreen are partners in an accounting firm. They do not have a partnership agreement. Identify **five** details that will apply in the absence of a partnership agreement.

14 Sundeep and Mihai are in partnership running a car rental business. They share their profits and losses in the ratio of 2 : 1.

Interest is paid on capital invested at 5% per annum; however, no interest is charged on drawings.

Mihai is entitled to a salary of $20000 per annum.

The following balances remained in the books of the partnership after preparation of the partnership's income statement for the year ended 30 November 2018.

	$
Profit for the year	52950
Trade payables	5000
Cash in hand	1500
Provision for doubtful debts	3800
Capital account: Sundeep	30000
Capital account: Mihai	17000
Drawings: Sundeep	18100
Drawings: Mihai	28000
Non-current assets	50000
Provision for depreciation of non-current assets	32000
Other receivables (prepaid expenses)	7000
Accrued income	3500
Bank overdraft	17000
Loan repayable May 2019	7000
Current account: Sundeep	750 Cr
Current account: Mihai	300 Dr
Trade receivables	57100

Prepare Sundeep and Mihai's appropriation account for the year ended 30 November 2018 and the statement of financial position as at 30 November 2018.

15 Li and Piao are in partnership sharing profits and losses in the ratio 2:1. The balances on their capital accounts are $150 000 and $100 000, respectively. Li is entitled to a salary of $15 000. Drawings for the year are as follows:

Li $5500

Piao $3400.

Their current account balances are: Li $36 000 and Piao $18 000 (both in credit). Interest is allowed on capital at 5%.

During the year, Li wanted to reduce his role in the business, so it was decided that from 1 July 2016, Li would reduce his share of the profit to an equal share, and that he would no longer receive his salary. Operating profit for the full year ended 31 December 2018 was $68 000 and was earned evenly through the year

Prepare an appropriation account for the year ended 31 December 2018 for the partnership and the current accounts as at 31 December 2018.

Check your progress

Read the unit objectives below and reflect on your progress in each.

▲ (light)	I struggle with this and need more practice.
▲▲	I can do this reasonably well.
▲▲▲	I can do this with confidence.

- Explain the advantages and disadvantages of forming a partnership

- Outline the importance and contents of a partnership agreement

- Explain the purpose of an appropriation account

- Prepare income statements, appropriation accounts and statements of financial position

- Record interest on partners' loans, interest on capital, interest on drawings, partners' salaries and the division of the balance of profit or loss

- Make adjustments to financial statements as detailed in 5.1 (sole traders)

- Explain the uses of, and differences between, capital and current accounts

- Draw up partners' capital and current accounts in ledger account form and as part of a statement of financial position.

Limited companies

Learning objectives

By the end of this unit, you should be able to:

- explain the advantages and disadvantages of operating as a limited company
- understand the meaning of the term limited liability
- understand the meaning of the term equity
- understand the capital structure of a limited company comprising preference share capital, ordinary share capital, general reserve and retained earnings
- understand and distinguish between issued, called-up and paid-up share capital
- understand and distinguish between share capital (preference shares and ordinary shares) and loan capital (debentures)
- prepare income statements, statements of changes in equity and statements of financial position
- make adjustments to financial statements as detailed in Unit 5.1 (sole traders).

Starting point

Answer these questions in pairs.

1 Explain the difference between a sole trader and partnership.

2 Explain what is meant by the term unlimited liability.

3 Discuss the reasons for a sole trader taking a partner into their business.

Exploring

Discuss these questions in pairs.

1 Explain why a business owner may not want to invest in a business that has unlimited liability.

2 Explain why investors may purchase shares in large businesses.

3 Discuss the difference between ownership and management in a business.

Developing

Introduction

A limited company has a unique status in legal terms. Limited companies are **incorporated**, which means that they have their own legal identity and can sue and own assets in their own name.

Key term

Limited company: A business that has a separate legal identity from its shareholders.

Owners of a limited company hold shares in the company. The ownership of a limited company is divided into equal parts, each part is known as a **share**. The individuals that own one or more shares in a limited company are known as shareholders. The total value of the shares that have been issued by the limited company is known as equity.

A limited company can continue even if the business's management or shareholders die or become bankrupt.

As a limited company has its own legal identity, the shareholders (owners) of the limited company are not personally responsible for the debts of the business.

In the case where a company goes into liquidation or becomes bankrupt, the shareholders would not be asked to pay the debts. They would, however, lose the money that they have paid for their shares. If they had not paid in full for the shares that they owned they would be required to pay the balance.

Key terms

Limited liability: Shareholders of limited companies are not personally liable for the debts of the business.

Equity (of a limited company): The value of the shares issued by a limited company.

Key knowledge

Unlike a sole trader and partnerships:

- a limited company has limited liability
- the owners of a limited company may not be involved in the day-to-day running of the business. A board of directors runs the day-to-day activities of a limited company.

Types of limited company

There are two main types of limited company:

- Private limited company (Ltd) – usually smaller businesses that will sell shares to family and friends only. Their shares are not traded on the stock exchange.

- Public limited company (plc) – usually large businesses that offer their shares for sale on the stock exchange.

1 Identify **three** private limited companies and **three** public limited companies.

Setting up a limited company

When forming a limited company, two key documents have to be produced:

- **Memorandum of Association** – this states the business's name, address and main purpose. It also describes the liability and amount of equity invested.

- **Articles of Association** – this includes details of the internal workings of the limited company, for example:
  - the number of company directors to be appointed
  - the process to elect company directors
  - the role of the company directors
  - how profits will be shared and distributed as dividends to shareholders.

In addition to the accounting records that would be maintained by a sole trader or partnership, limited companies are required to publish their financial statements annually.

Key term

Stock exchange: A market where shares are bought and sold.

Discuss the benefits to a shareholder of having limited liability.

Advantages and disadvantages of operating as a limited company

Private limited companies

Advantages	Disadvantages
Easy and inexpensive to set up.	Lack of capital as no external share issue can be offered.
Ownership and control of the business are closely connected. For example, the board of directors are usually the main shareholders.	When compared to a public limited company, a private limited company will not benefit from economies of scale, for example bulk buying or cheaper loans.
Decisions can be taken more speedily than in a public limited company. A private limited company is smaller and less bureaucratic.	Has to comply with more legal requirements than sole traders and partnerships.

Public limited companies

Advantages	Disadvantages
Public limited companies have the ability to raise large amounts of capital via share issues.	Public limited companies that become too large may have issues with employee relations.
Benefit from economies of scale, due to their size, public limited companies are able to bulk buy products and employ specialist staff as required.	Conflicts of interest can occur between shareholders and the board of directors.
Due to their size, public limited companies are able to produce goods at lower unit costs.	There is a possibility of a takeover or merger as shares are freely available on the stock market.

 Explain how a shareholder of a limited company is rewarded for their investment.

Capital structure of a limited company

Share capital

A sole trader invests money into their business, known as capital or owner's equity. In a partnership, this capital is invested by the partners in the organisation. However, in a limited company the capital is invested by the shareholders. Each shareholder purchases shares in the company. Capital in a limited company is known as **share capital**.

When a limited company is formed, the total amount of its share capital is usually stated. This is known as authorised share capital. It is the maximum amount of share capital that the limited company is allowed to issue.

Limited companies may not issue all of the share capital that they are authorised to. They will issue the number of shares that are required to meet the capital needs of the business. This is known as issued share capital.

A limited company may not require all of the money due from its shares immediately. In this case, the limited company may allow shareholders to pay the amount they owe in instalments. The total amount of money that will be due to the limited company is known as called-up share capital. The amount of money that has actually been received by the limited company is known as the paid-up share capital.

Key terms

Authorised share capital: The maximum amount of share capital that can be issued by a limited company. It is stated in the Memorandum of Association.

Issued share capital: The amount of share capital that has actually been raised by the company by the sale of shares.

Called-up share capital: The total amount of money that will be due to a limited company from the issue of shares.

Paid-up share capital: The amount of money that has actually been received by a limited company from the issue of shares.

Worked example 1

Johansson Limited was formed by two brothers on 1 March 2017. The company produced a Memorandum of Association that stated it could issue 250 000 shares of $1.50 each. The company decided to offer 200 000 shares for sale at $1.50 each. The terms of the issue were:

50% of the amount due was to be paid immediately.

50% to be paid on 1 December 2017.

On 1 November 2017, the shareholders of 175 000 shares had paid the amount due.

State, for Johansson Limited:

1 The authorised share capital on 1 November 2017

2 The issued share capital on 1 November 2017

3 The called-up share capital on 1 November 2017

4 The paid-up share capital on 1 November 2017.

---

1 250 000 shares × $1.50 = **$375 000**

2 200 000 shares × $1.50 = **$300 000**

3 200 000 shares × $0.75 = **$150 000**

4 175 000 shares × $0.75 = **$131 250**

Types of share

There are two main types of share in a limited company:

- Preference shares
- Ordinary shares

Shareholders of preference shares	Shareholders of ordinary (equity) shares
receive a fixed percentage rate of dividend	receive a variable dividend each year or may not receive one at all
are not entitled to vote at a limited company's annual general meeting	are entitled to vote at shareholder meetings – one vote per share
receive their dividends before ordinary shareholders receive their dividends	receive their dividend payment after the preference shareholders have received their dividend payment
receive capital before ordinary shareholders in the event of the limited company going bankrupt	are the last people to receive their share capital in the event of the limited company going bankrupt

There are two main types of preference shares:

- Redeemable preference shares – these are preference shares which are repayable by the company at a specified future date. On this date, the shares are cancelled and the shareholders are repaid.

These shares have the characteristics of a debt. They are classified as a liability in the statement of financial position.

- Non-redeemable preference shares – these are preference shares that are not redeemable. They remain in existence indefinitely. These shares are classified as equity in the statement of financial position.

4 Identify **two** benefits of holding preference shares rather than ordinary (equity) shares.

The shares of a limited company have a par value, for example, $0.5, $1, $5. A limited company may decide to sell its shares for a value in excess of the par value. The extra amount charged for the shares is known as share premium.

The shareholders of a limited company are only liable for the debts of the business up to the amount that they have agreed to pay for their shares.

Annual profits and losses belong to the company and not to the owners. The shareholders will be paid dividends out of the profits that the company has made. A proportion of the annual profit is retained for use within the company.

The dividend due to each shareholder is often stated as a percentage of the face value of the shares.

There are two types of dividend: interim and final.

- Interim dividends are declared by the board of directors.

- The board of directors propose final dividends for shareholders. The shareholders have the opportunity to vote on whether to accept them at the company's annual general meeting.

- Interim dividends are declared before the company has prepared its financial statements.

- Final dividends are only declared once the financial statements have been prepared and profit for the year calculated.

- Interim dividends relate to a part year (usually six months), while final dividends apply to a full year.

Key terms

Par value: The issue price of the shares. This is also called the nominal value of the shares.

Share premium: The difference between the par value and the sale price of the share.

Worked example 2

Meyvesi Limited has the following capital structure:

300 000 ordinary shares of $3 each.

Shareholders will receive a dividend of 5%.

1   Calculate the total amount Meyvesi Limited will need to pay in dividends.

2   Calculate the amount payable per share.

---

1   Value of shares = 300 000 × $3 = $900 000

    Total amount to pay in dividends = $900 000 × 5% = **$45 000**

2   Dividend = 5% of $3 = $0.15 per share

An alternative way to calculate this is:

Dividend per share
= $45 000 ÷ 300 000 = $0.15

Debentures

Debentures provide an alternative method of financing a business instead of an issue of ordinary shares. They are long-term loan capital and increase the debt capital of the company. Debenture holders receive a fixed rate of interest and the amount borrowed is charged on the assets of the company. This means that in the event that a business fails to repay the debenture in accordance with the terms agreed, the assets of the company would be used to settle the debt.

A debenture is one of the most common forms of long-term loan that a limited company takes. Sole traders and partnerships are not able to raise finance from debentures. Debenture holders are paid a fixed interest rate and need to be repaid on a specific date.

Debentures are higher risk than offering ordinary shares as the debenture interest must be paid regardless of the profitability of the company. The debenture interest is an expense in the income statement of the limited company. In contrast, ordinary share dividends are only paid if there is sufficient profit. Debenture holders do not have voting rights, unlike ordinary shareholders.

Key knowledge

- Debenture holders are liabilities of a company. They are not owners and do not have any voting rights.
- Debenture interest must be paid regardless of whether the company has made a profit or a loss.
- Debenture interest is paid at a fixed rate.
- Debentures due to be repaid within one financial year are recorded as current liabilities.
- Debentures due to be repaid after one financial year are recorded as non-current liabilities.
- In the event that a limited company is closed down, debenture holders receive their money before shareholders.

Ordinary Shares	Debentures
Owners	Liability (loan)
More speculative	Less speculative
Right to vote	No voting rights
No guaranteed dividend	Fixed rate of interest
Can be held long term	Redemption date

Reserves

A limited company rarely distributes all of its profit to its shareholders. It will usually keep part of the profit earned each year in the form of reserves. This allows the business to use the retained profit for other purposes within the business.

Even if a limited company would like to distribute all of the profit it has available to its shareholders, it is very unlikely that there would be sufficient cash available in the business to pay the dividends.

Any profit that is remaining after preparing a statement of changes of equity is carried forward to the next financial year. This profit is known as retained profit or retained earnings. Retained earnings remains as a balance in the statement of changes of equity section of the company's income statement and is carried forward to the next financial year to fund business plans. This figure appears in the statement of financial position as part of share capital and reserves.

General reserve

In addition to leaving a balance of undistributed profit in the income statement, many companies will transfer an amount to a general reserve. This is another way of keeping profit in the company to help fund both known and unknown future obligations. The general reserve can be used to pay dividends to company shareholders.

Income statement

The income statement of a limited company is prepared in the same way as for a sole trader or partnership.

Name of the limited company	
Income statement for the year ended	
	$
Revenue	X
Cost of sales	(x)
Gross profit	X
Distribution costs	(x)
Administrative expenses	(x)
Profit from operations	X
Finance income	X
Finance costs	(x)
Profit for the year	X

Key terms

Retained earnings: This is the profit that is not appropriated (used) to pay shareholder dividends and forms part of the company's share capital and reserves.

General reserve: A reserve created for general purposes in the future. It forms part of the capital of the company.

Key knowledge

Limited companies need to prepare a statement of changes in equity to show how they use their profit for the year. There are detailed legal regulations for public limited companies; however, these are beyond the scope of this course.

In Unit 5.2, you learned how to prepare an income statement and appropriation account for a partnership business. This showed how the profit or loss is divided between the partners. In a similar way, a limited company must prepare a statement to show how its profit for the year is being used. For a company, this is known as a statement of changes in equity. This is added at the end of the income statement to complete the financial statement for a limited company.

Statement of changes in equity

A limited company prepares a statement of changes in equity to show the movements during a financial year.

The following is an exemplar template for a statement of changes in equity.

	Name of the company				
	Statement of changes in equity for the year ended				
	Ordinary share capital	Preference share capital	General reserve	Retained earnings	Total
	$	$	$	$	$
Opening balance	X	X	X	X	X
Profit for the year				X	X
Dividend paid				(X)	(X)
Transfer to general reserve			X	(X)	-
Share issue	X	X			X
Closing balance	X	X	X	X	X

Statement of financial position

A statement of financial position for a company has a similar layout to that for a sole trader or partnership. However, alterations need to be made to include items that do not feature in unincorporated businesses. For example, debentures will be included as non-current liabilities and the capital and reserves section needs to include ordinary shares, preference shares and retained earnings.

The following is an exemplar template for a statement of financial position for a limited company.

	Name of the company	
	Statement of financial position as at	
		$
		Net book value
Non-current assets		
Premises		X
Fixtures and fittings		X
Equipment		X
Motor van		X
		X
Current assets		
Inventory	X	
Trade receivables	X	
	X	
	X	
Cash and cash equivalents	X	
Accrued income	X	

Name of the company		
Statement of financial position as at		
Other receivables (prepaid expenses)	X	
		X
Total assets		X
Capital and reserves		
Ordinary share capital		X
% Non-redeemable preference share capital		X
General reserve		X
Retained earnings		X
		X
Non-current liabilities		
% Debentures (year)		X
% Redeemable preference share capital		X
		X
Current liabilities		
Trade payables		X
Bank overdraft and loans		X
Other payables (accrued expenses)		X
Prepaid income		X
		X
Total liabilities		X

Worked example 3

Bungee Jumps Ltd formed the company on 1 January 2016.

The company issued 100000 ordinary shares of $1 each and 50000 7% non-redeemable preference shares of $1 each.

The company has provided the following information:

Profit for the first two years of the business was:

Year ended 31 December 2016 $30800

Year ended 31 December 2017 $43800

Finance costs amounted to:

Year ended 31 December 2016 $10400

Year ended 31 December 2017 $12600

Transfers to general reserve totalled:

Year ended 31 December 2016 $2000

Year ended 31 December 2017 $6000

The full amount of dividend due to preference shareholders was paid in 2016 and 2017.

Ordinary shareholders received a dividend of 4% in 2016 and 5% in 2017.

Prepare:

1 An extract from the income statement, to calculate retained profit carried forward for the years ended 31 December 2016 and 31 December 2017.

2 An extract from the statement of financial position to show the company's equity as at 31 December 2016 and 31 December 2017.

3 A statement of changes in equity for the years ended 31 December 2016 and 31 December 2017.

Bungee Jumps Ltd	
Income statement (extract) for the year ended 31 December 2016	
	$
Profit from operations	30800
Other operating income	0
Finance costs	10 400
Profit for the year	20 400
Dividends	(7 500)
Transfer to general reserve	(2 000)
Retained earnings	10900
Retained profit brought forward	0
Retained profit carried forward	10900

Preference share dividends
= 7% of $50 000 = $3500

Ordinary share dividends
= 4% of $100 000 = $4000

Total dividends
= $3500 + $4000 = $7500

Bungee Jumps Ltd	
Income statement (extract) for the year ended 31 December 2017	
	$
Profit from operations	43 800
Other operating income	0
Finance costs	12 600
Profit for the year	31 200
Dividends	(8500)
Transfer to general reserve	(6000)
Retained earnings	16 700
Retained profit brought forward	10 900
Retained profit carried forward	27 600

Preference share dividends
= 7% of $50 000 = $3500

Ordinary share dividends
= 5% of $100 000 = $5000

Total dividends
= $3500 + $5000 = $8500

Bungee Jumps Ltd	
Statement of financial position (extract) as at 31 December 2016	
Capital and reserves	$
Ordinary share capital (100 000 $1 shares)	100 000
Preference share capital (50 000 7% non-redeemable preference shares $1)	50 000
General reserve	2000
Retained earnings	10 900
	162 900

From the statement of changes of equity.

Bungee Jumps Ltd	
Statement of financial position as at 31 December 2017	
Capital and reserves	$
Ordinary share capital (100 000 $1 shares)	100 000
Preference share capital (50 000 7% non-redeemable preference shares $1)	50 000
General reserve	8000
Retained earnings	27 600
	185 600

General reserve = $2000 from the year ended 2016 + $6000 from the year ended 2017

From the statement of changes of equity.

$10 900 from the year ended 2016 + $16 700 from the year ended 2017

Bungee Jumps Ltd Statement of changes in equity for the year ended 31 December 2016					
	Ordinary share capital	Preference share capital	General reserve	Retained earnings	Total
	$	$	$	$	$
Opening balance	100000	50000	0	0	150000
Profit for the year				20400	20400
Dividend paid				(7500)	(7500)
Transfer to general reserve			2000	(2000)	
Share issue	0	0			
Closing balance	100000	50000	2000	10900	162900

Bungee Jumps Ltd Statement of changes in equity for the year ended 31 December 2017					
	Ordinary share capital	Preference share capital	General reserve	Retained earnings	Total
	$	$	$	$	$
Opening balance	100000	50000	2000	10900	162900
Profit for the year				31200	31200
Dividend paid				(8500)	(8500)
Transfer to general reserve			6000	(6000)	–
Share issue	0	0			0
Closing balance	100000	50000	8000	27600	185600

Worked example 4

At 1 February 2017, Kirov Ltd had the following shares and debentures:

250000 ordinary shares of $0.50 each

100000 8% preference shares of $1 each

$50000 6% debentures (2022)

The following balances were extracted from the books on 31 January 2018.

	$
Retained earnings	130000
Equipment (at book value)	368000
Motor vehicles (at book value)	174000
Trade payables	186000
Trade receivables	114000
Inventory	126000
Cash at bank	4000 Dr
Long-term bank loan (5%) taken out in 2016	195000

Prepare the statement of financial position as at 31 January 2018.

Kirov Ltd	
Statement of financial position as at 31 January 2018	
	$
Non-current assets	
Equipment	368 000
Motor vehicles	174 000
	542 000
Current assets	
Inventory	126 000
Trade receivables	114 000
Cash at bank	4 000
	244 000
Total assets	786 000
Capital and reserves	
Ordinary share capital	125 000
8% preference share capital	100 000
Retained earnings	130 000
	355 000
Non-current liabilities	
6% debentures (2022)	50 000
Bank loan	195 000
	245 000
Current liabilities	
Trade payables	186 000
Total liabilities	786 000

Worked example 5

The following information is also available for Kirov Limited.

- Retained earnings at 1 February 2017 were $55 500
- The interim ordinary dividend paid during the year was $0.04 per share
- All preference dividends were paid.

For the year ended 31 January 2018, calculate the:

(a) Profit for the year

(b) Profit before interest.

(a)

	$
Retained profit as at 31 January 2018	130000
Retained profit as at 1 February 2017	55500
	74500
Add back:	
Ordinary share dividend	10000
Preference share dividend	8000
Profit for the year	**92500**

(b)

	$
Profit for the year	92500
Add back:	
Bank loan interest	9750
Debenture interest	3000
Profit before interest	**105250**

Applying

Complete this task in pairs.

Task

Flower Power Florists Limited expanded during the late 2000s as a result of various acquisitions and mergers.

The following information has been provided for Flower Power Florists Limited for the year ended 30 April 2018.

	$m
Non-current assets	482.25
Inventory	186.3
Trade receivables	72.7
Short-term investments	1.95
Cash at bank	119.15
Trade payables	327.75
Loan repayable December 2018	12.4
Loan repayable 2021	164.4
Called-up share capital	82.3
General reserve	167.65
Profit and loss account	107.95

1   Prepare a statement of financial position for Flower Power Florists Limited for the year ended 30 April 2018.

2   Identify and describe three possible examples of non-current assets for Flower Power Florists Limited.

Knowledge check

1   Which of the following is an appropriation of profit on the income statement of a limited company?

A   Transfer to general reserve
B   Interest on drawings
C   Interest on loans
D   Administration expenses

2   In which section of the statement of financial position would a debenture be recorded?

A   Current assets
B   Current liabilities
C   Non-current assets
D   Non-current liabilities

3   Shares which are repayable by a company at a specified future date, when the shares are cancelled, are known as

A   Redeemable ordinary shares
B   Non-redeemable ordinary shares
C   Redeemable preference shares
D   Non-redeemable preference shares

4   Explain **three** advantages and **three** disadvantages of forming a public limited company.

5   Explain the difference between ordinary and preference shares.

6   Describe how a debenture is used by a limited company.

7   Explain the meaning of the term equity in relation to a limited company.

8   Differentiate between issued, called-up and paid-up share capital.

9   Define the term limited liability.

10 Explain the advantages to a business owner of having limited liability.

11 Explain the meaning of the terms general reserve and retained earnings.

12 Polish Bakers Limited has the following capital structure:

500000 ordinary shares of $2.50 each.

Shareholders will receive a dividend of 10%.

(a) Calculate the total amount Polish Bakers Limited will need to pay in dividends.
(b) Calculate the amount payable per share.

13 Maclean Limited was founded on 1 March 2018. The company prepared a Memorandum of Association that stated it could issue 550000 shares of $2 each. The company decided to offer 500000 shares for sale at $2 each. The terms of the issue were:

50% of the amount due was to be paid immediately

50% to be paid on 1 December 2018.

On 1 November 2018, the shareholders of 475000 shares had paid the amount due.

State, for Maclean Limited:

(a) the authorised share capital on 1 November 2018

(b) the issued share capital on 1 November 2018

(c) the called-up share capital on 1 November 2018

(d) the paid-up share capital on 1 November 2018.

14 Ahmed Ltd was formed on 1 January 2017.

The company issued 100000 ordinary shares of $1 each and 50000 7% non-redeemable preference shares of $1 each.

The company has provided the following information:

(a) Profit for the year for the year ended 31 December 2017 $87600

(b) Finance costs for the year ended to 31 December 2017 $25200

(c) Transfers to general reserve for the year ended 31 December 2017 $12000

The full amount of dividend due to preference shareholders was paid in 2017.

Ordinary shareholders received a dividend of 5% in 2017.

Prepare an extract from the statement of financial position to show the company's equity as at 31 December 2017.

15 Tiga Stadium Supplies Ltd provides football equipment to professional football clubs around the world. The company has provided the following information for the year ended 30 April 2018.

	$ 000s
Non-current assets	1446.75
Inventory	558.90
Trade receivables	218.10
Short-term investments	5.85
Cash at bank	357.75
Trade payables	983.25
Loan repayable December 2018	37.20
Loan repayable 2021	493.20
Called-up share capital	246.90
General reserve	502.95
Profit and loss account	323.85

Prepare a statement of financial position for Tiga Stadium Supplies Ltd for the year ended 30 April 2018.

Check your progress

Read the unit objectives below and reflect on your progress in each.

▲ I struggle with this and need more practice.

▲ I can do this reasonably well.

▲ I can do this with confidence.

- Explain the advantages and disadvantages of operating as a limited company

- Understand the meaning of the term limited liability

- Understand the meaning of the term equity

- Understand the capital structure of a limited company comprising preference share capital, ordinary share capital, general reserve and retained earnings

- Understand and distinguish between issued, called-up and paid-up share capital

- Understand and distinguish between share capital (preference shares and ordinary shares) and loan capital (debentures)

- Prepare income statements, statements of changes in equity and statements of financial position

- Make adjustments to financial statements as detailed in Unit 5.1 (sole traders).

Clubs and societies

Learning objectives
By the end of this unit, you should be able to:
- distinguish between receipts and payments accounts and income and expenditure accounts
- prepare receipts and payments accounts
- prepare accounts for revenue-generating activities, for example refreshments, subscriptions
- prepare income and expenditure accounts and statements of financial position
- make adjustments to financial statements as detailed in Unit 5.1 (sole traders)
- define and calculate the accumulated fund.

Starting point

Answer these questions in pairs.

1 Explain how irrecoverable debts are treated in the financial statements of a business.

2 Identify five expenses that would need to be paid when operating a small café.

3 Describe how an accrual of income is accounted for in a statement of financial position.

Exploring

Discuss these questions in pairs.

1 Discuss why some organisations do not operate with the intention of making a profit.

2 Identify three clubs and societies in your local area. Discuss what services each of these offer to their members.

3 Choose a charity that exists in your local area. Consider how this charity raises the money it uses to provide its services.

Developing

Non-profit-making organisations

Many businesses have the main aim of making a profit. Non-profit-making organisations (third sector organisations) exist to provide services to their members or to promote a 'good cause'.

Examples include:

- clubs
- societies
- charities

① List **five** non-profit-making organisations that exist in your local area.

Key knowledge

Non-profit-making organisations receive income in the form of:

- subscriptions or membership fees
- donations
- life memberships
- grants
- revenue received from activities, for example sale of refreshments, equipment
- money received from events, for example raffles, fairs, car boot sales.

The income generated by the non-profit-making organisation needs to be used to pay the running expenses of the organisation. These may include rent, staff wages, advertising.

② Identify the expenses that may need to be paid by a local sports club.

Clubs and societies are run by a committee. A treasurer will be elected by the committee to prepare the financial records of the organisation. Charities often call members of their committee 'Trustees'. These are usually unpaid roles but may be reimbursed their expenses. The type of annual accounts prepared by the non-profit-making organisation will vary depending on its size.

The treasurer of a non-profit-making organisation prepares annual financial statements that are presented to the members.

Depending on the activities of the organisation, the financial statements may include:

- receipts and payments account
- income statement (also known as a trading account)
- subscriptions account
- income and expenditure account
- statement of financial position.

Key term

Non-profit-making organisation: An organisation formed by groups of individuals to pursue a common not-for-profit goal. They exist with the intention of distributing their revenue to achieve their purpose or mission.

Receipts and payments account

A receipts and payments account is a summarised cash book. The account applies double entry procedures:

- The debit side of the receipts and payments account details the **money received by** the organisation.

- The credit side of the receipts and payments account details the **money paid out by** the organisation.

- The balance carried down at the end of the period is transferred to the next financial period.

- A **debit** balance represents money that is owned by the organisation and is recorded as an **asset** in the statement of financial position.

- A **credit** balance represents money that is owed by the organisation and is recorded as a **liability** in the statement of financial position. This is also known as an overdrawn balance.

Key knowledge

Receipts and payments accounts do not:

- account for accruals and prepayments

- include any non-cash transactions, for example depreciation

- differentiate between capital and revenue income and expenditure.

Clubs and societies will prepare receipts and payments accounts at the end of each financial period. The following shows the format for a receipts and payments account. Please note that the items included in the format are examples only.

Receipts and payments account					
Date	Narrative	$	Date	Narrative	$
	Balance b/d (opening bank balance)	x		Purchase of new equipment	x
	Subscriptions	x		Officials' expenses	x
	Refreshment sales	x		Travelling expenses	x
	Dinner dance tickets	x		Purchase of refreshment investments	x
				Event expenses	x
				Dinner dance expenses	x
				Rates and insurance	x
				General expenses	x
				Refreshment staff wages	x
				Balance c/d	x
		<u>xx</u>			<u>xx</u>
	Balance b/d	x			

Worked example 1

Huncoat bowling club was formed in 1949 to provide sporting and social facilities to its members. The club has a café that provides refreshments and a shop that sells sports equipment.

On 1 March 2017, the club had $5250 in its bank account.

For the year ended 28 February 2018, the treasurer provided the following list of receipts and payments:

	$
Subscriptions received	17 520
Revenue from sales of sports equipment	2 250
Café revenue	1 870
Purchases of sports equipment for resale	920
Wages – bowling coach	1 500
Wages – sales assistant	750
Wages – café staff	3 500
Rent and rates	1 210
Heat and light	2 575
General expenses	1 355
Purchase of sports equipment	5 650
National bowling competition: entrance fees received	3 375
National bowling competition: cost of prizes	995

All of the receipts were paid into the bank account and all payments were made by cheque.

Prepare the receipts and payments account of Huncoat bowling club for the year ended 28 February 2018.

Receipts and payments account			
	$		$
Balance b/d	5 250	Purchases of sports equipment for resale	920
Subscriptions received	17 520	Wages – bowling coach	1 500
Revenue from sales of sports equipment	2 250	Wages – sales assistant	750
Café revenue	1 870	Wages – café staff	3 500
National bowling competition: entrance fees received	3 375	Rent and rates	1 210
		Heat and light	2 575
		General expenses	1 355
		Purchase of sports equipment	5 650
		National bowling competition: cost of prizes	995
		Balance c/d	11 810
	30 265		30 265
Balance b/d	11 810		

Opening bank balance for the year commencing 1 March 2018

Revenue-generating activities

Non-profit-making organisations raise most of their income from subscriptions or membership fees paid to the organisation.

Subscriptions received need to be adjusted in accordance with the matching principle to calculate the amount to be included in the financial statements.

The subscriptions total needs to be adjusted for members who have not paid their subscriptions on time or have paid in advance for their membership.

The production of a **subscriptions account** allows the club or society to adjust the amount received for prepayments and accruals at both the start and end of the financial period.

Clubs and societies prepare a subscriptions account at the end of each financial period. This calculates the amount of subscriptions to be included in the income and expenditure account.

Subscriptions			
	$		$
Balance b/d (accrued)	X	Balance b/d (prepaid)	X
Income and expenditure account	X	Bank/cash	X
		Irrecoverable debts	X
Balance c/d (prepaid)	X	Balance c/d (accrued)	X
	X		X
Balance b/d	X	Balance b/d	X

Balance to be transferred to the income and expenditure account.

Worked example 2

Azerbaijan sports club has provided the following information relating to its subscriptions for the year ended 31 March 2018.

	Balances as at 1 April 2017	Balances as at 31 March 2018
	$	$
Subscriptions in arrears	50	20
Subscriptions paid in advance	30	70

During the year, the sports club received $522 in subscriptions.

Prepare a subscriptions account for the Isle of Mull sports club for the year ended 31 March 2018.

Subscriptions account as at 31 March 2018			
	$		$
Balance b/d (accrued)	50	Balance b/d (prepaid)	30
Income and expenditure account	**452**	Bank/cash	522
Balance c/d (prepaid)	70	Balance c/d (accrued)	20
	572		572
Balance b/d	20	Balance b/d	70

Missing figure: $572 – $50 – $70 = $452

Worked example 3

Mountain and Hill Walking society has provided the following information relating to its subscriptions for the year ended 30 April 2018.

	Balances as at 1 May 2017	Balances as at 30 April 2018
	$	$
Subscriptions in arrears	120	250
Subscriptions paid in advance	350	500

During the year, the Mountain and Hill Walking society received $3595 in respect of subscriptions.

The society has been informed that $100 owing at 1 May 2017 will not be recovered. The amount is to be treated as an irrecoverable debt.

Prepare a subscriptions account for the Mountain and Hill Walking society for the year ended 30 April 2018.

Subscriptions account as at 30 April 2018			
	$		$
Balance b/d (accrued)	120	Balance b/d (prepaid)	350
Income and expenditure account	**3675**	Bank/cash	3595
		Irrecoverable debts	100
Balance c/d (prepaid)	500	Balance c/d (accrued)	250
	4295		4295
Balance b/d	250	Balance b/d	500

Missing figure: $4295 – $120 – $500 = $3675

 3 Explain the benefits to a non-profit-making organisation of members prepaying their subscriptions.

Life membership schemes

A number of organisations have a system of life membership. This system allows a new member to pay a substantial one-off fee for use of all of the organisation's facilities for the remainder of their life. No further money is paid.

These payments are accounted for using the matching principle. The money received from the member is not all placed into the accounts in the year in which it has been received. Instead it is split into equal annual instalments and entered into the income and expenditure account. The organisation will decide over how many years to spread the life membership payment.

CASE STUDY

Baxenden golf club is a private members golf club. Members have access to an eighteen-hole golf course and use of the club house.

Due to the economic recession, the number of club members has decreased. This has made it increasingly difficult to meet the costs required to maintain and develop the golf course.

The committee decided to open up a life membership scheme asking members for a lump sum payment to allow the course to be redesigned. The club would like to bid to host a professional golf tournament but the course doesn't currently meet the requirements.

In return for the lump sum payment, the members received life membership to the club. This allows them to use the facilities of the golf club for the remainder of their lives.

Donations

Donations received during the financial year will be included as income in the year that they are received. They will be included in the income and expenditure account.

Fund-raising and trading activities

Non-profit-making organisations also use other fund-raising and trading activities to increase their annual income. Examples include:

- raffles
- social events
- refreshment sales, for example a coffee shop
- trading activity, for example sales of fishing equipment at a fishing club.

Key knowledge

Usual accounting practice is to include net proceeds from fund-raising events in the income and expenditure account.

Where a club or society has a trading part to its association, an income statement will be required. The profit or loss made during the period is transferred to the income and expenditure account.

The income statement of a non-profit-making organisation is prepared in the same way as for a sole trader or other trading business. Expenses that directly relate to the running of the trading organisation are deducted from the gross profit to calculate the profit on the trading activity that will be transferred to the income and expenditure account.

Worked example 4

Powerplay computer games club operates a shop selling computer games for its members.

Prepare an income statement for Powerplay computer games club shop for the year ended 31 December 2018 based on the following financial information.

	$
Computer games club shop takings	15955
Payments to computer games club shop suppliers	7525
Computer games club shop staff wages	3200

	Balance as at 1 January 2018	Balance as at 31 December 2018
	$	$
Computer games inventory	2750	1995

Powerplay computer games club shop Income statement for the year ended 31 December 2018		
	$	$
Revenue		15955
Less cost of sales		
Opening inventory	2750	
Purchases	7525	
	10275	
Closing inventory	1995	
Cost of sales		8280
Gross profit		7675
Less expenses		
Computer games club shop staff wages	3200	
		3200
Profit for the year		4475

Worked example 5

Springtime gardening club operates an organic food store for its members.

Prepare an income statement for the food store for the year ended 31 July 2018 based on the following information:

	$
Food store takings	3865
Payments to food store providers	1563
Food store wages	1100

	Balances as at 1 August 2017	Balances as at 31 July 2018
	$	$
Food store trade payables	352	277
Food store inventories	190	97

Springtime gardening club organic food store Income statement for the year ended 31 July 2018		
	$	$
Revenue		3865
Less cost of sales		
Opening inventory	190	
Purchases	1488	
	1678	
Closing inventory	97	
Cost of sales		1581
Gross profit		2284
Less expenses		
Food store wages	1100	
		1100
Profit for the year		1184

The purchases figure is calculated based on the payments to food store providers and then adjusted for the amount owing at the start and end of the financial year.

$1563 + $277 – $352 = $1488

Income and expenditure account

An income and expenditure account is the equivalent of a profit-making organisation's income statement. It includes non-cash transactions and adjustments made in accordance with the matching principle and for other items, for example irrecoverable debts and depreciation.

Total expenditure is subtracted from total income. If income is greater than expenditure then the organisation will make a **surplus**. However, if expenditure exceeds income, the organisation will make a **deficit**.

The following shows the format for a club or society's income and expenditure account. Please note that the items included in the format are examples only.

Name of club or society		
Income and expenditure account for the year ended		
	$	$
Income		
Profit from income statement	x	
Profit on events	x	
Subscriptions	x	
Life subscriptions	x	
		x
Expenditure		
Loss from income statement	x	
Loss on events	x	
Officials' expenses	x	
Travelling expenses	x	
Rates and insurance	x	
General expenses	x	
Loss on sale of equipment	x	
Depreciation	x	
		(x)
Surplus or deficit		x

From the subscriptions account

For working out the profit or loss

Statement of financial position

Non-profit-making organisations with a significant number of non-current assets need to include these in a statement of financial position.

> ### Key knowledge
>
> The format of the statement of financial position is similar to that for a sole trader.
>
> However, capital is replaced with **accumulated fund**.
>
> Instead of profit or loss, surplus or deficit is used in the statement of financial position.

Key term

Accumulated fund: Represents the difference in value between the assets and liabilities of the organisation.

Worked example 6

Mosslands watersports club has provided the following details of its assets and liabilities at 1 January 2017.

	$
Bank	6300 Dr
Motor van at valuation	4000
Subscriptions outstanding	500
Rent owing	100

The treasurer of the club has provided the following information about the receipts and payments for the year ended 31 December 2017.

	$
Receipts	
Subscriptions	21300
Proceeds of sale of motor van	3500
Competition entrance fees	1600
Payments	
Purchase of new motor van	20000
Competition prizes	420
General expenses	5290
Travelling expenses	1660
Rent	5200

The following information is also available:

1 The motor van is used to transport the water sports equipment to various tournaments and competitions.

The motor van owned on 1 January 2017 was sold in March 2017.

No depreciation is provided in the year of sale.

On the same day, a new motor van was purchased. At 31 December 2017, this motor van was valued at $17000.

2 On 31 December 2017:

- Members subscriptions paid in advance amounted to $800
- Rent prepaid amounted to $200.

(a) Prepare the income and expenditure account of Mosslands watersports club for the year ended 31 December 2017.

(b) Prepare the statement of financial position for Mosslands watersports club at 31 December 2017.

(a) Subscriptions workings:

Subscriptions			
	$		$
Balance b/d (accrued)	500	Bank/cash	21300
Income and expenditure account	20000		
Balance c/d (prepaid)	800		
	21300		21300
		Balance b/d	800

Mosslands watersports club		
Income and expenditure account for the year ended 31 December 2017		
	$	$
Income		
Subscriptions	20000	
Competition income	<u>1180</u>	
		21180
Expenditure		
General expenses	5290	
Travelling expenses	1660	
Rent	4900	
Loss on sale of motor van	500	
Depreciation of motor van	<u>3000</u>	
		15350
Surplus for the year		<u>**5830**</u>

Competition fees less cost of prizes = $1600 − $420 = $1180

$5200 − $100 − $200 = $4900

$4000 − $3500 = $500

$20000 − $17000 = $3000

b)

Mosslands watersports club			
Statement of financial position as at 31 December 2017			
	$	$	$
	Cost	Depreciation	Net book value
Non-current assets			
Motor van	20000	3000	17000
	20000	3000	17000
Current assets			
Bank		130	
Other receivables (rent)		<u>200</u>	
			330
Total assets			<u>17330</u>
Accumulated fund			10700
Add surplus for the year			<u>5830</u>
			16530
Current liabilities			
Subscriptions prepaid		800	
			800
Total liabilities			<u>17330</u>

Bank balance + total receipts − total payments = $6300 + $26400 − $32570 = $130

Key differences between the accounting records of profit-making and non-profit-making organisations

Profit-making organisations	Non-profit-making organisations
Income statement	Income and expenditure account
Capital	Accumulated fund
Profit	Surplus
Loss	Deficit
Cash book	Receipts and payments account

Applying

Complete this task in pairs.

Task

The Traditional theatre group was formed 20 years ago. Currently it has 80 members.

On 1 March 2017, the Traditional theatre group had the following assets:

	$
Theatre props and equipment (book value)	400
Cash at bank	4420
Subscriptions due from members	2000
Prepayment of rent	560

The treasurer provided the following information relating to the year ended 28 February 2018.

All receipts were paid into the bank account and all payments were made by cheque.

	$
Subscriptions received from members:	
For the year ended 28 February 2017	2000
For the year ended 28 February 2018	4000
For the year ending 28 February 2019	800
Receipts from theatre performances	3800
Theatre performance expenses	2500
Rent of premises	
For the year ended 28 February 2018	2800
For the year ending 28 February 2019	840
General expenses	430
Insurance	650
Proceeds of sale of theatre props and equipment	1400
Purchase of new theatre props and equipment	6700

1   Prepare the income and expenditure account of the Traditional theatre group for the year ended 28 February 2018.

2   Prepare the statement of financial position for the Traditional theatre group as at 28 February 2018.

Knowledge check

1   Which of the following will appear in a receipts and payments account?

   A   Accrued income   C   Depreciation
   B   Bank balance   D   Other receivables

2   Which of the following will appear as a current liability in a statement of financial position for a club or society?

   A   Subscriptions due and unpaid   C   Subscriptions paid in advance
   B   Subscriptions irrecoverable   D   Subscriptions received

3 What is the equivalent of an income statement for a club or society?

    A Accumulated fund account   **C** Receipts and payments account

    B Income and expenditure account   **D** Statement of financial position

4 Define the term accumulated fund.

5 Explain the difference between a receipts and payments account and an income and expenditure account.

6 Describe how an accrual of income is treated in a club's statement of financial position.

7 Explain how an association accounts for an expense that has been paid in advance in its annual accounts.

8 Snow Island ski club has provided the following information relating to its subscriptions for the year ended 30 September 2018.

	Balances as at 1 October 2017	Balances as at 30 September 2018
	$	$
Subscriptions in arrears	320	350
Subscriptions paid in advance	550	510

During the year, the Snow Island ski club received $6795 in respect of subscriptions.

The society has been informed that $210 owing at 1 October 2017 will not be recovered. The amount is to be treated as an irrecoverable debt.

Prepare a subscriptions account for Snow Island ski club.

9 Western organic food association provides refreshments and has a shop that sells organic food.

On 1 March 2017, the association had $7250 in its bank account.

For the year ended 28 February 2018, the treasurer provided the following list of receipts and payments:

	$
Subscriptions received	19855
Revenue from sales of organic food	12375
Café revenue	6250
Purchases of gardening equipment for resale	3150
Wages – sales assistant	2770
Wages – café staff	3158
Rent and rates	2579
Heat and light	1235
General expenses	795
Purchase of gardening equipment	1650
Entrance fees received	978
Cost of prizes	357

All of the receipts were paid into the bank account and all payments were made by cheque.

Prepare the receipts and payments account of Western organic food association for the year ended 28 February 2018.

10 The following information is available for Birkdale Snooker Club for the year ended
31 December 2018.

Assets and liabilities	1 Jan 2018	31 Dec 2018
	$	$
Sports equipment	3500	6850
Snack bar inventory	87	95
Payables on snack bar	225	118
Subscriptions owing	32	56
Subscriptions received in advance	27	22
Bank	295	(43)
Cash	76	55
Bank loan	–	4000

The bank loan was taken during 2018 and was used entirely to purchase new sports equipment.
As a special arrangement, the bank has agreed to provide the loan interest-free in the first
year only.

(a) Calculate the depreciation on sports equipment that would appear in the Income and
expenditure account for the year ended 31 December 2018.

(b) Prepare a Statement of financial position as at 31 December 2018 – showing the surplus or
deficit as the figure needed to balance the statement. There is no need to prepare an Income
and expenditure account.

Check your progress

Read the unit objectives below and reflect on your
progress in each.

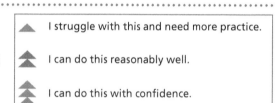

- I struggle with this and need more practice.
- I can do this reasonably well.
- I can do this with confidence.

- Distinguish between receipts and payments accounts and
income and expenditure accounts

- Prepare receipts and payments accounts

- Prepare accounts for revenue-generating activities,
for example refreshments, subscriptions

- Prepare income and expenditure accounts and statements of financial position

- Make adjustments to financial statements as detailed in Unit 5.1 (sole traders)

- Define and calculate the accumulated fund.

Manufacturing accounts

Learning objectives

By the end of this unit, you should be able to:

- distinguish between direct and indirect costs
- understand direct material, direct labour, prime cost and factory overheads
- understand and make adjustments for work in progress
- calculate factory cost of production
- prepare manufacturing accounts: income statements and statements of financial position
- make adjustments to financial statements as detailed in Unit 5.1 (sole traders).

Starting point

Answer these questions in pairs.

1 What is meant by the recovery of debts written off?

2 How are journal entries used to record the sale of non-current assets?

3 How is the revaluation method of depreciation applied to loose tools?

Exploring

Discuss these questions in pairs.

1 Consider the businesses in your local area. Identify **three** that produce the goods that they sell.

2 Identify a car manufacturer, for example Nissan. Discuss the components that will be used by your chosen car manufacturer to produce its motor vehicles.

3 What are the potential problems of a business making all of the products that it sells in its retail shop?

Developing

Introduction

The previous four units have considered the financial statements of sole traders, partnerships, limited companies and clubs and societies. In all of these examples, the businesses have purchased inventory and then sold this inventory to their customers. These businesses aim to sell the goods for a price that is higher than the cost so that they will make a profit.

There are a number of businesses that produce the goods that they sell. They purchase the raw materials and convert these into finished goods. If a business produces the goods that they sell there is no 'purchases' figure to include in the trading section of the income statement.

The costs incurred in the production of goods appear instead and these are calculated in a manufacturing account. A **manufacturing account** shows the cost of producing the goods that are sold during an accounting period.

A manufacturing account is split into two main sections:

- prime cost
- factory overhead costs.

Prime cost

The prime cost includes the **direct costs** of physically making the products and is related to the level of output.

Direct costs include:

- **Direct material:** The raw materials that are required to make the finished goods. The type of raw material varies depending on the type of business. For example, a window manufacturer requires glass, a baker needs flour and a machinery production company requires metal.

  Calculation of the cost of raw materials consumed:

  Opening inventory of raw materials

  Add purchases of raw materials

  Add carriage inwards on raw materials

  Less purchases returns of raw materials

  Less closing inventory of raw materials

  Equals cost of raw materials consumed

- **Direct labour:** This is often referred to as direct wages. Direct labour is the cost of the wages that are paid to individuals who are employed to make the goods being produced.

  > **Key knowledge**
  >
  > The direct labour category only applies to workers who are actually involved in the production of the goods. Supervisors, cleaners and maintenance engineers are not included.

- **Direct expenses:** These are the expenses that a manufacturer can link directly to the goods that are being produced. Examples include royalties and packaging costs.

Key term

Manufacturing account: An account in which it is calculated how much it has cost a business to manufacture the goods produced in a financial year.

Key terms

Prime cost: The total of direct costs of goods produced in terms of the materials, labour and expenses involved in its production.

Royalties: A fee that is paid to the individual who originally invented the product being manufactured.

Direct costs: The costs incurred in physically making the products; they are related to the level of output.

Indirect costs: The costs involved in the operation of a factory that cannot be directly linked to the goods that are being produced.

Factory overhead costs

Factory overhead costs, also known as **indirect costs** or indirect manufacturing costs, are the costs involved in the operation of a factory that cannot be directly linked to the goods that are being produced.

This section includes all other expenses concerned with the production of output but not in a direct way. This means that if the level of production increases, these expenses may also increase but not by the same proportion.

Key knowledge

Factory overhead costs include:

- Factory supervisor's salaries and other Indirect labour
- Factory rent and rates
- Depreciation of factory machinery

 Explain the difference between direct and indirect labour.

Manufacturing accounts

The cost of manufacturing the products is the totals of the prime cost and the overhead costs added together.

This total cost of production is then transferred to the trading section of an income statement where it will appear instead of the purchases figure in the accounts you have seen so far.

Key knowledge

Direct materials + direct labour + direct expenses = Prime cost

Prime cost + factory overhead = cost of production

The production cost is adjusted for goods that are not yet finished.

 Explain why a manufacturing account needs to be prepared by some businesses.

Allocation of expenses

A number of expenses will be split within the accounts of a business.

For example, an expense may be split between the prime cost and the overhead costs. Similarly, expenses may be split between the manufacturing account and the income statement.

The term office expense is often used to describe an expense that will be allocated to the income statement.

Key knowledge

Any adjustments need to be completed before the split between the sections of the financial statements.

Inventory

There are three main types of inventory in a manufacturing organisation:

- **Raw materials** – the purchases of these are adjusted for opening inventory and closing inventory in the prime cost.
- **Work in progress** – partly completed goods are dealt with at the end of the manufacturing account.
- **Finished goods** – opening and closing inventory is dealt with in the same way as for sole traders, partnerships and limited companies. The inventory of finished goods is included in the trading section of an income statement.

3 How will inventory for a manufacturing business differ from that for a trading business?

Key knowledge

Closing inventory values of raw materials, work in progress and finished goods appear as current assets in a statement of financial position.

4 Identify **three** examples of finished goods for a manufacturing business.

Work in progress

Goods which are not finished are known as work in progress.

The opening balance of work in progress is added to the production cost and the work in progress left at the end of the year is subtracted to give the cost of the goods completed during the period being dealt with.

Manufacturing account format

Businesses use a manufacturing account to calculate prime cost of manufacturing and cost of goods completed. The following format may be used.

Business name Manufacturing account for the year ended		
	$	$
Raw materials		
Opening inventory	x	
Purchases	x	
Carriage inwards	x	
Less returns	(x)	
	x	
Less closing inventory	(x)	
Cost of raw materials consumed		x
Direct wages/labour		x

Business name Manufacturing account for the year ended		
	$	$
Direct expenses		x
PRIME COST		x
Add factory overheads (examples include:)		
Rent and insurance	x	
Salaries	x	
Machinery repairs	x	
Indirect wages	x	
Light and power	x	
Depreciation of machinery	x	
		x
		x
Add: Opening work in progress		x
		x
Less: Closing work in progress		(x)
Manufacturing cost of goods completed		x

Worked example 1

Bali manufacturers has provided the following details of its factory costs for the year ended 30 November 2018.

	$
Opening inventory of raw materials	2000
Raw materials purchased	24000
Direct wages	48000
Royalties paid	600
Depreciation of factory equipment	1000
Factory rent	1700
General indirect expenses	1100
Closing inventory of raw materials	2600
Work in progress: 1 December 2017	8000
30 November 2018	12000

Prepare the manufacturing account for Bali manufacturers for the year ended 30 November 2018.

Clearly show the prime cost **and** manufacturing cost of goods completed.

Bali manufacturers Manufacturing account for the year ended 30 November 2018		
	$	$
Raw materials		
Opening inventory	2000	
Purchases	24000	
	26000	
Less closing inventory	(2600)	

Batley manufacturers		
Manufacturing account for the year ended 30 November 2018		
	$	$
Cost of raw materials consumed		23400
Direct wages/labour		48000
Royalties paid		600
PRIME COST		**72000**
Add factory overheads		
Factory rent	1700	
Depreciation of factory equipment	1000	
General indirect expenses	1100	
		3800
		75800
Add: Opening work in progress		8000
		83800
Less: Closing work in progress		(12000)
Manufacturing cost of goods completed		**71800**

Worked example 2

Chittagong manufacturers has provided the following details of its costs for the year ended 31 December 2018.

	$
Opening inventory of raw materials	48646
Raw materials purchased	246422
Direct wages	175372
Royalties paid	10686
Supervisor's salaries	50904
Factory heat and light	24764
Insurance	19616
Closing inventory of raw materials	53352
Work in progress: 1 January 2018	68648
31 December 2018	106906

Additional information

Insurance is to be split equally between the factory and the office.

Prepare the manufacturing account for Chittagong manufacturers for the year ended 31 December 2018. Clearly identify the prime cost **and** manufacturing cost of goods completed.

Chittagong manufacturers		
Manufacturing account for the year ended 31 December 2018		
	$	$
Raw materials		
Opening inventory	48646	

Chittagong manufacturers		
Manufacturing account for the year ended 31 December 2018		
	$	$
Purchases	246422	
	295068	
Less closing inventory	(53352)	
Cost of raw materials consumed		241716
Direct wages/labour		175372
Royalties paid		10686
PRIME COST		427774
Add factory overheads		
Supervisor's salaries	50904	
Factory heat and light	24764	
Insurance	9808	
		85476
		513250
Add: Opening work in progress		68648
		581898
Less: Closing work in progress		(106906)
Manufacturing cost of goods completed		474992

Insurance split equally between the factory and office: $19616 ÷ 2

$9808 to the manufacturing account

$9808 to the income statement

Worked example 3

Chirkunda manufacturing limited has a financial year that ends on 31 March.

The following information has been made available by the business.

	$
At 1 April 2017	
Machinery at cost	188000
Office fixtures at cost	68000
Loose tools at valuation	5300
Provision for depreciation: machinery	67680
Provision for depreciation: office fixtures	24480
Inventories:	
Raw materials	47000
Work in progress	22040
Finished goods	36200
For the year ended 31 March 2018	
Revenue	1078000
Purchases	
Raw materials	249200
Finished goods	33800
Purchases returns (finished goods)	400
Wages and salaries	
Factory workers	272000
Factory managers	62800

	$
Administrative and sales employees	123000
Expenses	
Direct expenses	32600
General factory expenses	38416
General office expenses	17800
Rates and insurance	12720

Additional information

- On 31 March 2018:

	$
Inventory: Raw materials	52200
Work in progress	24120
Finished goods	38600
Direct wages due and unpaid	4400
Administrative and sales employees accrued	760
Rates and insurance prepaid	240

- Rates and insurance are to be apportioned between the factory and the office in the ratio of 3 : 1.

- The machinery and office fixtures are being depreciated at 20% per annum using the reducing balance method.

- During the year ended 31 March, loose tools costing $620 were purchased.

  On 31 March 2018, loose tools were valued at $5480.

1   Prepare the manufacturing account of Chirkunda manufacturing limited for the year ended 31 March 2018.

2   Prepare the trading section of the income statement of Chirkunda manufacturing limited for the year ended 31 March 2018.

3   Prepare an extract from the statement of financial position of Chirkunda manufacturing limited as at 31 March 2018 to show the inventories being held.

Chirkunda manufacturing limited Manufacturing account for the year ended 31 March 2018		
	$	$
Raw materials		
Opening inventory	47000	
Purchases	249200	
	296200	
Less closing inventory	52200	
Cost of raw materials consumed		244000

Direct wages		276 400
Direct expenses		32 600
PRIME COST		**553 000**
Add factory overheads		
Factory managers salaries	62 800	
General factory expenses	38 416	
Depreciation of machinery	24 064	
Depreciation of loose tools	440	
Rates and insurance	9 360	
		135 080
		688 080
Add: Opening work in progress		22 040
		710 120
Less: Closing work in progress		24 120
Manufacturing cost of goods completed		**686 000**

$272 000 + $4400 = $276 400

20% of ($188 000 − $67 680) = $24 064

$5300 + $620 − $5480 = $440

($12 720 − $240) × 3/4 = $9360

Chirkunda manufacturing limited				
Income statement for the year ended 31 March 2018				
		$	$	$
Revenue			1 078 000	
Less	Sales returns		0	
				1 078 000
	Opening inventory	36 200		
Add	Purchases	686 000		
Add	Carriage inwards	0		
Less	Purchases returns	400		
			721 800	
Less	Closing inventory		38 600	
Cost of sales				683 200
Gross profit (or loss)				394 800

From the manufacturing account.

Chirkunda manufacturing limited		
Statement of financial position (extract) as at 31 March 2018		
	$	$
Current assets		
Inventory		
Raw materials	52 200	
Work in progress	24 120	
Finished goods	38 600	114 920

Applying

Complete this task in pairs.

Task

Morella Bakery Equipment Manufacturers has provided the following details of its costs for the year ended 31 December 2018.

	$
Opening inventory of raw material	25 000
Raw materials purchased	120 000
Direct wages	63 000
Royalties paid	2 500
Supervisor's wages	15 000
Factory electricity	7 250
Insurance	7 500
Closing inventory of raw materials	21 000
Work in progress: 1 January 2018	5 500
31 December 2018	7 650

Additional information

Insurance is to be split equally between the factory and the office.

1 Prepare the manufacturing account of Morella Bakery Equipment Manufacturers for the year ended 31 December 2018.

2 Prepare an extract from the statement of financial position of Morella Bakery Equipment Manufacturers as at 31 December 2018 to show the inventories being held.

Knowledge check

1 Which of the following calculates prime cost?

   A Direct materials + direct labour – direct expenses
   B Direct materials + direct labour + direct expenses
   C Indirect materials + indirect labour – indirect expenses
   D Indirect materials + indirect labour – indirect expenses

2 Which of the following would **not** appear in a manufacturing account?

   A Carriage inwards   C Raw material purchases
   B Carriage outwards   D Royalties

3 Which of the following is **not** used to calculate cost of production?

   A Inventory of finished goods   C Closing work in progress
   B Inventory of raw materials   D Opening work in progress

4 Define the term work in progress.

5   Explain what is meant by the term royalties.

6   Describe the two types of costs that exist in manufacturing accounts.

7   Describe the adjustments that are made for work in progress.

8   Define, with the use of practical examples, the following terms:

   (a) Direct materials

   (b) Direct labour

   (c) Prime cost

   (d) Factory overheads

9   Explain how to calculate the cost of raw materials consumed.

10   Opus manufacturers has provided the following details of its factory costs for the year ended
     30 April 2018:

	$
Opening inventory of raw materials	4000
Raw materials purchased	48000
Direct wages	96000
Royalties paid	1200
Depreciation of factory equipment	2000
Factory rent	3400
General indirect expenses	2200
Closing inventory of raw materials	4800
Work in progress: 1 May 2017	16000
30 April 2018	24000

     Prepare the manufacturing account for Opus manufacturers for the year ended 30 April 2018.

     Clearly show the prime cost and manufacturing cost of goods completed.

11   Saigon boat manufacturers has provided the following details of its costs for the year ended 31
     December 2018:

	$
Opening inventory of raw materials	97292
Raw materials purchased	492844
Direct wages	350744
Royalties paid	21372
Supervisor's salaries	101808
Factory lighting	49528
Rent and rates	39232
Closing inventory of raw materials	106704
Work in progress: 1 January 2018	137296
31 December 2018	213812

Additional information

Rent and rates is to be split equally between the factory and the office.

Prepare the manufacturing account for Saigon boat manufacturers for the year ended 31 December 2018. Clearly identify the prime cost and manufacturing cost of goods completed.

Check your progress

Read the unit objectives below and reflect on your progress in each.

- Distinguish between direct and indirect costs

- Understand direct material, direct labour, prime cost and factory overheads

- Understand and make adjustments for work in progress

- Calculate factory cost of production

- Prepare manufacturing accounts: income statements and statements of financial position

- Make adjustments to financial statements as detailed in Unit 5.1 (sole traders).

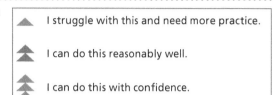

▲	I struggle with this and need more practice.
▲	I can do this reasonably well.
▲	I can do this with confidence.

Incomplete records

Learning objectives
By the end of this unit, you should be able to:
- explain the disadvantages of not maintaining a full set of accounting records
- prepare opening and closing statements of affairs
- calculate profit for the year from changes in capital over time
- calculate sales, purchases, gross profit, trade receivables, trade payables and other figures from incomplete information
- prepare income statements and statements of financial position from incomplete records
- make adjustments to financial statements as detailed in Unit 5.1 (sole traders)
- apply the techniques of mark-up, margin and inventory turnover to arrive at missing figures.

Starting point

Answer these questions in pairs.

1. What is the purpose of a sole trader's statement of financial position?

2. Discuss the usefulness to a sole trader of preparing an income statement.

3. How is their inventory valued?

Exploring

Discuss these questions in pairs.

1. Why is it important for a sole trader to maintain a full set of double entry accounting records?

2. Why is it important for a sole trader to accurately account for capital and revenue expenditure?

Developing

Introduction

Businesses are said to have incomplete records if they do not have a complete set of accounting records, books and ledger accounts. It may be that the records have been lost or damaged, for example during a flood or fire. However, the most common explanation is that the business has decided not to keep double entry accounting records.

For sole traders, it is not a legal requirement to keep comprehensive double entry accounting records; however, they do require accounts to ascertain the amount of tax that needs to be paid.

Many will employ an accountant to prepare their annual accounts based on a set of incomplete accounting records. From a business's point of view, the cost of employing an accountant is vastly increased if the business has very limited financial records.

A number of smaller businesses will prepare **single entry** accounts. This means that the business will record all payments, receipts and other transactions in one cash book. The records will be complete; however, there will be no matching entries in other books.

Key knowledge

A single entry system does not differentiate between items such as drawings, expenses, purchases, capital or revenue expenditure.

 Theo, a sole trader, does not have complete accounting records. Identify **three** pieces of information that Theo may not be able to provide to his accountant.

Calculation of profit from changes in capital

If a business does not have a cash book or a full record of transactions, it may not be possible for an accountant to prepare a set of financial statements. This means that they cannot prepare an income statement and statement of financial position. This will prevent the business owner from knowing their profit for the year.

As an alternative, it may be possible to calculate the annual profit using opening and closing capital figures. The following framework can be used:

Opening capital

Add

Capital introduced

Add

Profit for the year

Less

Drawings

Equals

Closing capital

Worked example 1

Iftikhar is a part-time taxi driver. He has not maintained accounting records and it has not been possible for his accountant to prepare an accurate set of financial statements.

Iftikhar has been able to ascertain the following details:

1 March 2017   Assets $57 080   Liabilities $4200

28 February 2018   Assets $67 400   Liabilities $6980

During the financial year, Iftikhar withdrew $29 000 for his own personal use. However, he did not add any further capital into the business.

Calculate:

1 The opening and closing capital for Iftikhar's taxi business.

2 The profit for the year of Iftikhar's taxi business.

---

1 Capital = assets – liabilities

Opening capital = 57 080 – 4200 = $52 880

Closing capital = 67 400 – 6980 = $60 420

2 Profit = closing capital – opening capital – capital introduced + drawings

Profit = 60 420 – 52 880 – 0 + 29 000 = $36 540

2 Explain **two** reasons why a sole trader may need to know the profit they have made during the year.

Key knowledge

A statement of affairs is similar to a statement of financial position and is set out formally.

Statement of affairs

A **statement of affairs** can be used to determine a business's capital. This can only be completed if the total amounts of assets and liabilities are known.

Key term

Statement of affairs:
A list of assets and liabilities at a given date; it is similar to a statement of financial position.

Worked example 2

Ati operates a small retail business. He has not maintained full accounting records; however, he has been able to supply the following details.

	As at 1 August 2017	As at 31 July 2018
	$	$
Motor vehicles	20 000	24 000
Fixtures and fittings	4700	3600

Inventory	7720	6860
Trade receivables	1020	660
Cash at bank	4360	2580
Cash in hand	840	900
Trade payables	2860	2420
Bank loan	6000	7000

During the financial year, Ati withdrew $24 000 from the business for his own use. Ati did not introduce any new capital during the year. The bank loan is due for repayment in six months' time.

1 Prepare a statement of affairs as at 1 August 2017 to calculate the opening capital of Ati's business.

2 Prepare a statement of affairs as at 31 July 2018 to calculate the closing capital of Ati's business.

3 Calculate Ati's profit for the year.

Ati			
Statement of affairs as at 1 August 2017			
	$		$
	Cost	Depreciation	Net book value
Non-current assets			
Motor vehicles	20000	0	20000
Fixtures and fittings	4700	0	4700
	24700	0	24700
Current assets			
Inventory		7720	
Trade receivables		1020	
Cash at bank		4360	
Cash in hand		840	
			13940
Total assets			38640
Capital			29780
Current liabilities			
Trade payables			2860
Bank loan			6000
			8860
Total liabilities			38640

> Missing figure = $38 640 – $8 860 = $29 780

Ati			
Statement of affairs as at 31 July 2018			
	$	$	$
	Cost	Depreciation	Net book value
Non-current assets			
Motor vehicles	24000	0	24000
Fixtures and fittings	3600	0	3600
	27600		27600

Current assets			
Inventory		6860	
Trade receivables		660	
Cash at bank		2580	
Cash in hand		900	
			11000
Total assets			38600
Capital			29180
Current liabilities			
Trade payables			2420
Bank loan			7000
			9420
Total liabilities			38600

Missing figure = $38600 – $9420 = $29180

Profit = closing capital – opening capital – capital introduced + drawings

Profit = 29180 – 29780 – 0 + 24000 = **$24300**

 Discuss **two** reasons why a sole trader may not have used a double entry book-keeping system to record financial transactions.

Calculation of financial figures from incomplete information

Even when a business does not maintain double entry accounting records, it may still be possible that the business can provide details of its assets, liabilities, money received and money paid.

With this information, it is possible to calculate missing figures and prepare a set of financial statements.

Credit sales and credit purchases totals for a financial year can be calculated as follows:

Credit Sales

Receipts from trade receivables

Less

Opening balance for trade receivables

Add

Closing balance for trade receivables

Equals

Credit sales for the year

Credit Purchases

Payments to trade payables

Less

Opening balance for trade payables

Add

Closing balance for trade payables

Equals

Credit purchases for the year

It is also possible to use a purchases ledger control account and sales ledger control account to calculate credit sales and credit purchases totals for a financial year.

The following formats are used:

Sales ledger control account					
Date		$	Date		$
	Balance b/d	x		Sales returns	x
	Credit sales	x		Bank	x
	Dishonoured cheques	x		Discounts allowed	x
	Interest on overdue trade receivables	x		Irrecoverable debts	x
	Refunds to customers	x		Balance c/d	x
		x			x
	Balance b/d	x			

> This is the missing figure to be calculated.

Purchases ledger control account					
Date		$	Date		$
	Cash book for credit purchases	x		Balances b/d	x
	Discounts received	x		Credit purchases for March	x
	Purchases returns	x		Interest on overdue trade payables	x
	Contra entries	x			
	Balances c/d	x			
		x			x
				Balance b/d	x

> This is the missing figure to be calculated.

It is very important to remember that businesses may have both credit and cash sales and purchases. Therefore, when calculating total sales revenue or total purchases, businesses need to include both the cash and credit elements.

Key knowledge

Total sales revenue = credit sales + cash sales

Total purchases = credit purchases + cash purchases

Worked example 3

Afiq operates as a sole trader. He has full bank account details but has not maintained full accounting records. He has been able to supply the following details.

	As at 1 July 2017	As at 30 June 2018
	$	$
Buildings at cost	120000	120000
Fixtures and fittings (cost $45 000)	36000	?
Inventory	56200	59600
Trade receivables	47600	53600
Trade payables	39400	40400
General expenses owing	400	
General expenses paid in advance		680
Cash at bank	25400	?

During the financial year, Afiq withdrew $8000 in goods from the business for his own use.

On 30 June 2018 fixtures and fittings are to be depreciated using the straight line method – 10% on cost.

The details for receipts and payments have been provided:

Receipts	$	Payments	$
Receipts from trade receivables	663200	Payments to trade payables	498800
Cash sales	24000	General expenses	39240
		Drawings	76800
		Wages	80000
		Heat and light	7600
		Insurance	3800
		Fixtures and fittings	16000

Prepare an income statement for the year ended 30 June 2018 **and** a statement of financial position as at 30 June 2018 for Afiq.

Afiq Statement of affairs as at 1 July 2017			
	$	$	$
	Cost	Depreciation	Net book value
Non-current assets			
Buildings	120000	0	120000
Fixtures and fittings	45000	9000	36000
	165000	9000	156000
Current assets			
Inventory		56200	
Trade receivables		47600	
Bank		25400	
			129200
Total assets			285200

Capital			245 400
Current liabilities			
Trade payables			39 400
Other payables			400
			39 800
Total liabilities			285 200

Missing figure = $285 200 – $39 800 = $245 400

Calculation of total sales and total purchases:

Credit sales	$
Receipts from trade receivables	663 200
Less	
Opening balance for trade receivables	47 600
Add	
Closing balance for trade receivables	53 600
Equals	
Credit sales for the year	**669 200**
Credit purchases	
Payments to trade payables	498 800
Less	
Opening balance for trade payables	39 400
Add	
Closing balance for trade payables	40 400
Equals	
Credit purchases for the year	**499 800**

Total Sales = $669 200 + $24 000 = **$693 200**

Total Purchases = $499 800 + $0 = **$499 800**

Calculation of bank balance:

Bank account	$		$
Balance b/d	25 400	Payments to trade payables	498 800
Receipts from trade receivables	663 200	General expenses	39 240
Cash sales	24 000	Drawings	76 800
Balance c/d	9 640	Wages	80 000
		Heat and light	7 600
		Insurance	3 800
		Fixtures and fittings	16 000
	722 240		722 240
		Balance b/d	9 640

Bank overdraft

Afiq		
Income statement for the year ended 30 June 2018		
	$	$
Revenue		693 200
Less cost of sales		
Opening inventory	56 200	
Purchases	491 800	
	548 000	
Closing inventory	59 600	
Cost of sales		488 400
Gross profit		204 800
Less expenses		
General expenses	38 160	
Wages	80 000	
Heat and light	7 600	
Insurance	3 800	
Depreciation: Fixtures and fittings	6 100	
		135 660
Profit for the year		69 140

$499\,800 - \$8000 = \$491\,800$

$39\,240 - \$400 - \$680 = \$38\,160$

$45\,000 + \$16\,000 = \$61\,000$
10% of $61\,000 = \$6100$

Afiq			
Statement of financial position as at 30 June 2018			
	$ Cost	$ Depreciation	$ Net book value
Non-current assets			
Buildings	120 000	0	120 000
Fixtures and fittings	61 000	15 100	45 900
	181 000	15 100	165 900
Current assets			
Inventory		59 600	
Other receivables		680	
Trade receivables		53 600	
			113 880
Total assets			279 780
Capital			
Capital			245 400
Profit for the year			69 140
			314 540
Less drawings (76 800 + 8000)			84 800
			229 740
Current liabilities			
Trade payables			40 400
Bank overdraft			9 640
			50 040
Total liabilities			**279 780**

Using ratios to calculate missing figures

Gross profit margin

The gross profit margin is the gross profit expressed as a percentage of the revenue generated by sales. By substituting into the formula, gross profit or revenue can be calculated.

$$\text{Gross profit margin} = \frac{\text{Gross profit}}{\text{Revenue}} \times 100$$

Profit margin

The profit margin is the profit for the year expressed as a percentage of the revenue generated by sales. This ratio shows how much profit the business has left over after the business has paid all their costs and expenses.

$$\text{Profit margin} = \frac{\text{Profit for the year}}{\text{Revenue}} \times 100$$

Mark-up

The mark-up is gross profit expressed as a percentage of cost of sales. This is the percentage by which the cost of an item has been increased to arrive at the selling price.

$$\text{Mark-up} = \frac{\text{Gross profit}}{\text{Cost of sales}} \times 100$$

Worked example 4

A business purchases an item of inventory for $80 and sells it for $100. The gross profit is $20.

(a) Calculate the gross profit margin.

(b) Calculate the mark-up.

$$
\begin{aligned}
\textbf{(a)} \ \text{Gross profit margin} \ &= \frac{\text{Gross profit}}{\text{Revenue}} \times 100 \\
&= \frac{20}{100} \times 100 \\
&= 20\% \\
&\text{or} \ \frac{1}{5}
\end{aligned}
$$

(b) Mark-up $= \dfrac{\text{Gross profit}}{\text{Cost of sales}} \times 100$

$\qquad\qquad = \dfrac{20}{80} \times 100$

$\qquad\qquad = 25\%$

$\qquad\qquad \text{or } \dfrac{1}{4}$

These ratios are used by accountants to calculate missing figures where businesses have incomplete records. It is possible to convert mark-up to margin and vice versa as required.

Worked example 5

Franco is a retailer who can supply the following information relating to the past trading year ended 31 December 2018.

Mark-up	25%
Purchases	$54000
Opening Inventory	$4890
Closing Inventory	$5210

Prepare an income statement for the year ended 31 December 2018.

Franco Income statement for the year ended 31 December 2018			
	$	$	$
Revenue			67100
Opening inventory	4890		
Purchases	54000		
		58890	
Closing inventory		5210	
Cost of sales			53680
Gross profit			13420

Revenue = cost of sales + gross profit

Cost of sales = opening inventory + purchases – closing inventory

By substituting into the formula for mark-up, it is possible to calculate gross profit.
$53680 \times 25\% = \$13420$

Inventory turnover

It is possible to use the inventory turnover ratio to calculate various missing figures when preparing financial statements from incomplete records. By substituting into the formula, it is possible to calculate cost of sales and average inventory. Once cost of sales has been calculated, it is possible to calculate purchases if inventory totals are known.

$$\text{Inventory turnover} = \frac{\text{Cost of sales}}{\text{Average inventory}}$$

$$\text{Average inventory} = \frac{\text{Opening inventory + closing inventory}}{2}$$

Worked example 6

Amolik has provided the following information from their books of account.

Inventory turnover	11 times
Opening inventory	$20000
Closing inventory	$50000

- Calculate Amolik's cost of sales to be included in their income statement.

- Calculate Amolik's purchases to be included in their income statement.

$$\text{Inventory turnover} = \frac{\text{Cost of sales}}{\text{Average inventory}}$$

$$= \frac{\text{Cost of sales}}{\text{Average inventory}}$$

$$11 = \frac{\text{Cost of sales}}{(20000 + 50000) \div 2}$$

Cost of sales = 11 × 35 000 = **$385000**

Amolik			
	$	$	$
Opening inventory	20000		
Purchases	**415000**		
		435000	
Closing stock		50000	
Cost of sales			385000

Complete this task in pairs.

Task

Anita operates a marketing agency. She operates her business from home; however, she does not keep full accounting records.

	31 October 2017	1 November 2018
	$	$
Motor vehicle	9000	10000
Office equipment	3200	4000
Fixtures and fittings	2500	300
Expenses paid in advance	800	700
Cash at bank	4860	1340
Cash in hand	240	300
Bank loan	6000	10000

During the year Anita withdrew $11000 from the business for her own private use.

The bank loan is due for repayment in six months' time. She did not introduce any new capital.

(a) Prepare a statement of affairs as at 31 October 2017.

(b) Prepare a statement of affairs as at 1 November 2018.

(c) Calculate Anita's profit for the year.

Knowledge check

1   Which of the following calculates profit for the year?

    A Profit = closing capital + opening capital – capital introduced + drawings

    B Profit = closing capital – opening capital + capital introduced + drawings

    C Profit = closing capital – opening capital – capital introduced – drawings

    D Profit = closing capital – opening capital – capital introduced + drawings

2   What is calculated as gross profit ÷ cost of sales × 100?

    A Capital employed

    B Margin

    C Mark-up

    D Profit for the year

3 Which of the following calculates inventory turnover as a number of times?

    A Average inventory ÷ cost of sales

    B Average inventory ÷ sales

    C Cost of sales ÷ average inventory

    D Revenue ÷ average inventory

4 Identify **and** explain **two** disadvantages of a business not maintaining a full set of accounting records.

5 Define the term statement of affairs.

6 Explain how a single entry accounting system may be used in small businesses.

7 Simonis runs a small coffee shop. He has not kept any accounting records and does not have sufficient information to prepare an income statement.

1 April 2017   Assets $89080   Liabilities $5120

31 March 2018   Assets $77400   Liabilities $7890

During the financial year, Simonis withdrew $29000 for his own personal use and added $10000 in capital to the business.

Calculate Simonis's profit for the year from the information supplied.

8 A retailer has supplied the following information relating to the past trading year ended 31 December 2018.

Gross profit margin	30%
Sales	$80000
Opening inventory	$2600
Closing inventory	$2800

Prepare the income statement for the year ended 31 December 2018.

9 Frederic owns an engineering wholesale business. He has supplied the following information relating to the past trading year ended 31 October 2018.

Mark-up	25%
Cost of sales	$880000
Opening inventory	$45000
Closing inventory	$65000

Prepare the income statement for the year ended 31 October 2018.

10 Agyei is a sole trader who owns a builders' supplies company. He has provided the following information to his accountant for the year ended 30 April 2018.

	1 May 2017	30 April 2018
	$	$
Trade receivables	7500	9000
Inventory at cost	8000	3200
Rent prepaid	200	150
Wages owing	300	350
Trade payables	6000	4000
Motor vehicles	8000	13500
Land and Buildings	60000	60000

Bank account summary for the year ended 30 April 2018			
	$		$
Balance b/d	6000	General expenses	12000
Trade receivables	135000	Wages	6000
Cash sales	10500	Rent	5000
		Trade payables	124000
		Motor vehicles	10000

Additional information

- Prior to paying the cash sales into his bank account, Agyei took $250 per week for 52 weeks as drawings.

- Tarkowski, a trade receivable, has recently been declared bankrupt. His outstanding debt of $280 is now irrecoverable and needs to be written off.

- Discounts received during the year amounted to $1200.

Prepare the income statement for Agyei for the year ended 30 April 2018.

Chapter review

1 Which of the following accurately represents the statement of financial position for a sole trader?
- **A** Assets = liabilities – capital
- **B** Capital = assets + liabilities
- **C** Capital = assets – liabilities
- **D** Liabilities = capital – assets

2 Which of the following groups only contains non-current assets?
- **A** Cash at bank, trade receivables, machinery
- **B** Inventory, prepaid expenses, motor vehicles
- **C** Machinery, accrued income, land and buildings
- **D** Motor vehicles, land and buildings, equipment

3 In which section of a statement of financial position would 'an item that can be quickly converted to cash' appear?
- **A** Current Assets
- **B** Current Liabilities
- **C** Non-current Assets
- **D** Non-current Liabilities

4 Ramanjeet and Jemina are in partnership.
They have agreed to take $25 000 drawings each year.
In which of the following financial statements would the drawings appear?
- **A** Appropriation account
- **B** Income statement
- **C** Ramanjeet and Jemina's fixed capital accounts
- **D** Ramanjeet and Jemina's current accounts

5 Which of the following appears in a limited company's income statement?
- **A** Administration expenses
- **B** Closing equity
- **C** General reserves
- **D** Interim dividends

6 Garden designs' financial year ended on 31 December 2017.
On 1 October 2017, $15 000 was paid for rent for the six months to 31 March 2018.
What is the correct entry in the statement of financial **position on 31 December 2017?**
- **A** Current asset $7500
- **B** Current asset $15 000
- **C** Current liability $7500
- **D** Current liability $15 000

7 Which of the following calculates average inventory?
- **A** [opening inventory + closing inventory] ÷ 2
- **B** [opening inventory + closing inventory] × 2
- **C** [opening inventory – closing inventory] ÷ 2
- **D** [opening inventory – closing inventory] × 2

8 What is an income statement?
- **A** A record of all assets and liabilities of a business at the year end.
- **B** A list of all the balances in the ledger accounts of a business at the year end.
- **C** A record of receipts and payments of a business for a financial year.
- **D** A summary of income and expenditure of a business for a financial year.

9   Which of the following is **not** a current asset in a statement of financial position?

   A   Cash in hand
   B   Cash at bank
   C   Money owed by a customer
   D   Money owed to a supplier

10 Which of the following is an intangible non-current asset?

   A   Cash at bank
   B   Closing inventory
   C   Goodwill
   D   Trade receivables

11 (a) Explain the reasons why a business prepares a manufacturing account in addition
       to an income statement.   [5]

   (b) Explain **each** of the following terms and show how they are calculated in manufacturing
       accounts:

       (i)   Prime cost   [2]
       (ii) Work in progress.   [3]

   (c) The financial year of Berenice manufacturing company ends on 31 August.

       The management have provided the following financial information:

Inventory	At 1 September 2017	At 31 August 2018
	$	$
Raw materials	14080	12440
Work in progress	1620	1900
Finished goods	11560	12200

For the year ended 31 August 2018:

	$
Sales of finished goods	361000
Purchases of raw materials	87640
Wages – factory workers	80380
Wages – factory managers	36800
Wages – office staff	74000
General expenses - factory	10680
General expenses – office	7200
Rates and insurance	15000

Additional information:
* The factory machinery cost $84000 and the office machinery cost $46000. Both non-current assets are depreciated using the straight line method of 20% on cost.
* Rates and insurance are to be apportioned – factory $\frac{4}{5}$ and office $\frac{1}{5}$.

Prepare the manufacturing account of Berenice manufacturing company for the year
ended 31 August 2018.   [10]

[Total 20]

12 Mathilda operates Somerton home designs. The business provides design services to residential customers. Mathilda has provided the following financial information for the year ended 30 June 2018.

	$
Premises	120000
Office equipment	89000
Advertising	4600
Trade payables	6300
Trade receivables	5900
Bank overdraft	790
Short-term loan	50000
Capital	?
Drawings	23000
Fees received	300000
Office expenses	165000
Heat and light	7000
Provision for depreciation: office equipment	8900
Discounts allowed	3200
General expenses	73890

The following information is also available:

- A general provision for doubtful debts is to be introduced at 20% of closing trade receivables.

- Office expenses were prepaid: $575

- General expenses due but unpaid: $555

- Depreciation is to be provided as follows:

  – Office equipment   10% per annum using the straight line method.

Prepare:

(a) the income statement of Somerton home designs for the year ended 30 June 2018.   [10]

(b) the statement of financial position as at 30 June 2018, clearly showing the capital value.   [10]

[Total 20]

13 Melissa and Cristofor are in partnership. Their financial year ends on 31 October.

After preparing their income statement for the year ended 31 October 2018, the following balances remained on the books of account:

	$
Capital account: Melissa	100000
Capital account: Cristofor	60000
Current account: Melissa	30000 Cr
Current account: Cristofor	10000 Dr
Non-current assets at cost	170000
Provision for depreciation of non-current assets	20000
Inventory	16000
Trade receivables	28000
Bank balance	10000 Dr
Trade payables	24000

(a) Prepare the statement of financial position for the partnership as at 31 October 2018. **[12]**

(b) State and explain three advantages of operating as a partnership. **[6]**

(c) Identify two items that Melissa and Cristofor will have included in their deed of partnership. **[2]**

[Total 20]

14 Akira, Eito and Fumihiro are in partnership. Their partnership agreement states:

- Profits and losses will be shared in the ratio of 3 : 2 : 1

- Interest on all forms of capital is allowed at 10% per annum on the year-end balances

- Akira will receive a partnership salary of $15000 per annum

- Interest on all forms of drawings is charged at 5% on balances at the end of the year.

At 30 November 2018, the following balances were extracted from the books of account.

	$
Profit for the year	131500
Capital account balances	
Akira	160000
Eito	120000
Fumihiro	100000
Drawings	
Akira	12000
Eito	14750
Fumihiro	16000

In addition, Akira took a car out of the partnership for her own personal use. The car was valued at $7000. Elito took goods out of the business for personal use and these were valued at $1250. Fumihiro introduced a van into the partnership for business use. This van was to be treated as a further capital contribution by Fumihiro and had not been included in the balances from the books of account. The van was valued at $20000.

(a) Prepare the appropriation account for Akira, Eito and Fumihiro for the year ended 30 November 2018. **[12]**

(b) Identify four situations when adjustments will be required to a partner's capital account. **[4]**

(c) Describe the difference between fixed capital and fluctuating capital accounts. **[4]**

Total [20]

15 Oceana Golf Club has provided details of its assets and liabilities on 1 January 2018.

Bank	$12 600
Motor van at valuation	$8 000
Subscriptions outstanding	$1 000
Rent owing	$200

The treasurer of the club has provided the following information about the receipts and payments for the year ended 31 December 2018.

Receipts	
Subscriptions	$42 600
Proceeds of sale of motor van	$7 000
Competition entrance fees	$3 200
Payments	
Purchase of new motor van	$40 000
Competition prizes	$840
General expenses	$10 580
Travelling expenses	$3 320
Rent	$10 400

The following information is also available:

1 The motor van is used to transport the golf equipment to various competitions

The motor van owned on 1 January 2018 was sold in March 2018

No depreciation is provided in the year of sale

On the same day, a new motor van was purchased. At 31 December 2018, this motor van was valued at $34 000.

2 On 31 December 2018:

- Members subscriptions paid in advance amounted to $1 600

- Rent prepaid amounted to $400.

(a) Prepare the income and expenditure account of the Oceana Golf Club for the year ended 31 December 2018. **[14]**

(b) Prepare the statement of financial position for the Oceana Golf Club at 31 December 2018. **[6]**

16 Gumia Manufacturing Ltd has extracted the following balances from its books of account at 28 February 2018.

	$
Inventory: 1 March 2017	
Raw materials	42 500
Work in progress	84 600
Finished goods	52 500
Purchases of raw materials	620 000
Direct expenses	73 100
Indirect wages and salaries	41 000
Direct wages and salaries	153 200
Revenue	1 500 000
Trade receivables	95 000
Sales returns	4 000
Loan interest	1 200
Rent	20 000
Insurance	2 000
Office expenses	140 500
Buildings (Cost)	130 000
Provision for depreciation – Buildings	26 000
Plant and equipment (Cost)	90 000
Provision for depreciation – Plant and equipment	44 000
Irrecoverable debts	1 100
Provision for doubtful debts	4 500
Loan (10% interest per year)	24 000

Additional information

1 Closing inventory on 28 February 2018:

  Raw materials $39 300

  Work in progress $37 550

  Finished goods $78 750

2 Provision for doubtful debts to be provided at 5% of closing trade receivables.

3 Rent is to be apportioned in the ratio 4 : 1 between the factory and the office

  Rent of $5000 is outstanding at the year end.

4 Insurance is to be apportioned in the ratio 5 : 1 between the factory and the office

  Insurance of $200 is prepaid at the year end.

5 Provision for depreciation:

  Buildings: 5% on cost – apportioned in the ratio 4 : 1 between the factory and the office

  Plant and equipment: 20% using the reducing balance method – apportioned in the ratio 7 : 1 between the factory and the office.

Prepare a manufacturing and trading account for the year ended 28 February 2018. [20]

17 Owl Traditional Toys Ltd was formed on 1 January 2017. The company issued 100 000 ordinary shares of $1 each and 50 000 7% non-redeemable preference shares of $1 each.

The company has provided the following information for the year ending 31 December 2017:

Operating profits	$92 400
Finance costs	$31 200
Transfer to general reserve	$2 000

The full amount of dividend due to preference shareholders was paid in 2017.

Ordinary shareholders received a dividend of 4% in 2017.

(a) Explain the term 'non-redeemable preference share'. [2]

(b) Prepare an extract from the income statement to calculate retained profit carried forward for the year ending 31 December 2017. [7]

(c) Prepare a statement of changes in equity for the years ending 31 December 2017 and 31 December 2018. [5]

(d) Owl Traditional Toys Ltd was formed from a successful partnership that had existed for over 10 years. Explain two advantages and one disadvantage of the conversion of the business from a partnership to a limited company. [6]

6 Analysis and interpretation

6.1 Calculation and understanding of ratios

6.2 Interpretation of accounting ratios

6.3 Inter-firm comparison

6.4 Interested parties

6.5 Limitations of accounting statements

This chapter explains the basics of ratio analysis. It provides the ratio formulae required to make an analysis of a business's performance.

Numerical examples and tasks will enable you to practise ratio calculations and understand the importance of ratio analysis for businesses.

Calculation and understanding of ratios

Learning objectives
By the end of this unit, you should be able to calculate and explain the importance of the following ratios:
• Gross margin
• Profit margin
• Return on capital employed (ROCE)
• Current ratio
• Liquid (acid test) ratio
• Rate of inventory turnover (times)
• Trade receivables turnover (days)
• Trade payables turnover (days)

Starting point

Answer these questions in pairs.

1 Why might a sole trader want to analyse their accounts?

2 How can an income statement be used to review the profitability of a business?

3 What does the term 'liquidity' mean?

Exploring

Discuss these questions in pairs.

1 A local bakery would like to analyse its current financial performance. What types of business could the bakery compare itself with?

2 How can an income statement and statement of financial position be used to review whether a business has grown?

3 A partnership decides to apply to a bank for a long-term loan. What financial information would the bank want to review?

Developing

Introduction

Ratio analysis is an accounting technique that allows financial accounts to be analysed.

Numerical data and numbers in isolation have very little meaning. For example, an annual profit of $1 000 000 could be outstanding for a small local business but mean potential business failure for a large public limited company. The calculation of ratios allows financial information to be related to other data to allow for analysis.

CASE STUDY

Theba owns a local sports shop. It specialises in football and cricket equipment. Last year, her business made an annual profit of $500 000. Theba is very happy with the profit. It will allow her to expand and purchase a new warehouse. She also plans to set up an online shop.

Last week, Theba was talking to a representative of the sportswear company adidas. In 2016, adidas made approximately $1.110 billion in profit. He thought her annual profit was very small in comparison. He said that if the annual profit of a large business such as adidas declined to $500 000 the business would not be able to continue to operate.

Accounting ratios are easy to calculate and can be used to measure a business's solvency, profitability and financial strength. They are calculated from information found in the financial statements of the business. They allow the business to identify areas of financial weakness and enable management to decide if immediate action is required.

There are several categories of accounting ratio:

- Profitability ratios
- Activity or efficiency ratios
- Liquidity or solvency ratios.

Profitability ratios

These ratios assess whether a business has met its financial aims and objectives. Profitability ratios review the profit made by the business over the last financial year. They relate financial profitability to other financial indicators such as sales revenue and capital invested.

They include:

- Gross margin
- Profit margin
- Return on capital employed (ROCE).

Gross margin

Key knowledge

$$\text{Gross margin (\%)} = \frac{\text{gross profit}}{\text{revenue}} \times 100$$

The **gross margin** expresses the gross profit of a business as a percentage of the revenue generated by sales. This ratio shows how much profit a business has earned in relation to the cost of the products being sold.

Businesses aim to increase their gross margin from one year to the next.

Profit margin

Key knowledge

$$\text{Profit margin (\%)} = \frac{\text{profit for the year}}{\text{revenue}} \times 100$$

The **profit margin** expresses the profit for the year of a business as a percentage of the revenue generated by sales. This ratio shows how much profit the business has left over after the business has paid all its costs and expenses. The profit margin allows businesses to assess more effectively how efficient they are at turning products or services into revenue for the business. Businesses compare their gross margin with their profit margin to assess how well they are managing their expenses.

The profit margin is lower than the gross margin as all business expenses are deducted from the gross profit. As with the gross margin, businesses aim to increase their profit margin from one year to the next.

Return on capital employed

Key knowledge

$$\text{Return on capital employed (\%)} = \frac{\text{profit for the year}}{\text{capital employed}} \times 100$$

For a limited company:

$$\text{Return on capital employed (\%)} = \frac{\text{profit before interest}}{\text{capital employed}} \times 100$$

where capital employed = issued shares + reserves + non-current liabilities.

The **return on capital employed (ROCE)** expresses a business's profit for the year as a percentage of the capital employed. For a sole trader or partnership this is the amount of money invested by the owners plus non-current liabilities. For limited companies, the capital employed is the total of issued shares, reserves and non-current

Key terms

Gross margin: The gross profit of a business expressed as a percentage of revenue generated by sales.

Profit margin: The profit for the year of a business expressed as a percentage of revenue generated by sales.

Return on capital employed: The profit for the year expressed as a percentage of the capital employed. It informs a business of the profits that have been made based on the resources made available to them.

liabilities. This ratio shows how much profit is made as a proportion of the capital that has been invested into the business.

Once calculated, the higher the answer, the greater the return earned by the investor. A higher result indicates greater efficiency and ensures that the owners or investors are getting a greater return for their investment. Investors often compare the results of different businesses in order to decide which one to invest in.

Activity or efficiency ratios

These ratios analyse the financial efficiency of a business. They measure how efficiently a business uses its resources in generating its revenue from sales. For example, a finance department can use the trade receivables turnover to measure how quickly debts from credit customers are being collected. They include:

- Rate of inventory turnover (times)
- Trade receivables turnover (days)
- Trade payables turnover (days).

Rate of inventory turnover

Key knowledge

$$\text{Rate of inventory turnover} = \frac{\text{cost of sales}}{\text{average inventory}}$$

where $\text{average inventory} = \frac{\text{opening inventory} + \text{closing inventory}}{2}$.

The **rate of inventory turnover** measures how quickly a business uses or sells its inventory. This ratio considers how efficiently a business converts its inventory into sales.

The rate of inventory turnover depends on the type of business being considered. For example, a supplier of luxury cars such as Bentley has a lower inventory turnover than a supplier of lower-priced cars such as Ford. Due to the high price of luxury cars, fewer cars are sold. However, the profit per car is much greater than for a lower priced vehicle.

In general, high inventory turnover is considered preferable and means inventory is being sold quickly. A low inventory turnover means that inventory is not being sold or is being sold at a slow rate. This could be due to poor quality of goods or services, ineffective advertising and marketing or poor customer service.

Key term

Rate of inventory turnover: A measure of how quickly a business uses or sells its inventory.

Trade receivables turnover

Key knowledge

$$\text{Trade receivables turnover (in days)} = \frac{\text{trade receivables}}{\text{credit sales}} \times 365$$

The trade receivables turnover measures the average number of days that it takes a business to collect its debts from its credit customers (trade receivables).

A lower trade receivables turnover means that a business is collecting its debts more quickly. Businesses that offer credit terms to gain new customers experience an increase in the trade receivables turnover period.

 1 What are the benefits to a business of offering 90 days' credit to customers?

Trade payables turnover

Key knowledge

Trade payables turnover (in days) = $\frac{\text{trade payables}}{\text{credit purchases}} \times 365$

The trade payables turnover measures the average number of days that it takes a business to pay its debts to its credit suppliers (trade payables).

Businesses aim to have a trade payables turnover period that exceeds their trade receivables turnover period. They receive the money from their trade receivables before they need to pay their trade payables.

 2 Explain why businesses, from a financial point of view, want to collect their debts as quickly as possible and pay the money they owe as slowly as possible?

Liquidity or solvency ratios

These ratios measure the liquidity or solvency of a business. They measure a business's ability to pay its short-term debts. They focus on the short-term assets and liabilities of the business. They include:

* the current ratio
* the liquid (acid test) ratio.

Current ratio

Key knowledge

Current ratio = $\frac{\text{current assets}}{\text{current liabilities}}$

The current ratio measures the liquidity of a business. It compares current assets to current liabilities. The ratio assesses a business's ability to meet its short-term debts.

For most businesses a ratio in excess of 2 : 1 is generally considered to be acceptable. A lower ratio, for example 1 : 1, means that a business may not be able to pay its debts if required.

Key terms

Trade receivables turnover: The average number of days that it takes a business to collect its debts from its credit customers (trade receivables).

Trade payables turnover: The average number of days that it takes a business to pay its debts to its credit suppliers (trade payables).

Liquidity (of a business): A measure of the ability of a business to pay its short-term debts.

Current ratio: A measure of the liquidity of a business which compares current assets to current liabilities.

A higher ratio, for example 5 : 1, may mean that a business is inefficient and has too much money tied up in inventory.

Liquid (acid test) ratio

Key knowledge

$$\text{Liquid (acid test) ratio} = \frac{\text{current assets} - \text{closing inventory}}{\text{current liabilities}}$$

The liquid or acid test ratio measures the liquidity of a business. It compares current assets excluding closing inventory to current liabilities. This ratio is a more severe test of a business's liquidity and its ability to pay short-term debts. The ratio assumes that inventory may be perishable, go out of date or become obsolete (due to changes in fashion or technology). This would mean that the business would be left with inventory that it cannot sell and therefore could not be used to pay the business's short-term debts.

For most businesses a ratio in excess of 1 : 1 is generally considered to be acceptable.

Key term

Liquid (acid test) ratio: A measure of the liquidity of a business which compares current assets excluding closing inventory to current liabilities.

Worked example 1

The owner of Riverside car sales and repairs has provided the business's financial statements for the year ended 31 March 2018.

All sales and purchases during the year were on credit.

Riverside car sales and repairs Income statement for the year ended 31 March 2018			
	$	$	$
Revenue		18462	
Less returns Inwards		0	
			18462
Less cost of sales			
Opening inventory	1274		
Purchases	13355		
		14629	
Closing inventory		2548	
Cost of sales			12081
Gross profit			6381
Less expenses			
Wages and salaries		2150	
Motor expenses		520	
Rent		1670	
Insurance		111	
General expenses		105	
			4556
Profit for the year			1825

	Cost	Depreciation	Net book value
Riverside car sales and repairs **Statement of financial position as at** **31 March 2018**			
	$	$	$
Non-current assets			
Equipment	2000	500	1500
Motor vehicles	2100	900	1200
	4100	1400	2700
Current assets			
Closing inventory		2548	
Trade receivables		1950	
Cash at bank		654	
Cash in hand		40	
			5192
Total assets			7892
Capital			
Capital			5424
Profit for the year			1825
			7249
Drawings			(895)
			6354
Current liabilities			
Trade payables			1538
			1538
Total liabilities			7892

Calculate the following ratios based on the financial information that has been provided (to 2 decimal places). All of the business's sales and purchases during the year were on credit.

- Gross margin
- Profit margin
- Return on capital employed (ROCE)
- Rate of inventory turnover
- Trade receivables turnover
- Trade payables turnover
- Current ratio
- Liquid (acid test) ratio

Gross margin $= \dfrac{\text{gross profit}}{\text{revenue}} \times 100$

$\qquad\qquad = \dfrac{6381}{18\,462} \times 100 = 34.56\%$ (to 2 decimal places)

Profit margin $= \dfrac{\text{profit for the year}}{\text{revenue}} \times 100$

$\qquad\qquad = \dfrac{1825}{18\,462} \times 100 = 9.89\%$

Return on capital employed $= \dfrac{\text{profit for the year}}{\text{capital employed}} \times 100$

$\qquad\qquad = \dfrac{1825}{6354} \times 100 = 28.72\%$

Rate of inventory turnover $= \dfrac{\text{cost of sales}}{\text{average inventory}}$

$\qquad\qquad = \dfrac{12\,081}{1911} = 6.32 \text{ times}$

Trade receivables turnover $= \dfrac{\text{trade receivables}}{\text{credit sales}} \times 365$

$\qquad\qquad = \dfrac{1950}{18\,462} \times 365 = 38.55 \text{ days}$

Trade payables turnover $= \dfrac{\text{trade payables}}{\text{credit purchases}} \times 365$

$\qquad\qquad = \dfrac{1538}{13\,355} \times 365 = 42.03 \text{ days}$

Current ratio $= \dfrac{\text{current assets}}{\text{current liabilities}}$

$\qquad\qquad = \dfrac{5192}{1538} = 3.38 : 1$

Liquid (acid test) ratio $= \dfrac{\text{current assets} - \text{closing inventory}}{\text{current liabilities}}$

$\qquad\qquad = \dfrac{5192 - 2548}{1538} = 1.72 : 1$ (to 2 decimal places)

Average inventory $= \frac{1}{2} \times$ (opening inventory + closing inventory)

Average inventory $= \dfrac{1274 + 2548}{2} = 1911$

Applying

Complete this task in pairs.

Task

The finance manager of Turf Moor retail outlet has provided its financial statements for the year ended 31 January 2018.

All of the business's sales and purchases during the year were on credit.

Turf Moor retail outlet Income statement for year ended 31 January 2018			
	$	$	$
Revenue		414 640	
Less sales returns		7 384	
			407 256
Less cost of sales			
Opening inventory	21 442		
Purchases	192 552		
Less returns outwards	19 596		
		194 398	
Closing inventory		23 004	
Cost of sales			171 394
Gross profit			235 862
Less expenses			
Carriage outwards		21 300	
Advertising		11 644	
Electricity and gas		17 608	
Insurance		5 822	
Motor expenses		26 980	
Rent and rates		27 832	
Salaries and wages		52 824	
Depreciation – Fixtures and fittings		25 624	
Depreciation – Motor vehicles		13 561	
Provision for doubtful debts		256	
			203 451
Profit for the year			32 411

Turf Moor retail outlet Statement of financial position as at 30 January 2018			
	Cost	Depreciation	Net book value
	$	$	$
Non-current assets			
Fixtures and fittings	170 826	115 084	55 742
Motor vehicles	59 640	18 957	40 683
	230 466	134 041	96 425

Current assets			
Closing inventory		23 004	
Trade receivables		33 398	
Cash in hand		4 970	
			61 372
Total assets			**157 797**
Capital			
Capital			118 996
Profit for the year			32 411
			151 407
Drawings			(32 518)
			118 889
Current liabilities			
Trade payables		29 110	
Bank overdraft		7 952	
Other payables (accrued expenses)		1 846	
			38 908
Total liabilities			**157 797**

Calculate the following ratios based on the financial information that has been provided:

- Gross margin

- Profit margin

- Return on capital employed (ROCE)

- Rate of inventory turnover (times)

- Trade receivables turnover (days)

- Trade payables turnover (days)

- Current ratio

- Liquid (acid test) ratio.

Knowledge check

1 Junaid's statement of financial position showed the following assets and liabilities.

	$
Non-current assets	90000
Current assets	12000
Current liabilities	6000
Non-current liabilities	36000

Calculate Junaid's current ratio.

A 0.5 : 1
B 2.0 : 1
C 2.4 : 1
D 2.5 : 1

2 Paula commences trading as a sole trader with capital of $50000. She obtains a ten-year loan of $25000 to purchase non-current assets for her business.

Calculate Paula's capital employed.

A $25000
B $50000
C $75000
D $100000

3 Alexandre supplies goods on credit to Salma.

Which of Salma's accounting ratios would Alexandre be interested in?

A Gross margin
B Rate of inventory turnover
C Trade payables turnover
D Trade receivables turnover

4 The following information has been provided for three small retail stores.

	Store 1	Store 2	Store 3
	$	$	$
Revenue	130000	250000	150000
Gross profit	50000	75000	100000
Profit for the year	35000	60000	55000
Capital employed	55000	125000	35000

Calculate the following ratios for each of the three stores (to 2 decimal places):

(a) Gross margin
(b) Profit margin
(c) Return on capital employed (ROCE).

5 A small business has provided the following information from its financial statements.

	$
Revenue	300000
Opening inventory	30000
Purchases	200000
Closing inventory	20000

Calculate the rate of inventory turnover.

6 The following data has been provided for three small retail stores.

	Store 1	Store 2	Store 3
	$	$	$
Current assets	50000	130000	310000
Closing inventory	10000	30000	50000
Current liabilities	25000	50000	250000

Calculate the following ratios for each of the three stores.

(a) Current ratio

(b) Liquid (acid test) ratio.

7 Describe the difference between the current ratio and the liquid (acid test) ratio.

8 What is the difference between profitability and liquidity ratios?

9 What does the return on capital employed ratio (ROCE) measure?

10 How can a statement of financial position be used to assess the liquidity of a business?

Check your progress

Read the unit objectives below and reflect on your progress in each.

Calculate and explain the importance of the following ratios:

- Gross margin
- Profit margin
- Return on capital employed (ROCE)
- Current ratio
- Liquid (acid test) ratio
- Rate of inventory turnover (times)
- Trade receivables turnover (days)
- Trade payables turnover (days).

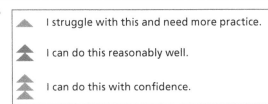

I struggle with this and need more practice.

I can do this reasonably well.

I can do this with confidence.

Interpretation of accounting ratios

Learning objectives

By the end of this unit, you should be able to:

- prepare and comment on simple statements showing comparison of results for different years
- make recommendations and suggestions for improving profitability and working capital
- understand the significance of the difference between the gross margin and the profit margin as an indicator of a business's efficiency
- explain the relationship of gross profit and profit for the year to the valuation of inventory, rate of inventory turnover, revenue, expenses, and equity.

Starting point

Answer these questions in pairs.

1 Explain what is meant by 'working capital'.

2 Describe the difference between gross profit and profit for the year.

3 Explain what the current ratio and the liquid (acid test) ratio show about a business.

Exploring

Discuss these questions in pairs.

1 A local coffee shop wants to improve its profitability. Identify two actions the coffee shop could take to increase its current profit levels.

2 A business has calculated its return on capital employed (ROCE) as 5.5%. The current base interest rate is 1.5%. Discuss how the business may interpret its performance.

3 Adi, a sole trader, needs to review his current liquidity. Identify the most appropriate method for Adi to use.

Developing

Ratio analysis

Ratio analysis is an excellent tool that can be used by individuals both inside and outside of a business to review financial performance.

It is useful to have a structured approach to any analysis. This could involve the following steps:

- Review the economy that the business operates within.
- Assess the industry in which the business operates.
- Identify the business's local, national and international competitors.
- Evaluate the strengths and weaknesses of the business using financial statements and ratios.

The goal of ratio analysis is to identify issues within a business and their possible causes. For example, it would not be appropriate for a business to reduce its cost of sales to bring it into line with local competition if the underlying problem relates to the business holding too much inventory.

 Explain how an income statement and statement of financial position can be used to assess whether a business has grown financially over a period of time?

A financial analyst reviewing financial statements and ratios needs to act as a detective. Ratios are the clues which can then be reviewed and explained.

A business prepares simple statements of its financial results and ratio calculations in order to show a comparison of results for different financial years. This allows management to undertake trend analysis and interpret the financial statements of the business in order to assess its performance and progress.

Key terms

Economy: The system by which goods and services are produced, sold and purchased in a particular area.

Competitor: A business that is engaged in commercial competition with other businesses.

Financial analyst: An individual whose job is to review the financial performance of a business to assess whether it is a sound investment.

Trend analysis: This is where a business compares its ratio results against benchmarks or industry averages and previous years' results.

Interpretation (of financial ratios): Comparing financial results with benchmarks or targets, previous years or similar businesses.

CASE STUDY

Teresa owns a retail store and has been in business for several years. She wants to expand her store and purchase a warehouse for storage.

Teresa approached her local bank for a mortgage. The bank asked for the business's financial statements for the last three years.

The bank advisor reviewed the financial statements, identified key trends over the three years and calculated a number of profitability, liquidity and efficiency ratios.

She found that Teresa's gross profit had declined considerably in the second year. She asked Teresa for additional information to explain why the gross profit had fallen. Teresa was able to show that her store had been closed for three months due to local flooding and she had made no sales. Following this, the bank offered Teresa a mortgage.

All businesses aim to maximise profits and maintain an appropriate level of working capital.

Businesses review their ratio results and then analyse their financial performance.

Profitability ratios

Gross margin

Gross margin shows the gross profit that is earned for every $100 of sales revenue. There are no set benchmarks for gross margin as different industries and trades have different gross margins. A business usually has a similar gross margin year on year. The higher the gross margin, the more profitable the business is.

Key knowledge

To improve the gross margin of a business, it could:

- increase its selling prices
- use cheaper suppliers
- increase business advertising and sales promotions to support a change in selling price or move to cheaper suppliers.

These actions could have an adverse effect on the business's performance. For example, increasing selling prices may reduce the number of customers purchasing the goods. The use of cheaper suppliers may mean that customers choose to purchase from elsewhere, due to poorer quality goods or services.

A business should investigate a fall in gross margin. There are a number of potential causes. These include:

- failing to pass on cost increases to customers
- reduction in selling prices
- offering a higher rate of trade discount.

2 Explain how a small retail outlet may increase its gross margin.

Worked example 1

Tian Tian owns a retail business. She has calculated her gross margin as 30%.

A local business enterprise group has calculated the sector average as 40%.

1 Explain whether Tian Tian should be satisfied with her result.

2 Describe how Tian Tian could improve her gross margin.

1   Tian Tian will be disappointed that her gross margin is 10% lower than that of the local retail sector average.

    To improve sales, Tian Tian may have to reduce her profit mark-up to encourage customers to purchase her goods. Alternatively, Tian Tian may have purchased goods for resale that are higher priced.

2   Tian Tian needs to consider:

    •   Increasing her selling price. This may encourage customers to go to another retail store.

    •   Using a cheaper supplier for her goods. This may cause customers to shop elsewhere as the quality of her products may decrease.

Profit margin

Profit margin shows the profit for the year that is earned for every $100 of sales revenue. There are no set benchmarks for profit margin as different industries and trades have different profit margins.

The higher the profit margin, the more profitable the business is. The profit margin indicates how well a business controls its operating expenses.

Key knowledge

Businesses need to consider the difference between gross margin and the profit margin. This indicates a business's efficiency. Any changes in gross margin have a direct effect on profit margin. The profit margin is affected by different types of business expense.

Expenses that change in proportion to the sales made, such as commission paid, have no effect on the profit margin. Other expenses that are unrelated to the sales made, for example heat and light, affect the profit margin.

Key knowledge

To improve the profit margin, a business could:
• reduce its expenses, for example:
  (a) lower staff wages
  (b) reduce expenditure on heating and lighting
• increase its gross profit, for example by reducing the purchase price of goods for resale.

Worked example 2

Yang Guang operates as a hairdresser. He has provided the following information from his accounts for the last two years.

Yang Guang		
	31 January 2017	31 January 2018
	$	$
Revenue	200 000	210 000
Gross profit	110 000	125 000
Expenses	75 000	90 000

1   Calculate, for the two years, the gross margin **and** profit margin ratios for Yang Guang.

2   Explain whether Yang Guang should be satisfied with his financial performance.

3   Describe how Yang Guang could improve his profitability.

---

1   Gross margin $= \dfrac{\text{gross profit}}{\text{revenue}} \times 100$

Year ended 31 January 2017:

Gross margin $= \dfrac{110\,000}{200\,000} \times 100 = 55\%$

Year ended 31 January 2018:

Gross margin $= \dfrac{125\,000}{210\,000} \times 100$

$\qquad\qquad = 59.52\%$ (to 2 decimal places)

Profit margin $= \dfrac{\text{profit for the year}}{\text{revenue}} \times 100$

Year ended 31 January 2017:

Profit margin $= \dfrac{(110\,000 - 75\,000)}{200\,000} \times 100 = 17.5\%$

Year ended 31 January 2018:

Profit margin $= \dfrac{(125\,000 - 90\,000)}{210\,000} \times 100$

$\qquad\qquad = 16.67\%$ (to 2 decimal places).

2   Yang Guang will be satisfied that his gross margin has increased from 55% to 59.52%. This shows that his profitability has improved. However, he will be concerned that his profit margin has decreased from 17.5% to 16.67%. This has been caused by the large increase in expenses.

3   Yang Guang needs to control his expenses in order to increase his profit margin. He could reduce the amount he spends on advertising, and heating and lighting his premises, or consider reducing the amount he spends on wages.

Return on capital employed

The **return on capital employed (ROCE)** is a very important ratio. The higher the value of the ratio, the more efficiently the capital invested into the business is being employed. In order to maximise the return on capital employed a business needs to increase its profit for the year.

Worked example 3

Ariella owns an electrical store and operates as a sole trader. She has extracted the following balances from her books at 31 March 2018.

	$
Revenue	300 000
Inventory – 1 April 2017	18 000
Inventory – 31 March 2018	22 000
Purchases	244 000
Closing capital employed	500 000
Expenses	36 000

1 Prepare an income statement for Ariella's electrical store for the year ended 31 March 2018.

2 Calculate the following profitability ratios based on the financial information that has been provided:

- Gross margin

- Profit margin

- Return on capital employed (ROCE).

3 Analyse the profitability of Ariella's business.

1

Ariella electrical store Income statement for the year ended 31 March 2018			
	$	$	$
Revenue			300 000
Less cost of sales			
Opening inventory	18 000		
Purchases	244 000		
		262 000	
Closing inventory		22 000	
Cost of Sales			240 000
Gross profit			60 000
Less expenses			
Total expenses		36 000	
			36 000
Profit for the year			24 000

2 Gross margin $= \dfrac{\text{gross profit}}{\text{revenue}} \times 100$

$= \dfrac{60\,000}{300\,000} \times 100 = 20\%$

Profit margin $= \dfrac{\text{profit for the year}}{\text{revenue}} \times 100$

$= \dfrac{24\,000}{300\,000} \times 100 = 8\%$

Return on capital employed $= \dfrac{\text{profit for the year}}{\text{capital employed}} \times 100$

$= \dfrac{24\,000}{500\,000} \times 100 = 4.8\%$

3
- The gross margin is 20% and the profit margin is 8%. The profit margin is less than half of the gross margin, which means expenses are particularly high. Ariella needs to review her expenditure in order to increase her profit margin.

- The return on capital employed at 4.8% is very low. There is a risk involved in running any business and such a low return does not compensate for this risk. It is likely that an investor could receive a higher return with no risk by saving in a bank.

Activity or efficiency ratios
Rate of inventory turnover
The rate of inventory turnover calculates the number of times a business sells and replaces its inventory over a period of time.

The rate of inventory turnover will vary depending on the type of business.

A business selling luxury cars, for example Bentley motors, has a low rate of inventory turnover. However, a business that sells day-to-day essentials, for example bread and milk, has a much higher rate of inventory turnover. Usually, businesses have a similar rate of inventory turnover year on year. An increase in the rate of inventory turnover indicates that the business has become more efficient.

A decrease in the rate of inventory turnover implies that the business has too much inventory stored or that sales have fallen.

Key knowledge

A low rate of inventory turnover could be caused by:
- business inefficiency
- a reduction in business activity
- falling demand in the current market
- a significant increase in selling prices
- the business purchasing too much inventory
- lower sales.

Worked example 4

Aloysius owns a local patisserie, selling luxury cakes and pastries.

He has calculated his rate of inventory turnover for the last year as 335 times.

The industry average for the rate of inventory turnover is 300 times.

1 Explain whether Aloysius should be satisfied with his rate of inventory turnover.

2 Describe how Aloysius could improve his rate of inventory turnover.

---

1 Aloysius will be satisfied with his rate of inventory turnover. His turnover rate is higher than the industry average. This means that he will not be left with out of date inventory, which is important due to the type of business that Aloysius is operating.

2 Aloysius could consider:
   - Using a cheaper supplier for raw materials. However, this may cause customers to shop elsewhere as the quality of his products may decrease.
   - Increasing the amount of advertising that he does to enhance his brand image.

Trade receivables turnover

The **trade receivables turnover** measures the average time it takes credit customers to pay their accounts. This needs to be compared with the credit terms that were offered to the customers when they made their purchases. For example, a furniture retailer may offer customers 90 days to pay for goods. If the trade receivables turnover period is 85 days, then the business is efficiently collecting its debts. However, if the trade receivables turnover period is 150 days, then the business needs to investigate.

The quicker customers pay their debts, the better this is for the business. It can then use this money to pay other debts and for day-to-day operations. If a debt is outstanding for a considerable amount of time, there is more chance that the debt will remain unpaid and become an **irrecoverable debt**.

If the trade receivables turnover period decreases from one year to the next, it implies that the business is maintaining effective credit control. If the trade receivables turnover period increases from one year to the next, it may indicate that credit control is ineffective. It could also mean that the business has needed to offer extended credit terms to customers so as to remain competitive.

Key knowledge

A business could improve its trade receivables turnover period by:

- improving the credit control, for example by sending regular statements to all credit customers, chasing overdue accounts, reducing the length of the credit period offered to credit customers
- offering cash discounts for early payment
- charging interest on overdue accounts
- offering cash sales only
- refusing further supplies until all accounts have been settled
- **debt factoring**.

Key term

Debt factoring: Occurs when a business sells its outstanding customer accounts to a debt factoring company. The factoring company pays the business a set percentage of the value of the debts (80–90%) and then collects the full amount of the debts. Once collected the business receives the remaining amount less a charge.

Trade payables turnover

The **trade payables turnover** measures the average time that it takes a business to pay its credit suppliers. The same business may have a similar trade payables turnover period from one year to the next. If the trade payables turnover period decreases, the business pays its credit suppliers more quickly. If the trade payables turnover period increases, the business may be short of liquid assets and unable to pay its debts.

It is important that the trade payables turnover period is compared with the trade receivables turnover period. If credit customers do not pay their debts on time, then the business will be unable to pay its credit suppliers as it has insufficient funds.

Delaying payment to credit suppliers allows a business to use the money for other purposes.

Key knowledge

Negative effects of delaying payment to a credit supplier:

- Damaging business reputation with the supplier
- Loss of any cash discount offered for early payment
- Suppliers refusing to offer business credit terms in the future
- Suppliers refusing to supply goods to a business in the future.

Worked example 5

The owner of Jo's Pet Warehouse has provided the following balances from their books of account at 30 April 2018.

	$
Credit sales	530 000
Credit purchases	250 000
Trade receivables	15 000
Trade payables	30 000

1   Calculate the following ratios based on the financial information that has been provided.

- Trade receivables turnover

- Trade payables turnover

2   Analyse the efficiency of Jo's Pet Warehouse.

---

1   Trade receivables turnover $= \dfrac{\text{trade receivables}}{\text{credit sales}} \times 365$

$$= \dfrac{15\,000}{530\,000} \times 365$$

$$= 10.33 \text{ days (to 2 decimal places)}$$

$$\text{Trade payables turnover} = \frac{\text{trade payables}}{\text{credit purchases}} \times 365$$

$$= \frac{30\,000}{250\,000} \times 365$$

$$= 43.80 \text{ days (to 2 decimal places)}$$

2 The trade receivables turnover period is relatively short, with trade receivables settling their accounts within 11 days. Usual credit terms are 30, 60, or 90 days.

The trade payables turnover period is in excess of the trade receivables turnover period. This is beneficial as it allows Jo's Pet Warehouse to pay its debts after receiving payment from customers. To ensure loyalty with suppliers, Jo's Pet Warehouse should consider paying its debts within 30 days.

Liquidity or solvency ratios

Current ratio

The current ratio can be referred to as the working capital ratio. Although the benchmark for this ratio is 2 : 1, a ratio between 1.5 : 1 and 2 : 1 may be considered satisfactory depending on the type of business being considered. A ratio in excess of 2 : 1 requires investigation. Typically, it indicates poor management of current assets. For example, the business could be holding too much inventory or the value of trade receivables is too high. It is vital that the working capital of a business is adequate to finance its day-to-day trading activities. A shortage of working capital means that a business could not meet its liabilities when they were due. As a consequence, suppliers may not offer trade credit to the business.

Worked example 6

Worldwide travel plc is a commercial airline, providing transportation for business goods.

The finance director has provided the business's statement of financial position for the years ended 31 December 2017 and 31 December 2018.

Worldwide travel plc Statement of financial position for the years ended 31 December 2017 and 31 December 2018		
	2018	2017
	$'000	$'000
Non-current assets	5426	5377
Current assets		
Inventory	32	27
Trade receivables	973	926
Cash at bank	340	550
Other	129	182

	1474	1685
Total assets	900	7062
Share capital	91	86
Reserves	1651	1634
	1742	1720
Non-current liabilities	1773	1154
	1773	1154
Current liabilities		
Trade payables	1821	1904
Short-term loans	1564	2284
	3385	4188
Total liabilities	6900	7062

1   Calculate the current ratio, for Worldwide travel plc, for the years ended 31 December 2017 **and** 31 December 2018.

2   Analyse the liquidity of Worldwide travel plc.

1   **31 December 2017**

Current ratio $= \dfrac{\text{current assets}}{\text{current liabilities}}$

$= \dfrac{1685000}{4188000} = 0.40 : 1$ (to 2 decimal places)

31 December 2018

Current ratio $= \dfrac{\text{current assets}}{\text{current liabilities}}$

$= \dfrac{1474000}{3385000} = 0.44 : 1$ (to 2 decimal places)

2   • The current ratios of 0.40 : 1 and 0.44 : 1 are very low.

   • A satisfactory current ratio for this type of business is 2 : 1. Worldwide travel plc's ratios are considerably lower than the expected level, which indicates a liquidity problem. It is likely that the business will be unable to pay its debts if these needed to be paid immediately.

   • Worldwide travel plc needs to continue to reduce the amount of money that it owes to its trade payables and for its short-term loans.

Liquid (acid test) ratio

The liquid (acid test) ratio compares assets that are in the form of money or those which can be quickly converted into money, for example trade receivables with current liabilities. A satisfactory liquid (acid test) ratio is 1 : 1. As with the current ratio, this depends on the type of business being considered. A liquid (acid test) ratio in excess of 1 : 1 may indicate poor management of liquid current assets. For example, a business should investigate whether there is too high a balance on the current account, in which case the money should be used to pay the business's debts.

Key knowledge

It is possible to improve the working capital position of a business by:

- obtaining a short-term loan or overdraft
- selling any surplus non-current assets, for example spare machinery or vehicles
- reducing the amount of drawings taken by the business owner(s)
- the owner(s) introducing additional capital into the business
- improving the amount of cash in the business by:
  (a) delaying payment to trade payables
  (b) decreasing the credit period offered to customers
  (c) increasing the number of cash sales.

3 Identify **three** disadvantages of a shortage of working capital for a business.

Worked example 7

Dakshina operates as a sole trader. She has extracted the following balances from her books at 30 April 2018.

	$
Inventory – 31 March 2018	22 000
Trade receivables	56 000
Trade payables	64 000
Cash at bank	7 000
Closing capital employed	500 000

1 Calculate the following ratios based on the financial information that has been provided:

- Current ratio

- Liquid (acid test) ratio.

2 Analyse the liquidity of Dakshina's business.

---

1 Current ratio = $\dfrac{\text{current assets}}{\text{current liabilities}}$

$= \dfrac{(22\,000 + 56\,000 + 7000)}{64\,000}$

$= \dfrac{85\,000}{64\,000} = 1.33 : 1 \text{ (to 2 decimal places)}$

$$\text{Liquid (acid test) ratio} = \frac{\text{current assets} - \text{closing inventory}}{\text{current liabilities}}$$

$$= \frac{(85\,000 - 22\,000)}{64\,000}$$

$$= 0.98 : 1 \text{ (to 2 decimal places)}$$

2
- The current ratio of 1.33 : 1 is lower than expected for a general trading business. The standard expected in this sector is usually 2 : 1. This appears to have been caused by high levels of trade receivables and trade payables.

- The liquid (acid test) ratio is at an acceptable level of 1 : 1. This means that Dakshina would be able to pay all of her debts should they need repaying. However, Dakshina owes a large amount of money to her trade payables.

- Dakshina has very little cash available at the bank to be able to meet the debts that are due to be paid.

The relationship of gross profit and profit for the year to the valuation of inventory, rate of inventory turnover, revenue, expenses and equity is shown in the table below.

	Gross profit	Profit for the year
Calculation	Gross profit = sales revenue – cost of sales	Profit for the year = gross profit – expenses
Valuation of inventory	Opening and closing inventory are used to calculate cost of sales. Cost of sales = opening inventory + purchases – closing Inventory. An increase or decrease in the value of inventory will alter the cost of sales which in turn will affect the gross profit. For example, an increase in cost of sales will decrease the gross profit of a business. You met this in Unit 4.5.	Inventory valuation will affect the gross profit value which will then have an impact on the profit for the year.
Rate of inventory turnover	Rate of inventory turnover = $\dfrac{\text{cost of sales}}{\text{average inventory}}$ Profit is connected to but not directly related to the rate of inventory turnover of a business.	
Revenue	Assuming the cost of sales does not change: • an increase in sales revenue will increase the gross profit of a business • a decrease in sales revenue will decrease the gross profit of a business.	Revenue will affect the gross profit value which will then have an impact on the profit for the year.
Expenses	The expenses of a business do not have any impact on the gross profit.	Assuming the gross profit does not change: • an increase in expenses will decrease the profit for the year • a decrease in expenses will increase the profit for the year.
Equity	The value of a business's equity is calculated using the accounting equation: Equity = assets – liabilities Profit and equity are connected. However, this depends on whether profit is taken out of the business by the owner(s) as drawings. Profit that is not taken as drawings will add to equity. In this way equity increases with profit, and equity decreases with losses.	

Applying

Complete this task in pairs.

Task

Dover and Sole new car sales has provided the following balances from its accounts for the financial years ended 31 January 2017 and 31 January 2018.

	31 January 2017	31 January 2018
	$	$
	'000	'000
Revenue	12900	13250
Opening inventory	650	980
Closing inventory	980	870
Purchases	1550	2750
Total expenses	770	990
Trade receivables	810	930
Trade payables	570	710
Cash at bank	53	235
Closing capital employed	3050	2950

1 Calculate the following ratios to review the financial results of 'Dover and Sole new car sales' for the years ended 31 January 2017 **and** 31 January 2018:

- Gross margin
- Profit margin
- Return on capital employed (ROCE)
- Rate of inventory turnover
- Trade receivables turnover
- Trade payables turnover
- Current ratio
- Liquid (acid test) ratio.

2 Comment on 'Dover and Sole new car sales' financial performance.

Knowledge check

1 Janna has calculated her current ratio for the last two years:

2017:   2.5 : 1

2018:   2 : 1

Her current liabilities remained the same in 2017 and 2018.

Which of the following could be a reason for the decrease in Janna's current ratio?

A   Decrease in trade payables
B   Increase in trade payables
C   Decrease in trade receivables
D   Increase in trade receivables

2 Westwell Commercial's profit margin has decreased over the last two years.

Which of the following could be a reason for the decrease?

A   Decrease in business assets
B   Increase in business assets
C   Decrease in business expenses
D   Increase in business expenses

3 Which of the following ratios allows a business to assess its current profitability in order to make improvements?

A   Gross margin
B   Rate of inventory turnover
C   Trade payables turnover
D   Trade receivables turnover

4 Explain why the liquid (acid test) ratio is more effective than the current ratio as a measure of a business's liquidity.

5 Explain how the valuation of inventory affects the gross profit of a business.

6 A sole trader has been offered trade credit of 90 days. They always settle invoices within 50 days. Explain **one** advantage and **one** disadvantage of paying before the 90 days.

7 Identify **two** ratios that would allow a business owner to assess the liquidity of their business.

8 Make **two** recommendations of how a small retail business could improve its profit margin.

9 Describe **two** reasons why the rate of inventory turnover of a business may fall.

10 An office furniture supplier allows customers 60 days' credit. The collection period is currently 75 days. Explain whether the supplier should be satisfied with this result.

11 Suggest **two** actions a business can take in order to improve its working capital.

12 Farnoud owns and runs a large furniture business. He has provided the following balances from his accounts for the financial years ended 31 January 2017 and 31 January 2018.

	31 January 2017	31 January 2018
	$	$
	'000	'000
Revenue	4000	4600
Opening inventory	690	910
Closing inventory	910	435
Purchases	2015	1825
Total expenses	755	1310
Trade receivables	470	1230
Trade payables	650	620
Cash at bank	50	940
Closing capital employed	2218	1733

(a) Calculate the following ratios based on the financial information that has been provided.

- Gross margin
- Profit margin
- Return on capital employed (ROCE)
- Rate of inventory turnover
- Trade receivables turnover
- Trade payables turnover
- Current ratio
- Liquid (acid test) ratio

(b) Comment on Farnoud's business's performance.

Check your progress

Read the unit objectives below and reflect on your progress in each.

- Prepare and comment on simple statements showing comparison of results for different years
- Make recommendations and suggestions for improving profitability and working capital

 I struggle with this and need more practice.

 I can do this reasonably well.

I can do this with confidence.

- Understand the significance of the difference between the gross margin and the profit margin as an indicator of a business's efficiency
- Explain the relationship of gross profit and profit for the year to the valuation of inventory, rate of inventory turnover, revenue, expenses, and equity.

Inter-firm comparison

Learning objectives
By the end of this unit, you should be able to:
- understand the problems of inter-firm comparison
- apply accounting ratios to inter-firm comparison.

Starting point

Answer these questions in pairs.

1 Identify three ratios that could be reviewed to assess the efficiency of a business.

2 What are the benefits of comparing this year's ratio results with those of previous years?

3 Describe three items included in a statement of financial position that would be useful to a business considering expansion.

Exploring

Discuss these questions in pairs.

1 Discuss the benefits of a business being able to compare its financial results with those of similar businesses.

2 Identify a suitable business that a local butcher's store could use to compare financial results.

Developing

Problems of inter-firm comparison

The previous unit considered how businesses may compare their ratio results against benchmarks or industry averages and previous years' results, known as trend analysis.

This unit considers how businesses may compare their ratio results against other businesses, for example local competitors. This is known as inter-firm comparison.

It is a meaningless activity to compare one business's performance with another unless they are similar. For example, it is inappropriate to compare a local takeaway with a large multinational business such as McDonald's. Ideally, both businesses should be of a similar size and operating in the same

Key term

Inter-firm comparison: This is where a business compares its financial performance with another business of a similar size in the same business sector.

industry in order to obtain information that could be used for analysis and evaluation.

Business size can be measured in terms of sales revenue or capital employed. This form of comparison and industry analysis allows a business to assess how other businesses are dealing with external factors that also affect them. For example, a top league football club could compare itself against another club competing in the same league. It could then review how both clubs are managing changes in television rights and funding.

A business is able to obtain important information by comparing its accounting ratios with those of another business. However, the business must be aware that there are a number of limitations to using inter-firm comparison. Every business is different, uses different accounting principles and procedures and has different requirements. For example:

- A business may apply different accounting principles when preparing its financial statements.

- Financial statements are based on historical data and historic cost. They do not account for the effects of inflation. When using the information from an inter-firm comparison, a business needs to consider the current economic climate and what may happen in the future.

1 Describe **two** different depreciation methods that could be used by businesses. Explain how the use of these depreciation methods would affect a business's profit for the year.

- Non-monetary items do not appear in the accounting records of a business. For example, goodwill and the skills of the workforce do not appear in the financial statements. They are, however, vital to the success of any business.

- The information provided for another business may be for one year only. Therefore, there is no opportunity to calculate business trends. When comparing ratio results, a business must remember that the results being used for comparison are only a 'snapshot' and may not be a typical year.

- Different businesses may apply different operating policies. This may include renting premises in preference to purchasing premises, and obtaining long-term finance from business owners only rather than equity from business owners and long-term loans. The choice of policy may have an impact on both the profit for the year and the statement of financial position.

2 Identify **three** business situations that would mean a business is not operating in a typical manner.

Key term

Accounting principles: Specific rules that are used by a business to prepare its financial statements.

- It is not always possible to gain all of the information about another business that is required for a comprehensive comparison. For example, a statement of financial position provides a net book value for non-current assets. It does not inform the reader when they were purchased, how old each asset is or when it is planned to sell these assets.

- Different businesses have different financial year-ends. For example, one business may have a year end on 30 April and another business may have a year end on 31 December. This makes comparison difficult. Depending on the type of business, inventory levels may be lower at certain times of the year and this is reflected in the financial statements. This is particularly relevant for seasonal businesses. For example, an ice cream business has considerably more inventory during the summer months than during the winter period.

CASE STUDY

During 2016, Sainsbury's, one of the UK's largest supermarket chains, reviewed its financial performance in order to stay competitive.

Sainsbury's total sales revenue fell by 1.1% to £25.8bn due to falling food prices and intense competition from low-cost supermarkets Aldi and Lidl.

Inter-firm comparison is important for supermarket chains in this highly competitive market to help them make informed management decisions. Supermarkets may compare themselves against the total market share or against competitors.

For the 12 weeks to 24 April 2016, the following till roll values were declared by a number of supermarket chains in Great Britain. These results can be used to measure market share, analyse current performance and allow for targets to be set for the future.

	£ millions
Tesco	7122
Sainsbury's	4182
Asda	4069
Morrisons	2690
Co-op	1571
Aldi	1529
Waitrose	1322
Lidl	1118

Profitability ratios

Businesses often compare their profitability with other businesses in the same industry. However, it is meaningless to compare absolute figures in isolation.

 A sole trader, selling kitchen appliances, has decided to review their year-end financial ratios against the results of a multinational business. Explain why this is not appropriate.

Gross margin

The gross margin, which shows the amount of gross profit earned for every $100 of sales revenue, could meaningfully be compared with other businesses.

Key knowledge

Differences between two businesses' gross margins could be caused by differences in:

- selling prices
- organisational advertising and sales promotions
- supplier costs
- level of trade discounts
- sales revenue.

Profit margin

Similarly, the profit margin, which shows the profit for the year earned for every $100 of sales revenue, can also be compared.

Key knowledge

Differences between two businesses' profit margins could be caused by differences in:

- cost of sales
- gross margin
- expenses, for example staff wage rates
- accounting principles, for example depreciation method
- sales revenue.

Return on capital employed (ROCE)

The return on capital employed (ROCE) ratio of one business can be compared effectively with the result of another business. However, it is important to remember that businesses may calculate their capital employed in different ways. This ratio highlights the return that is being earned for every $100 of capital employed in the business.

Worked example 1

Trinity plc has provided the following information relating to its financial performance:

Gross margin	20%
Profit margin	15%
Return on capital employed	11%

Trinity plc's local competitor Fleetwood plc has provided the following financial information:

Gross margin	35%
Profit margin	20%
Return on capital employed	15%

1 Compare Trinity plc's ratio results with those of Fleetwood plc.

2 Advise the management of Trinity plc how they could improve the company's ratio results.

---

1 Trinity plc will be disappointed that its gross margin is 15% lower than that of its competitor. This may have been as a result of Trinity plc reducing its mark-up in order to encourage sales. Alternatively, Trinity plc may have purchased goods for resale that cost more to buy.

   Although Trinity plc's profit margin is lower than that of Fleetwood plc, the difference is smaller than that of the gross margin. The difference in profit margins is 5%.

   This means that Trinity plc is managing its expenses more effectively.

   Trinity plc's return on capital employed is 4% lower than its competitor's. It may find it difficult to encourage individuals to invest in its business.

2 Trinity plc needs to consider:

   - Increasing its selling price. However, this may mean that customers will go to a competitor.

   - Purchasing goods from a cheaper supplier. However, this may mean that the quality of goods being sold may decline, causing customers to buy elsewhere.

   - Increasing the amount of advertising and marketing to encourage more sales, but this will increase expenses.

Worked example 2

Zeki is the management accountant of SPG plc. He is preparing a report on the profitability of the company.

Zeki has provided the following information for SPG plc and the profitability ratios for its local competitor.

SPG plc Financial information for the year ended 30 April 2018	
	$
Revenue	1 500 000
Gross profit	870 000
Expenses	375 000
Capital employed	950 000

SPG's competitor ratio data:

Gross margin	31%
Profit margin	19%
Return on capital employed	17%

1 Calculate the following ratios for SPG plc for the year ended 30 April 2018.

- Gross margin
- Profit margin
- Return on capital employed (ROCE).

2 Analyse the profitability of SPG plc.

---

1 Gross margin $= \dfrac{\text{gross profit}}{\text{revenue}} \times 100$

$= \dfrac{870\,000}{1\,500\,000} \times 100 = 58\%$

Profit margin $= \dfrac{\text{profit for the year}}{\text{revenue}} \times 100$

$= \dfrac{(870\,000 - 375\,000)}{1\,500\,000} \times 100 = 33\%$

Return on capital employed $= \dfrac{\text{profit for the year}}{\text{capital employed}} \times 100$

$= \dfrac{(870\,000 - 375\,000)}{950\,000} \times 100$

$= 52.11\%$ (2 decimal places)

2 SPG plc will be satisfied with its gross margin of 58%. This is considerably higher than the local competitor's gross margin. SPG plc's ratio is 27% higher than the competitor's.

SPG plc will also be satisfied with its profit margin. This is considerably (14%) higher than the local competitor's.

However, the difference between gross margin and profit margin is 12% for the local competitor but 25% for SPG plc. This implies that SPG plc is not managing its expenses efficiently.

SPG plc will be extremely satisfied with its return on capital employed of 52.11%. This is considerably higher than the local competitor's. In comparison to other investment opportunities, 52.11% is very high. SPG plc will have no problem in attracting an investor to purchase shares or to invest in its business.

Activity or efficiency ratios

Rate of inventory turnover

The rate of inventory turnover of a business can be successfully compared against another business's result to measure its efficiency. However, it is vital that the business used for comparison operates in the same industry. The rate of inventory turnover varies considerably from one industry to another. For example, comparing a luxury car manufacturer's inventory turnover with a budget car manufacturer's turnover would be inappropriate and lead to misleading results.

Key knowledge

Differences between two businesses' rate of inventory turnover could be caused by differences in:

- cost of sales
  - opening inventory
  - purchases
  - closing inventory
- average inventory values.

Worked example 3

Shailyn operates a business that manufactures engineering components.

He has calculated his rate of inventory turnover for the last twelve months as 90 times.

Shailyn has downloaded the published accounts for a local competitor that also manufactures engineering components. It has a rate of inventory turnover of 73 times.

1   Explain whether Shailyn should be satisfied with his rate of inventory turnover.

2   Describe how Shailyn could improve his rate of inventory turnover.

1   Shailyn should be satisfied with his rate of inventory turnover as his current turnover rate is higher than the rate of the local competitor.

2   Shailyn could consider using a cheaper supplier for his raw materials. However, this may cause customers to shop elsewhere as the quality of his products may decrease. He could also ask his current supplier for a trade discount to reduce his purchase costs if he buys in bulk.

Trade receivables turnover

The trade receivables turnover calculates the average time it takes a business to collect the money that is owed from its trade receivables.

Businesses need to compare their result with the trade credit period that has been offered to their customers and also against other local businesses in the same line of trade.

Trade payables turnover

The trade payables turnover calculates the average time it takes a business to pay the money that it owes to its trade payables.

As with the trade receivables turnover period, businesses need to compare their result with the trade credit period that has been offered by their suppliers and also against other local businesses in the same line of trade.

Key knowledge

Differences between two businesses' trade payables turnover could be caused by differences in the:

- amount owing to trade payables
- value of credit purchases.

Worked example 4

Aref and Aya garden centre has been operating for a number of years. The owners are looking to diversify and are reviewing the financial statements. They have calculated the financial ratios based on the latest financial statements. The owners have obtained the results of a local competitor, Outdoor Plants garden centre, to use for comparison.

	Aref and Aya garden centre	Outdoor Plants garden centre
Gross margin	30%	40%
Profit margin	5%	20%
Return on capital employed	3%	12%
Current ratio	2 : 1	1.9 : 1
Liquid (acid test) ratio	0.6 : 1	1 : 1
Rate of inventory turnover	13 times	8 times

Use the ratio information provided to analyse the financial performance of Aref and Aya Garden Centre.

- The current ratio of Aref and Aya garden centre is marginally higher than the result for Outdoor Plants garden centre.

- The liquid (acid test) ratio of Aref and Aya garden centre is considerably below the result of Outdoor Plants garden centre. This could be caused by a high level of inventory. It may lead to problems if Aref and Aya garden centre is unable to pay its credit suppliers in a timely manner.

- The gross margin of Aref and Aya garden centre is 10% lower than the competitor's. This could have been caused by a reduction in selling price or mark-up in an attempt to attract more customers. Alternatively, Aref and Aya garden centre may have paid a higher purchase price for its goods for resale.

- The inventory turnover rate of Aref and Aya garden centre is higher than the competitor's. This implies that the garden centre has reduced its selling price in order to increase sales.

- The profit margin of Aref and Aya garden centre is considerable lower than Outdoor Plants garden centre. This implies that expenses are very high and need to be controlled. A review of marketing and selling costs should be undertaken.

- The return on capital employed of Aref and Aya garden centre is considerably lower than Outdoor Plants garden centre's. The current rate does not provide investors with an adequate return. There are alternative investments available that would have higher returns with less risk.

Liquidity or solvency ratios

Businesses often compare their liquidity with other businesses in the same industry. However, it is meaningless to compare absolute figures in isolation.

Liquidity is essential to any business to ensure that they are able to meet all of their short-term debts.

 4 What issues does a business need to consider when comparing its results with those of another business.

Current ratio

The current ratio compares a business's current assets with its current liabilities. 2 : 1 is usually acknowledged as the benchmark figure for this ratio.

The current ratio of a business can be meaningfully compared both against the benchmark and also against another business's result.

Key knowledge

Differences between two businesses' current ratios may be caused by differences in:

- current assets totals:
  - closing inventory values
  - amount of cash and money at the bank
  - amount owing from trade receivables
- current liabilities totals:
  - amount owing to trade payables
  - amount of money owing to the bank – overdrafts
  - amount of money owing for short-term loans.

Liquid (acid test) ratio

Similarly, the liquid (acid test) ratio, which compares a business's current assets less its closing inventory with the current liabilities, can be compared. 1 : 1 is considered a satisfactory ratio, so businesses can compare against the benchmark and also against other businesses.

Key knowledge

Differences between two businesses' liquid (acid test) ratios may be caused by differences in:

- current assets totals:
  - amount of cash and money at the bank
  - amount owing from trade receivables
- current liabilities totals:
  - amount owing to trade payables
  - amount of money owing to the bank – overdrafts
  - amount of money owing for short-term loans.

Worked example 5

Yoo Sang is considering purchasing shares in a public limited company. Yoo Sang is keen to invest in a company that does not have any liquidity issues.

She has downloaded the following financial information about the two companies she is considering.

	Pabna plc	Jamalpur plc
	$	$
Closing inventory	30 000	85 000
Trade receivables	55 000	125 000
Trade payables	95 000	63 000
Cash at bank	100 000	
Bank overdraft		25 000

1 Calculate the following ratios for Pabna plc **and** Jamalpur plc:
   - Current ratio
   - Liquid (acid test) ratio.

2 Analyse the liquidity of both businesses to allow Yoo Sang to make an informed investment decision.

---

1 Current ratio $= \dfrac{\text{current assets}}{\text{current liabilities}}$

Pabna plc:

Current ratio $= \dfrac{(30\,000 + 55\,000 + 100\,000)}{95\,000} = 1.95 : 1$

Jamalpur plc:

Current ratio $= \dfrac{(85\,000 + 125\,000)}{(63\,000 + 25\,000)} = 2.39 : 1$

Liquid (acid test) ratio $= \dfrac{\text{current assets} - \text{closing inventory}}{\text{current liabilities}}$

Pabna plc:

Liquid (acid test) ratio $= \dfrac{(55\,000 + 100\,000)}{95\,000} = 1.63 : 1$

Jamalpur plc:

Liquid (acid test) ratio $= \dfrac{125\,000}{(63\,000 + 25\,000)} = 1.42 : 1$

2 The current ratio of Pabna plc, 1.95 : 1, is slightly lower than the benchmark of 2 : 1 and lower than the result for Jamalpur plc. This appears to have been caused by a high level of trade payables. Jamalpur plc's current ratio is considerably above the benchmark. It has a considerable amount of inventory and money owing from trade receivables. Jamalpur plc should try to reduce its inventory levels to prevent these going out of date and collect the money from its trade receivables.

Based on the ratio analysis and Yoo Sang's requirements, you might advise her to invest in Pabna plc. The liquid (acid test) ratio is a tougher test of a business's liquidity than the current ratio. Pabna plc's liquid (acid test) ratio is higher than that of Jamalpur plc's and meets Yoo Sang's requirements.

The liquid (acid test) ratio of Pabna plc of 1.63 : 1 is above the benchmark of 1 : 1. This means that it is able to pay all of its debts should they need repaying. Pabna plc's liquid (acid test) ratio value is above that of Jamalpur plc. However, Jamalpur plc's result is above the benchmark but is lower than Pabna plc's due to the high level of inventory and the bank overdraft that the business is currently using.

Applying

Complete this task in pairs.

Task

White Cliffs Outdoor Supplies provided the following ratios based on its accounts for the financial year ended 31 January 2018. A local business, Glencoe Mountain Warehouse has provided its ratios to allow for comparison.

	White Cliffs Outdoor Supplies	Glencoe Mountain Warehouse
Gross margin	50%	25%
Profit margin	30%	20%
Return on capital employed	15%	7%
Current ratio	3 : 1	2 : 1
Liquid (acid test) ratio	2 : 1	1 : 1
Rate of inventory turnover	20 times	15 times

Use the ratio information provided to analyse the financial performance of White Cliffs Outdoor Supplies.

Knowledge check

1   A sole trader compares his financial statements for the year with those of a similar business in the local area.

Which of the following will show how effectively the sole trader is controlling his expenses?

A   Cash at bank

B   Cost of sales

C   Gross profit

D   Profit for the year

2   A small coffee shop is to complete an inter-firm ratio comparison.

Which of the following would be most appropriate to use for the comparison?

A   A local coffee shop

B   A multinational coffee shop chain

C   A nationwide coffee shop provider

D   An overseas coffee shop supplier

3 Sinhala Ltd has calculated its accounting ratios for the year ended 30 January 2018.

Which of the following ratios would Sinhala Ltd compare with a local competitor, in order to review the efficiency of its operations?

A Current ratio

B Gross margin

C Liquid (acid test) ratio

D Rate of inventory turnover

4 Define the term inter-firm comparison.

5 Discuss **three** limitations of a business's use of inter-firm comparison to review its ratio results.

6 Zhongguo and Huaxia operate as a partnership, providing office lunches to local businesses. They plan to expand their operation and are reviewing their year-end financial accounts. They have calculated their ratios based on their year-end results and have also obtained the financial ratios of a similar business in the local area

	Zhongguo and Huaxia office lunches	Shenzhou lunch on the go!
Gross margin	50%	35%
Profit margin	25%	20%
Return on capital employed	30%	25%
Current ratio	2.5 : 1	1.85 : 1
Liquid (acid test) ratio	1.5 : 1	1 : 1
Rate of inventory turnover	360 times	300 times

(a) Explain whether Zhongguo and Huaxia should be satisfied with their profitability ratios.

(b) Identify **two** possible reasons for Zhongguo and Huaxia office lunches' current ratio being higher than that of Shenzhou lunch on the go!

(c) Explain whether Zhongguo and Huaxia should be satisfied with their efficiency ratio.

(d) Based on the inter-firm comparison, identify **three** actions that Zhongguo and Huaxia should consider in order to improve their business.

(e) Explain **two** benefits for Zhongguo and Huaxia of comparing their ratio results with those of Shenzhou lunch on the go!.

Check your progress

Read the unit objectives below and reflect on your progress in each.

Calculate and explain the importance of the following ratios:

- Understand the problems of inter-firm comparison
- Apply accounting ratios to inter-firm comparison.

I struggle with this and need more practice.

 I can do this reasonably well.

 I can do this with confidence.

Interested parties

Learning objectives

By the end of this unit, you should be able to:

- explain the uses of accounting information for decision-making by the following interested parties:
  - owners
  - managers
  - trade payables
  - banks
  - investors
  - club members
  - other interested parties such as governments and tax authorities.

Starting point

Answer these questions in pairs.

1. Identify three ratios that enable an owner to assess a business's efficiency.

2. Why would a business manager compare this year's ratio results with those of last year?

3. Explain the importance of the current ratio to a sole trader.

Exploring

Discuss these questions in pairs.

1. Discuss how an income statement of a sole trader can be used to review business growth.

2. How does a potential shareholder use the financial information produced by a public limited company?

3. How might a partner use the gross margin and profit margin of the business?

Developing

Stakeholders

Interested parties are known as business stakeholders.

Every business has many different stakeholder groups. Each of these groups may have very different objectives. For example, when a supermarket chain plans to open a 24-hour superstore in a small town, local residents may welcome the idea of having a superstore close to their homes and the opportunities for employment.

Key term

Stakeholder: An individual or group who has an interest in a business and may be directly affected by the activities of the business.

However, the residents may not welcome the extra traffic caused by deliveries and customers travelling from out of town. Other local businesses may object to the superstore as they will lose customers to the superstore. This is a financial risk as a small local business may not be able to continue to trade successfully.

There are two main types of business stakeholder:

- internal stakeholders
- external stakeholders

Businesses often categorise their stakeholders so that they can focus on the needs and wants of each group. Businesses will then be able to provide the relevant accounting information to allow the interested parties to make informed decisions.

 Identify **two** internal and **two** external stakeholders of a city centre hotel.

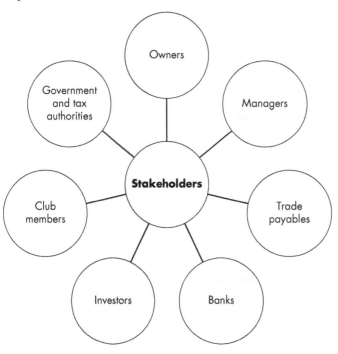

Stakeholders with an interest in financial information

Key terms

Internal stakeholder: Any individual or group that is directly involved with the business. For example, employees, managers, owners.

External stakeholder: Any individual or group who has an interest in a business but may not be directly involved with the business; for example, a local resident.

Owners

Business owners have an interest in all aspects of the operation. In particular, they are interested in the profitability, liquidity and efficiency of the business. This information allows individual owners to evaluate their business's performance and progress.

In a sole trader business, the owner is interested in the amount of profit for the year that is generated. This allows the owner to decide how much they can take out of the business as drawings.

Financial information allows an owner to make informed decisions about expansion, business growth or future opportunities.

Potential partners considering joining a partnership are interested in the profitability of a business. They will want to be assured that the business is likely to continue for the foreseeable future.

 Identify **three** ratios that may be of interest to a potential partner thinking of joining an existing partnership.

Managers

Managers and employees of any business need to be assured that it is likely to remain profitable and in operation for the foreseeable future. Any manager or employee of a business expects to be fairly paid, and have a long career with excellent working conditions.

Managers also have an interest in all aspects of the operation. In particular, they are interested in the profitability, liquidity and efficiency of the business.

A review of financial accounts and the use of ratio analysis allows managers to evaluate past performance, plan for the future and take action to solve problems if required.

Trade payables

Trade payables are the credit suppliers of a business. They provide the business with goods and services on credit and need to be repaid within the specified period.

Prior to offering credit, a supplier should review the liquidity position of the business. In particular, they may review the trade payables turnover to review current performance.

Following review, a supplier will decide on the credit limit and length of credit term that will be offered to a business.

For sole traders and partnerships, where financial statements are not publicly available, other means of checking credit-worthiness may need to be used.

Worked example 1

The owner of Al-Maseka chocolate house is considering supplying a retail store in the centre of Riyadh.

Al-Maseka chocolate house only offers customers 30 days' credit.

The retail store has provided its financial statements which show that the trade payables turnover period for the last two years has been 45 days and 41 days.

Advise the owner of Al-Maseka chocolate house as to whether they should supply the retail store.

The retail store's trade payables turnover period for the last two years implies that it is not able to meet the terms of Al-Maseka chocolate house.

It would be advisable for Al-Maseka chocolate house not to supply goods to the retail store on credit. It could offer to supply goods on a cash basis only.

Banks

Banks and other financial institutions use financial information to review the performance of a business prior to agreeing to lend money via an overdraft, loan or mortgage. A bank needs to know if a business has sufficient security to cover the amount of any loan. Banks also need to ensure that a business can repay any loan when it is due and that it has sufficient funds to pay the debt and any interest that has been charged.

When making a mortgage offer, a bank has to be sure that the non-current asset being purchased provides sufficient collateral in the unfortunate situation that the business cannot repay the debt.

Investors

Investors in limited companies are known as **shareholders**. Existing shareholders and individuals considering investment are interested in the profitability, liquidity and efficiency of the business. They need to know the amount of return they can expect to gain from their investment, whether their money is safe and the possible amount of dividends that they may earn.

 Identify **three** items in a public limited company's accounts that would be of interest to a potential investor.

Club members

Clubs, societies and associations are known as **third sector organisations**. These organisations exist to provide a service to their members and do not aim to make a profit.

Club members are individuals that have paid a subscription or membership fee to a club in order to benefit from their services. For example, an individual may pay an annual subscription to a gym and leisure centre. This will allow them to use the gym and all of the facilities at the leisure centre for a twelve-month period.

Club members expect their subscription money to be used appropriately. The financial statements show how subscription money has been used.

Key term

Collateral: An asset that is pledged as security for the repayment of a debt. In the event that the debt cannot be repaid, the asset will be taken by the lender.

Government and tax authorities

Central and local governments are key stakeholders of a business. The business is legally required to pay taxes on a regular basis and ensure that it complies with national and international laws. These include business laws, financial regulations and employment laws.

Government departments also compile business statistics for national review.

CASE STUDY

In 2016, a number of well-known multinational companies were in the news for making huge profits while paying relatively small amounts of corporation tax.

Following reviews by the UK government in 2016, it was discovered that:

In 2014, Facebook reported UK revenues of £105 million and paid £4327 in British corporation tax.

Apple made £34 billion in profit during the year to September 2014. Experts estimate that the UK accounted for £1.9 billion of that profit; the firm paid £11.8 million in British corporation tax.

Amazon announced profits of £34.4 million in the UK on sales of £5.3 billion and paid £11.9 million in British corporation tax.

The companies were able to use the tax regulations in various countries to their advantage to reduce the tax that they paid. Following the poor publicity, some companies agreed to pay more corporation tax.

Sources: *The Guardian*, 24 June 2015, 11 October 2015. *Daily Mail*, 4 July 2015

 Discuss the implications to a national government of companies paying smaller amounts of corporation tax than might be considered 'fair' in relation to their profits.

Stakeholders vs shareholders

There is an important difference between a stakeholder and a shareholder.

Shareholders hold shares in a limited company, which means that they own part of the business.

Stakeholders have an interest in a business but do not necessarily own it.

In many cases, the aims and objectives of the stakeholders are not the same as those of shareholders. This causes conflict.

For example, shareholders wish to maximise their investment and receive the highest possible dividend. This is possible if a business is able to maximise its profit for the year. By contrast, employees want a high wage, which reduces the profit for the year. This means that dividends to shareholders are reduced.

Accounting documentation requirements

Different types of businesses are required to prepare different accounting documentation, as shown in the table.

Type of business	Examples	Accounting documentation
Sole trader	Bakers Builders Butchers Painters and decorators Plumbers	Income statement Statement of financial position
Partnership	Accountants Architects Estate agents Solicitors Surveyors	Income statement Appropriation account Statement of financial position Current accounts Capital accounts
Private limited company	Wide range of businesses covering all industry sectors. Examples include: Dyson Harrods Group JCB Virgin Atlantic	Income statement Statement of financial position
Public limited company	British Airways plc Cadbury Schweppes plc Microsoft plc Nike plc Rolls-Royce plc	Annual report which includes: General corporate information Accounting policies Income statement Statement of financial position Statement of cash flows Notes to the financial statements Chairperson's and directors' reports Auditor's report
Third sector organisations	Associations Charities Clubs and societies	Receipts and payments account Income and expenditure account Bar/refreshments, etc. trading accounts Statement of financial position

Worked example 2

Highlight the features in the financial statements that would be of interest to the members of Daska golf and sports club.

1   Catering profit – the profit has decreased. Members may be concerned that the refreshment facilities may not continue to operate in the long term if profits keep declining.

2   Green fees from visitors – income has dramatically increased. Members will be happy that this brings money into the club which can be spent on improvements. However, it may prevent members being able to use the facilities.

3   Surplus of income over expenditure – the surplus has increased from 12530 to 16096. This will allow the club to spend money on improving facilities and maintaining the club.

Daska golf and sports club Income and expenditure account for the years ended 31 March 2017 and 2018				
	31 March 2018		31 March 2017	
	$	$	$	$
Income				
Catering profit	2142		3750	
Subscriptions	29604		26097	
Events	7830		5350	
Green fees from visitors	8300		5320	
		47876		40517
Expenditure				
Greenkeeper's wages	14000		12000	
Depreciation	2500		2500	
Rent and rates	8900		7800	
Printing	2500		2000	
Heat and light	3880		3687	
		31,780		27987
Surplus of income over expenditure		16096		12530

Applying

Complete this task in pairs.

Task

The following financial statements have been published by two 'international food stores':

- Reliance produce plc
- Grocery basket plc.

Income statements for the year ended 30 April 2018		
	Reliance produce plc	Grocery basket plc
	$	$
	'000	'000
Revenue	210	189
Cost of sales	133	117
Gross profit	77	72
Expenses	38	36
Profit for the year	39	36

Statements of financial position as at 30 April 2018		
	Reliance produce plc	Grocery basket plc
	$	$
	'000	'000
Non-current assets	99	81
Current assets		
Inventory	4	5
Trade receivables	24	16
Cash in hand	24	31
Other	2	2
	54	54
Total assets	153	135
Capital and reserves		
Share capital	51	31
Reserves	9	11
	60	42
Non-current liabilities		
Non-current liabilities	31	53
	31	53
Current liabilities		
Trade payables	29	32
Bank overdraft	33	8
	62	40
Total liabilities	153	135

Identify the items in the financial statements that would be of interest to the following interested parties:

1 Shareholders and owners

2 Managers

3 Employees

4 Bank

5 Potential investors

6 Government

7 Trade payables.

Knowledge check

1 Boris is considering investing in a public limited company.

 Which of the following ratios, would provide Boris with information about the company's profitability?

 A Gross margin
 B Rate of inventory turnover
 C Trade payables turnover
 D Trade receivables turnover

2 Which of the following best defines the term 'business stakeholder'?

 Any individual or group:

 A employed by a business
 B that owns a business
 C with an interest in a business
 D with shares in a business

3 Which of the following is an internal stakeholder of a business?

 A Customer
 B Employee
 C Lender
 D Supplier

4 Copy and complete the following table. The first one has been completed as an example.

Stakeholder group	Financial interest in a business
Government	Profitability Tax liabilities
Owner of a small retail store	
Manager in a private limited company	
Trade payable	
Bank	
Investor	
Member of a local football club	

5 Identify **three** individuals or groups who would be interested in the income statement of a sole trader.

6 Explain why a credit supplier would be interested in the financial statements of a business that they supply.

7 Discuss why a member of a local cricket club would be interested in the annual financial report provided at the club's annual general meeting.

Check your progress

Read the unit objectives below and reflect on your progress in each.

Explain the uses of accounting information for decision-making by the following interested parties:

- owners
- managers
- trade payables
- banks
- investors
- club members
- other interested parties such as governments and tax authorities.

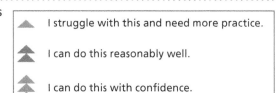

I struggle with this and need more practice.

I can do this reasonably well.

I can do this with confidence.

Limitations of accounting statements

Learning objectives
By the end of this unit, you should be able to:
* recognise the limitations of accounting statements due to such factors as:
  – historic cost
  – difficulties of definition
  – non-financial aspects.

Starting point

Answer these questions in pairs.

1 Explain what is meant by the term 'trend analysis' when reviewing published accounts.

2 What does the term 'profitability' mean?

3 Identify **three** limitations of ratio analysis.

Exploring

Discuss these questions in pairs.

1 A local hairdresser has been comparing their accounting statements with those of a local competitor. Discuss the problems with comparing accounting statements.

2 What non-financial factors, for example employee motivation, may affect the performance of a business?

Developing

Introduction

For most businesses, an income statement and statement of financial position provide the most useful information for anyone interested in how well the business is doing.

Interested parties analyse financial data and records to make informed judgements.

Interested parties may compare a business's performance:

- Over time. By only looking at one year's financial records the figures may hide a longer-term issue. Comparisons over several years allow interested parties to identify any key trends.

- Against other businesses. Interested parties may compare a business's financial records with those of a competitor. As long as the information that is available is detailed, meaningful comparisons can be made. It is possible to review questions such as:

  - Has the business's sales revenue increased as quickly as the competitor's?

  - How do expense costs compare with those of the competitor?

- Against a benchmark. Comparison against a benchmark can be useful for a business. However, the benchmark data may include very different businesses, making any comparison meaningless.

It is important to remember that there are a number of limitations in using accounting statements when analysing business performance and making informed decisions.

In particular, these limitations include:

- Historic cost – The only accepted way to record financial transactions is to use the original cost price. Financial statements are prepared using data from the past.

- Non-financial aspects – Only numerical data are included in the financial records of a business. Non-financial aspects are ignored.

- Difficulties of definition – Different businesses define accounting terms in different ways. Comparisons are only meaningful if like for like comparisons are made.

Historic cost

Information in accounting records is based on historic data.

Income statements contain numerical data from the past financial period. This is usually one year. A statement of financial position is based on a snapshot at a particular moment in time. This takes place on the last day of the financial year. At this time, a business values its assets and liabilities.

 Explain how non-current assets are recorded in a statement of financial position.

By the time that financial statements and records have been prepared and published, the material is out of date. This means

Key term

Historic data: This is financial data or information from the past. In an income statement, this is traditionally the last year.

that the financial statements may not be a reliable prediction of what may be happening currently or in the future.

For example, during the financial year, the business may have completed a 'one off' project earning a considerable amount of profit. This may not be repeated in future years. This inflates the amount of profit for the year, but will not impact on future years' accounts. This may give interested parties an incorrect view of the business's potential.

Worked example 1

Kariri supermarket has provided the following extract from its financial statements.

Kariri supermarket Statement of financial position as at 30 September 2018	
	$
	'000
Non-current assets	732
Current assets	
Inventory	188
Trade receivables	132
Cash in hand	80
	400
Current liabilities	
Trade payables	266
Bank overdraft	7
	273

Identify **three** items in the statement of financial position that are based on historic data.

1   All non-current assets are valued at their net book value – historic cost less depreciation.

2   Closing inventory is included in the current assets. This valuation is only valid at the time of the stocktake.

3   The bank overdraft is the value at 30 September 2018. On 1 October 2018, money could be paid into the account and the overdraft paid off. This is historic data after 30 September 2018.

Non-financial aspects

Only quantitative information is included in accounting statements and is expressed in monetary terms.

Qualitative information cannot be expressed in monetary terms and is therefore omitted from accounting statements.

Key terms

Quantitative information: Factual information and data that is not based on opinions.

Qualitative information: Information collected based on an individual's opinions and views.

Although qualitative information is not included in accounting statements, it is essential to have a clear understanding of it to get a true picture of the financial position and results of a business.

Workforce and management

The quality of individuals working in a business has a major impact on the overall performance of the business. A well-motivated, well-trained and loyal workforce is likely to be efficient and provide effective customer service resulting in better goods or services. This leads to increased sales revenue and eventually profit for the year.

 Discuss why it is difficult to value the quality of service offered by a workforce.

Location of the business

The location of a business is likely to be a major factor in its success. A well-located business attracts more customers and encourages customer loyalty.

CASE STUDY

During 2017, a large number of luxury hotels were under construction in the United Arab Emirates. The Grand Hyatt Abu Dhabi has:

- seven restaurants
- 428 rooms, 36 suites and 8 penthouses
- private beach
- two outdoor swimming pools, a gym and a spa.

All of these features are aimed at attracting customers, and help to increase sales revenue. However, none of the non-financial aspects of the hotel, for example its location and luxury features, will appear in the financial statements published annually.

Difficulties in definition

Accounting statements are meaningless to a reader, unless the definition of the contents is understood. Without an understanding of the definitions used by the business producing the accounting statements, the reader cannot have a complete picture of the performance and position of the business. Unless similar definitions have been used, comparisons are extremely difficult to make.

Key knowledge

Examples of conflicting accounting definitions include:

- the calculation of profit – some businesses adjust for loan interest, other businesses do not.
- valuation of inventory – there are different methods of valuing inventory.
- calculation of depreciation – one business may depreciate their motor vehicles using a reducing balance method at a rate of 20% per annum, whereas a competitor may use a reducing balance method at a rate of 25% per annum.

Applying

Complete this task in pairs.

Task

Amala Confectionery Ltd manufactures and sells a range of sweets and chocolates. These include halwa, baklawa and barfi.

The finance manager of Amala Confectionery Ltd prepares a comprehensive set of financial statements each year.

Explain the limitations of the financial statements that Amala Confectionery Ltd produces.

Knowledge check

1   Which of the following is a non-financial aspect of a business?

    A   Financial statements

    B   Customer loyalty

    C   Ratio analysis

    D   Working capital

2   How is the net book value of a non-current asset calculated?

    A   Current estimated value less depreciation

    B   Current estimated value plus depreciation

    C   Historic cost less depreciation

    D   Historic cost plus depreciation

3 Which of the following is a limitation of accounting statements?

    A All numerical data is estimated

    B Businesses can omit transactions

    C Financial statements include historic data

    D Financial records are incomplete

4 Identify **three** limitations of accounting statements.

5 Define the term historic data.

6 Explain the difference between financial and non-financial information.

Check your progress

Read the unit objectives below and reflect on your progress in each.

Recognise the limitations of accounting statements due to such factors as:

- historic cost
- difficulties of definition
- non-financial aspects.

 I struggle with this and need more practice.

 I can do this reasonably well.

 I can do this with confidence.

Chapter review

1 A business has provided the following information for the year ended 30 April 2018.

	$
Sales revenue	400 000
Cost of sales	300 000
Expenses	60 000

   What is the profit margin?

   A 10%

   B 15%

   C 25%

   D 75%

2 How is the current ratio calculated?

   A Current assets + current liabilities

   B Current assets – current liabilities

   C Current assets × current liabilities

   D Current assets ÷ current liabilities

3 Lynne has provided the following information about her business's assets and liabilities.

	$
Non-current assets	120 000
Current assets	80 000
Current liabilities	40 000
Non-current liabilities	37 000

   Calculate the current ratio.

   A 1 : 1

   B 2 : 1

   C 3 : 1

   D 4 : 1

4 The liquid (acid test) ratios of two local businesses have been calculated:

   Snowball Ltd   1.5 : 1

   Sunshine Ltd   0.5 : 1

   What does the inter-firm ratio comparison show?

   A Snowball Ltd controls its expenses more effectively than Sunshine Ltd

   B Snowball Ltd has a lower value of cost of sales than Sunshine Ltd

   C Snowball Ltd has less equity invested than Sunshine Ltd

   D Snowball Ltd has less liquidity than Sunshine Ltd

5 Which of the following ratio groups measures the liquidity of a business?

   A Current ratio   Gross margin

   B Current ratio   Liquid (acid test) ratio

   C Liquid (acid test) ratio   Return on capital employed

   D Return on capital employed   Current ratio

6 Which of the following ratios would be of **most** interest to the owner of a business reviewing profitability?

   A Current ratio

   B Liquid (acid-test) ratio

   C Trade receivables turnover

   D Return on capital employed

7 Gledhill Engineering's profit margin has increased over the last year.

Which of the following could explain the increase?

A Decrease in current assets

B Increase in current assets

C Decrease in annual expenses

D Increase in annual expenses

8 Which of the following is a limitation of using accounting statements for business decision-making?

A Inclusion of non-current assets at their historic cost

B Inclusion of irrecoverable debts as expenses

C The use of a provision for doubtful debts

D The use of straight line depreciation

9 The following financial information has been provided by a business.

	$
Sales revenue	150000
Cost of sales	120000
Opening inventory	12000
Closing inventory	18000

Calculate the rate of inventory turnover.

A 4 times

B 5 times

C 8 times

D 10 times

10 The partners in a solicitor's firm are reviewing their financial affairs.

Information regarding business _____ will be available in the income statement.

A assets

B equity

C expenses

D liabilities

11 The statement of financial position of Vedhika Engineering is given below with a number of words and figures missing.

Vedhika Engineering Statement of financial position as at 30 April 2018			
	Cost $	Depreciation $	Net book value $
Non-current assets			
Premises	93 000	7 460	(i)
Equipment	29 000	11 180	17 820
	122 000	18,640	103 360
Current assets			
Inventory		16 300	
Trade receivables		(ii)	
General expenses prepaid		550	
			39 684
Total assets			143 044
Capital			
Capital			110 000
(iii) _____			(3 556)
			106 444
Drawings			(iv)
			104 644
Current (v) _____			
Trade payables			26 200
Salaries outstanding			3 400
Bank charges owing			(vi)
Bank (vii) _____			8 200
			38 400
Total liabilities			143 044

(a) Identify the missing words and figures **(i)** to **(vii)** on the statement of financial position. [7]

(b) Calculate, showing your workings, Vedhika Engineering's:

   (i) Current ratio [3]

   (ii) Liquid (acid test) ratio [3]

(c) Calculate the working capital of Vedhika Engineering. Show your workings. [3]

(d) Explain **two** effects of a business **not** having sufficient working capital. [4]

[Total 20]

12 Reyansh is a sole trader. His financial year ends on 31 December. Each year he prepares his financial statements, calculates ratios and compares them with a similar local business. He is aware that comparisons can be meaningless.

(a) Explain why the liquid (acid test) ratio is a more reliable indicator of liquidity than the current ratio. [4]

(b) Identify **four** things that Reyansh should consider when comparing his results with those of a similar business. [4]

(c) State how **each** of the following may be regarded as a limitation of accounting statements.

   (i) Historic cost [2]

   (ii) Difficulties of definition [2]

   (iii) Non-financial aspects [2]

(d) In addition to Reyansh, various other individuals would be interested in the business's financial statements.

   Explain why **each** of the following would be interested in the financial statements of Reyansh.

   (i) Bank [2]

   (ii) Trade payables [2]

   (iii) Employees [2]

[Total 20]

13 Donaldo is a trader. All of his sales and purchases are made on credit terms.

He allows his trade receivables 60 days credit and is allowed 30 days credit by his trade payables.

At 31 March 2018, the following information is available:

For the year ended 31 March 2018:

Credit sales	$ 134 250
Credit purchases	$ 121 250

At 31 March 2018:

Trade receivables	$ 15 000
Trade payables	$ 10 100

(a) Calculate, showing your workings, Donaldo's:

   (i) Trade receivables turnover [3]

   (ii) Trade payables turnover [3]

(b) State **and** explain whether Donaldo will be satisfied with the ratio results calculated in part (a). [4]

(c) Explain how Donaldo could improve his:

   (i) Trade receivables turnover [3]

   (ii) Trade payables turnover [3]

(d) Explain how a business will try to organise its trade receivables turnover and its trade payables turnover. [2]

(e) Identify **two** limitations that Donaldo should be aware of when he is reviewing his financial statements. [2]

[Total 20]

     6

14 Jam Jar Organic Food Store has been operating for a several years. The owners want to expand their business and product range. To prepare for this, they are reviewing their financial statements. They have calculated some financial ratios based on the latest financial statements. The owners have obtained the results of a local competitor, Fresh!, to use for comparison.

	Jam Jar Organic Food Store	Fresh!
Gross margin	40%	50%
Profit margin	15%	30%
Current assets	$52 500	$70 000
Current liabilities	$25 000	$40 000
Inventory	$30 000	$10 000
Rate of inventory turnover	260 times	160 times

(a) Calculate (i) current ratio and (ii) acid test ratio for both businesses. [10]

(b) Explain two reasons why the gross margin of Jam Jar is lower than that of Fresh! [4]

(c) Explain two reasons why the acid test ratio may indicate liquidity problems for Jam Jar. [4]

(d) Explain one reason why the rate of inventory for Fresh! is lower than that of Jam Jar. [2]

15 Lang is the owner of LMN Stores. He is preparing a report on the profitability of his business. He has provided the following information for LMN Stores and the benchmark profitability ratios for the local area.

LMN Stores
Financial information for the year ended 30 April 2018

	$
Revenue	150 000
Gross profit	87 000
Expenses	37 500
Capital employed	95 000

Benchmark profitability ratios for the local area:

Gross margin	31%
Profit margin	19%
Return on capital employed	17%

(a) Calculate the following ratios for LMN Stores for the year ended 30 April 2018:
   (i) Gross margin [3]
   (ii) Profit margin [3]
   (iii) Return on capital employed (ROCE). [3]

(b) Explain **three** limitations of the financial information produced by businesses. [6]

7 Accounting principles and policies

7.1 Accounting principles

7.2 Accounting policies

This chapter explains the various accounting rules, known as accounting principles and policies. It considers how these accounting principles and policies can be applied to businesses, accounting procedures and financial transactions.

Accounting principles

Learning objectives
By the end of this unit, you should be able to explain and
recognise the application of the following accounting principles:

- matching
- business entity
- consistency
- duality
- going concern
- historic cost
- materiality
- money measurement
- prudence
- realisation.

Starting point

Answer these questions in pairs.

1. Identify **two** accounting methods that apply to the calculation of depreciation.

2. Explain why a business divides its useful life into accounting periods of one year.

3. Describe the difference between an accrual and a prepayment.

Exploring

Discuss these questions in pairs.

1. Why is it necessary for accountants to have a set of accounting rules to follow?

2. Why is it important for a business to use the same depreciation method from one year to the next?

3. Explain what is meant by the term 'double entry book-keeping'.

Developing

Introduction

The financial accounts of any business need to reflect a true and fair view of its current financial position.

Key term

True and fair view:
Describes financial records that are free from misinformation and accurately represent the financial position of a business.

In order to ensure this occurs, accountants apply a series of rules known as accounting principles.

International Accounting Standard Number 1 (IAS 1) provides details of the accounting principles that accountants should apply when preparing financial accounts. Applying these principles ensures that financial records are consistently prepared and can be compared.

If every business and accountant applied their own rules to the production of financial records, the records would become meaningless and make inter-firm comparisons impossible.

There are a number of accounting principles that are applied by businesses when recording their financial information.

 Explain **two** reasons why accounting principles are important for a public limited company.

Lego prepares an annual report each year.

The report includes financial statements which can be analysed by shareholders, investors, employees and other interested parties.

The information in the report contains clear evidence of the accounting policies and principles that have been used. This allows comparisons to be made with previous years and other businesses.

These include details of Lego's depreciation methods.

Lego calculates depreciation using the straight line method to allocate the cost of each asset to its residual value over its estimated useful life, as follows:

Buildings 40 years

Installations 10–20 years

Plant and machinery 5–15 years

Moulds 2 years

Furniture, fittings and equipment 3–10 years.

Figure 7.1.1 Accounting principles

Prudence

The prudence principle emphasises that a business should only recognise revenue and profit when they are achieved. This principle ensures that all business's accounting records present a realistic view of their financial affairs.

When applying the principle of prudence, accountants usually look for the worst case scenarios. Profits should only be recognised when a business is certain that the profit will be realised. All possible losses should be recorded as soon as they are known.

Key knowledge

In applying the prudence principle, profits will not be overstated and losses will be provided for as soon as they are recognised.

The prudence principle overrules all other principles. If the situation arises that the application of another principle would mean that the prudence concept would be contravened, then the prudence principle takes priority.

Matching

The matching principle determines when financial transactions should be entered into the accounts of a business. The principle ensures that incomes are matched to expenses in a particular accounting period. Income and expenses are entered into the financial statements as they are earned or incurred, not when the money is received.

Key knowledge

The revenue of the accounting period is matched against the costs of the same period.

The timing of receipts and payments is ignored.

To allow for meaningful comparisons, the data included in an income statement must relate to the time period covered by the statement.

Adjustments for prepayments and accruals of income and expenditure need to be made in a business's income statement and statement of financial position.

Expenses

- An accrued expense is added to the relevant expense in the income statement and shown as a current liability (other payables) in the statement of financial position.
- A prepaid expense is deducted from the relevant expense in the income statement and shown as a current asset (other receivables) in the statement of financial position.

Income

- A prepaid income is deducted from the relevant additional income in the income statement and shown as a current liability in the statement of financial position.
- An accrued income is added to the relevant additional income in the income statement and shown as a current asset in the statement of financial position.

Consistency

When an accountant is faced with a choice of method or policy, the consistency principle states that in the preparation of financial records, accounting policies should not be changed without good reason.

When a choice of method has been made by a business, for example a 20% straight line depreciation method for equipment, this should be used consistently from one year to the next.

Key term

Consistency principle: This principle states that, when faced with choice between different accounting techniques, an accountant should not change accounting policies without good reason.

Without consistent use of accounting methods and policies, it would be very difficult to complete trend analyses and compare one year's financial statements with another.

Changes in method can distort the value of the profit for the year. For example, an increase in depreciation would increase expenses and therefore reduce the profit for the year.

Going concern

The going concern principle states that a business's financial statements should be prepared on the assumption that the business will continue to trade in the foreseeable future. It should be assumed that there is no intention to make a significant reduction in size or close down.

Key knowledge

The going concern principle has a number of practical applications:

- Non-current assets, for example equipment and motor vehicles, will appear at their net book value (original cost less accumulated depreciation) in the statement of financial position.
- Inventory is valued at the lower of cost and net realisable value for inclusion in the financial statements.

In cases where a business is likely to cease operations in the near future, asset values will probably be lower and amended in the statement of financial position. Business assets would then be shown at their expected sales values rather than their net book values. This makes the value more meaningful when being reviewed.

Historic cost

The historic cost principle states that an asset should be recorded in the financial accounts at the cost for which it was purchased, not its current value.

The cost of an asset when purchased is a known fact and can be verified for accuracy. Current values are difficult to calculate because there is an element of subjectivity. It is rare that two people will agree on the current value of an asset.

To ensure the prudence principle is applied, the historic cost of a non-current asset is reduced by depreciation charges in the statement of financial position.

Key knowledge

The problem with the historic cost principle is that it ignores any increases in value due to inflation.

Key term

Going concern principle: This principle states that a business's financial statements should be prepared on the assumption that the business will continue to trade for the foreseeable future.

Key term

Historic cost principle: This principle states that an asset should be recorded in the financial accounts at the cost for which it was purchased, not its current value.

Materiality

The materiality principle states that accountants should not spend time trying to accurately record items that are immaterial. That is, those items that are of low value and not important to the operation of a business.

Another application of the materiality principle occurs when small expenses are entered into one account, for example general expenses, rather than having separate accounts for each item. Such items may include paper clips, light bulbs, pens, etc.

Key knowledge

The size of a business will determine what is considered material. For example, a $300 computer may be immaterial to a large public limited company but be of material value to a sole trader. The sole trader would record the computer as a non-current asset in the statement of financial position, whereas, the public limited company would record it as an expense.

Business entity

The business entity principle states that the financial affairs of a business should be kept completely separate from those of the owner. The financial records of a business **only** relate to the transactions of the business, for example rent of business premises, purchases of goods and sales revenue.

Key knowledge

The personal assets and liabilities of a business's owner(s) do not appear in the accounting records of their business.

The business's financial records are recorded from the viewpoint of the business and not the owner(s).

Key terms

Materiality principle:
This principle states that accountants should not spend time trying to accurately record items that are immaterial.

Business entity principle:
This principle states that the financial affairs of a business must be maintained separately from those of the owner.

Worked example 1

Yasmine, a sole trader, purchases two motor vehicles, one for her own personal use and one for use in the business. Each vehicle cost $30 000. Prepare the entries in the business's motor vehicle and capital accounts.

Motor vehicle					Motor vehicle			
Dr		Cr	$		Dr	$	Cr	$
Capital	30 000						Motor vehicle	30 000

The credit entry in the capital account represents the amount which is owed to the owner by the business. Only the motor vehicle that is being used by the business is recorded in the accounting system.

Duality

The duality principle, states that every transaction has two aspects and requires two entries in the accounts:

- one debit entry
- one credit entry.

Key term

Duality principle: This principle states that a business transaction always has two effects on the business and requires two entries, one debit and one credit, to be made in the accounts; also known as double entry.

Worked example 2

A business purchases a motor van for $20000, paying in cash.

What are the two aspects of this transaction?

Prepare the double entry accounts to show this transaction.

1   The amount of the business's motor van account has **increased** by $20000.
2   The amount of cash in the business's cash account has **decreased** by $20000.

Motor vehicle			
Dr	$	Cr	$
Capital	20000		

Motor vehicle			
Dr	$	Cr	$
		Motor vehicle	20000

The amount of cash in the business's cash account has **decreased** by $20000.

The amount of the business's motor van account has **increased** by $20000.

2   Show how the following transactions illustrate the duality principle.

A business:

(a) paid an insurance premium of $300 in cash
(b) purchased equipment for $2500 on credit from Bryn equipment supplies.

Money measurement

The money measurement principle states that only transactions that can be expressed in monetary terms should be recorded in a business's financial records. This includes the value of all transactions, assets, liabilities and capital.

Money is a recognised unit of value and is the most commonly accepted way of valuing transactions. It is objective because valuing in monetary terms does not rely on personal opinions. It is purely based on facts.

Key term

Money measurement principle: This principle states that only transactions that can be expressed in monetary terms should be recorded in a business's accounts.

Items that cannot be valued in monetary terms, include:

- workforce skills
- management competency
- local community residents
- staff morale.

Worked example 3

Magtanggol delivery services is known for its excellent customer service. The business would like to record its customer service in the financial statements at $50 000.

Explain whether customer service can be recorded in the financial statements.

According to the money measurement principle, only transactions that can be expressed in monetary terms can be recorded in a business's financial statements. It is not possible to objectively value the customer service of a business; $50 000 would only be one person's opinion of how much the customer service was worth.

Realisation

The realisation principle states that revenue should only be recognised when the exchange of goods or services takes place. Revenue should not be inflated by sales which have not yet happened.

Key term

Realisation principle: This principle states that revenue should be recognised when the exchange of goods or services takes place.

According to the realisation principle, profits should not be recorded until they have been earned.

Profit should only be claimed as earned once the legal title to the goods or services has passed from the seller to the buyer. The buyer then has a legal obligation to pay for the goods or services received.

Applying

In pairs, copy and complete the following sentences with the names of appropriate accounting principles.

1   The _____ principle states that income and expenses should be entered in the financial records when they are earned or incurred and not when the money is received.

2   A business thinks that a number of its credit customers may not pay the debts that they owe. The business needs to account for all potential losses in accordance with the _____ principle.

3   An accountant has informed a business owner that they only need to know the value of their drawings and not that the owner purchased a holiday with this money. This is in accordance with the _____ principle.

4   A business has taken an order for goods but the goods have not left the warehouse. According to the _____ principle, the business should not record the revenue from the sale.

5   The management of QNet are exceptionally well qualified. However, the skills cannot be recorded in the statement of financial position due to the _____ principle.

6   A business always uses the FIFO method to value its closing inventory. This meets the requirements of the _____ principle.

7   The _____ principle describes the concept of double entry book-keeping.

8   An accounting clerk is considering accounting for every sheet of paper that is used in the office. According to the _____ principle, items of a low value should not be accounted for.

9   Financial statements are prepared on the basis that the business is going to continue for the foreseeable future. This is in accordance with the _____ principle.

10 In the statement of financial position, a business needs to include its motor vehicles at their net book value. This meets the _____ principle.

1 The financial affairs of a business are treated separately from those of the owner.

Which principle does this define?

A   Business entity

B   Matching

C   Money measurement

D   Prudence

2 Prior to completing the financial statements for a local retail store, the accountant has asked the owner, Lisa, to confirm that her business is likely to continue for many years to come.

Which principle is the accountant applying?

A   Business entity

B   Matching

C   Going concern

D   Prudence

3 Hafeji retail store has purchased a pair of curtains costing $15. The curtains are expected to last for ten years. The retail store owner feels that they should record the curtains under non-current assets in the financial statements.

Which of the following principles prevents the curtains being recorded in this manner?

A   Consistency

B   Matching

C   Materiality

D   Prudence

4 Define the term 'accounting principles'.

5 Explain why accounting principles are required by a business preparing financial statements.

6 A business has not recorded in its accounting records the fact that a competitor has reduced its prices by 25%. Explain why this is the case.

7 Explain what is meant by the matching principle.

8 Laura owns a coach company. She would like to change the depreciation method that she uses for her coaches in order to increase her profit for the year.

Explain whether this is possible.

9 Riaz owns a clothing store. He has taken goods, originally costing $570, from the shop for his own personal use.

Which accounting principle explains how Riaz should account for this transaction?

10 A business should not 'overstate its profits'.

Which accounting principle is being described?

11 Explain how the principle of materiality would be applied to a desk calculator used in a public limited company.

12 Explain the meaning of the 'realisation' principle.

13 Identify the accounting principle which states that assets should be valued at their original cost and not their current value.

14 A business owner knows that his business is likely to close in the next twelve months. Does the owner need to inform the accountant preparing the business's financial statements?

Check your progress

Read the unit objectives below and reflect on your progress in each.

Explain and recognise the application of the following accounting principles:

*   matching
*   business entity
*   consistency
*   duality
*   going concern
*   historic cost
*   materiality
*   money measurement
*   prudence
*   realisation.

 I struggle with this and need more practice.

 I can do this reasonably well.

 I can do this with confidence.

Accounting policies

Learning objectives

By the end of this unit, you should be able to:

- recognise the influence of international accounting standards and understand the following objectives in selecting accounting policies:
  - comparability
  - relevance
  - reliability
  - understandability

Starting point

Answer these questions in pairs.

1. Why might a business compare its ratio results with those of a local competitor?

2. How does the consistency principle allow financial statements to be compared?

3. Why is the business entity principle important to a sole trader?

Exploring

Discuss these questions in pairs.

1. A local coffee shop manager would like to understand how efficiently the business is operating. Explain how the manager could assess its efficiency.

2. A partnership is looking for a new partner to join the business. Which items in the financial statements of the partnership would be of interest to the new partner?

3. Why might a supplier want to compare the financial statements of two businesses?

Developing

The International Accounting Standards Board

The International Accounting Standards Board (IASB) is an independent body that is responsible for the development, adoption and publication of International Financial Reporting Standards (IFRSs).

The IASB's main aim is to act as a standard-setting body of the International Financial Reporting Standards Foundation.

The International Financial Reporting Standards include:

- International Financial Reporting Standards (IFRSs) – developed by the International Accounting Standards Board

- International Accounting Standards (IASs) – adopted by the International Accounting Standards Board

- Interpretations originated from the International Financial Reporting Interpretations Committee (IFRIC).

Key knowledge

International Accounting Standards, known as IASs, have been introduced to standardise accounting practices around the world.

By using agreed accounting policies and principles, accountants can avoid confusion and inconsistencies. This allows accounting records to be effectively compared and analysed. The use of such policies and principles helps businesses present financial information that is 'true and fair' and ensure that none of the information is misleading.

Key term

International accounting standards: A set of internationally agreed principles and procedures that inform businesses how to present their accounts.

CASE STUDY

International Accounting Standards (IASs) were issued originally by the International Accounting Standards Council (IASC). These standards were endorsed and amended by the International Accounting Standards Board (IASB). When appropriate, the International Accounting Standards Board (IASB) will amend and reissue International Accounting Standards.

The following are a selection of the International Accounting Standards that are currently in operation:

IAS 1: Presentation of financial statements

IAS 2: Inventories

IAS 7: Statement of cash flows

IAS 16: Property, plant and equipment

IAS 33: Earnings per share

IAS 38: Intangible assets

IAS 1 requires that businesses should use accounting policies that are 'tailored to their particular information needs'. The quality of the data and information in the financial statements of a business will determine their usefulness to an interested party.

Policies should be judged against the policies of:

Comparability

Financial information can be useful if a business wants to compare its current year's financial statements with those of a previous year. It allows a business to complete a trend analysis. For example, an interested party can compare the 2018 financial statements of Shell Oil with its financial statements of 2017, providing the same accounting principles and policies have been used.

It is also useful for a business to compare its financial results with those of a similar business, known as inter-firm comparison.

For example, an interested party could compare the 2018 financial statements of Shell Oil with those of ExxonMobil, providing consideration is given to the accounting principles and policies used by both businesses.

 Identify **two** businesses that McDonald's could use to compare its financial statements against.

Key knowledge

In order to make meaningful comparisons, financial statement users need to:
- be aware of the accounting principles used by the businesses
- consider the accounting policies and principles applied when producing the statements
- identify similarities and differences between the businesses being compared.

Relevance

Financial statements prepared by a business provide information about its performance and position in the market. These statements are used to make informed business decisions.

It is vital that the information is provided on time to enable these important decisions to be made. If the information is too late, then the information is of no use to the user.

It is very important that the data and information contained in any financial statement is relevant to the user. This means the information contained in the statements must:
- confirm expectations of historic events
- correct prior expectations of historic events
- form, revise or confirm expectations for the future.

Key term

Comparability: Financial information is comparable when accounting principles and policies are consistency applied from one accounting period to the next and from one business to another.

Key term

Relevance: A non-numerical characteristic in accounting. Relevance is associated with accounting information that is timely, useful and will make a difference to an interested party when making a decision.

Reliability

Reliability refers to whether the financial statements of a business can be verified for accuracy and used consistently by all interested parties.

Key knowledge

In order to be reliable, financial statements should:

- be free from bias
- be free from errors
- be dependable for all interested parties
- represent a true and fair view
- be independently verifiable.

Understandability

Understandability is an accounting policy applied by all businesses. It is very important that financial statements can be understood by any interested party reading the information. It is assumed that interested parties will have a reasonable knowledge of business, finance, economic activities and accounting. It is also assumed that the interested parties will be willing to study the financial statements that have been prepared.

Businesses are not permitted to omit information from their financial statements simply because it is deemed to be too difficult for interested parties to understand.

Key knowledge

Understandability depends on:

- the clarity of the information provided by the business
- the ability of the interested party reading the information.

Key terms

Reliability: Relates to the trustworthiness of a business's financial statements.

Bias: Prejudice in favour of or against one thing, usually in a way that would be considered as unfair.

Key term

Understandability: An accounting policy that states that a business's financial information should be presented in a way that an individual with a reasonable knowledge of business and finance and a willingness to study the information provided should be able to understand.

Applying

Complete this task in pairs.

Task

Edfu Motors Ltd commenced operations on 1 April 2017. On 31 March 2018, the accountant of Edfu Motors Ltd is to prepare the company's annual accounting records.

Discuss the **four** objectives that Edfu Motors Ltd need to consider when selecting the accounting policies and principles to be applied.

Knowledge check

1   Which objective for selecting accounting policies does the following statement define?

    The trustworthiness of a business's financial statements.

    A   Comparability
    B   Relevance
    C   Reliability
    D   Understandability

2   Which of the following is an example of inter-firm comparison?

    A   Financial statements of a business being compared to the previous year's statements.
    B   Financial statements of a business being compared with a benchmark.
    C   Financial statements of one business being compared with those of a contrasting business.
    D   Financial statements of one business being compared with those of a similar business.

3   Why have International Accounting Standards been developed?

    A   To identify errors in accounting information prepared by businesses.
    B   To monitor accounting practices around the world.
    C   To standardise accounting practices around the world.
    D   To verify accounting information prepared by businesses.

4   Explain why a business's manager needs to be aware of any changes in accounting policies and principles when comparing the business's financial statements with those of last year.

5   Explain the meaning of the term 'relevance'.

6   The quality of information that is included in a set of financial statements determines how useful the accounting statements are. Identify the **four** objectives that must be considered when selecting accounting policies.

7   Explain the meaning of the term 'understandability'.

Check your progress

Read the unit objectives below and reflect on your progress in each.

Recognise the influence of international accounting standards and understand the following objectives in selection accounting policies:

- comparability
- relevance
- reliability
- understandability.

I struggle with this and need more practice.

I can do this reasonably well.

I can do this with confidence.

Chapter review

1 Which accounting principle requires businesses to provide for foreseeable losses?

   A Consistency

   B Duality

   C Matching

   D Prudence

2 Zan, a sole trader, uses the same depreciation method every year.

   Which accounting principle is Zan applying?

   A Consistency

   B Duality

   C Matching

   D Prudence

3 The business owner should not include their personal assets and liabilities in the business's statement of financial position.

   Which accounting principle is being applied?

   A Business entity

   B Going concern

   C Historic cost

   D Money measurement

4 Which of the following defines the money measurement principle?

   A Financial accounts only contain items that have a monetary value

   B Financial transactions are maintained on a double entry basis

   C Non-current assets are valued at cost less depreciation

   D Profit for the year is calculated by deducting expenses from gross profit

5 Which accounting principle is applied when accounting for an irrecoverable debt?

   A Matching

   B Materiality

   C Prudence

   D Realisation

6 Financial transactions have both a debit and a credit entry.

   Which accounting principle does this define?

   A Duality

   B Matching

   C Prudence

   D Realisation

7 A business would like to record its employees' skills in the statement of financial position.

   Which accounting principle prevents this inclusion?

   A Business entity

   B Going concern

   C Historic cost

   D Money measurement

8 Which of the following groups contains the four objectives in selecting accounting policies?

   A Comparability, understandability, reliability, relevance

   B Comparability, understandability, prudence, relevance

   C Consistency, understandability, reliability, relevance

   D Consistency, understandability, reliability, accruals

9 A business pays a credit supplier in cash. The transaction is recorded in the cash book and the supplier's personal account.

   Which accounting principle is being applied?

   A Business entity

   B Duality

   C Matching

   D Money measurement

10 When should a business recognise the income from a sale of goods on credit?

A   when the business sends a statement to the customer.

B   when the customer pays for the goods purchased.

C   when the goods are delivered to the customer.

D   when the goods are ordered by the customer.

11 Abdelrahman owns a retail store. His accountant has advised that the quality of the information in his financial statements can be measured in terms of comparability and reliability.

(a) Define the following terms:

(i)   Comparability   [2]

(ii) Reliability.   [2]

(b) Name **and** explain the accounting principle which states that Abdelrahman should only record the business's transactions in the financial statements of his retail store.

Give an appropriate example to support your answer.   [4]

Abdelrahman has started to sell goods on credit. He offers his credit customers a cash discount of 2.5% provided the account is settled within 30 days.

Abdelrahman has applied the accounting principle of prudence by maintaining a provision for irrecoverable debts.

(c) Describe what is meant by the term 'cash discount'.   [2]

(d) Explain why Abdelrahman has allowed his credit customers a cash discount.   [2]

(e) Define the prudence principle.   [2]

(f) State **two** effects on Abdelrahman's financial statements of not applying the prudence principle correctly.   [4]

(g) Name **and** explain **one** other accounting principle that Abdelrahman is applying by maintaining a provision for doubtful debts.   [2]

[Total 20]

12 Peter owns the Snuffie pet store.

1   During the last year, Peter took goods costing $250 from the business for his own use.

2   The pet store is known for its excellent customer relations. Peter would like to include this in his financial statements.

3   During the last year, the pet store bought shop fittings costing $20. Peter has included these in his statement of financial position as non-current assets.

(a) For **each** of the statements 1 to 3, identify **and** explain the accounting principle which should be applied to each transaction.   [6]

(b) List **four** objectives which Peter must consider when selecting accounting policies.   [4]

(c) Peter is unsure why items are recorded on the opposite side of the cash book to that on which they appear on the bank statement.

(i)   Explain why this is the case.   [3]

(ii) Define the duality concept.   [1]

(iii) Explain why recording items in a cash book is an example of the duality concept.   [2]

(d) Explain **two** advantages of Peter operating as a sole trader.   [4]

[Total 20]

13 Raman and Fatima started a business that supplies and repairs laptop computers. They have been advised by their accountant that they need to depreciate their non-current assets each year and apply the consistency accounting principle.

   (a) State **three** reasons why Raman and Fatima should depreciate their non-current assets. [3]

   (b) Explain the principle of consistency. [2]

   (c) Name **and** explain **one** application, other than depreciation, of the consistency principle. [2]

   (d) Describe the following objectives which Raman and Fatima must consider when selecting accounting policies:

      (i) Relevance [2]

      (ii) Understandability. [2]

   (e) Explain why it is important for a partnership to prepare an income statement and statement of financial position. [6]

   (f) Identify **three** items that would appear in a partnership agreement. [3]

   [Total 20]

GLOSSARY

Accounting: The process of recording financial transactions, producing financial statements and analysing financial performance of a business.

Accounting period: The time period for which financial statements are prepared.

Accounting principles: Specific rules that are used by a business to prepare its financial statements.

Accrued expenses: Expenses relating to the current accounting period that remain unpaid at the end of the period. Also known as Other payables.

Accrued incomes: Incomes earned but not yet received by the business at the end of the period.

Accumulated fund: Represents the difference in value between the assets and liabilities of the organisation.

Appropriation account: An account that shows how a partnership's profit or loss for the year is shared out between the partners.

Asset disposal: The selling or scrapping of a non-current asset.

Asset disposal account: The ledger account used to record asset disposal and to calculate the profit or loss on the disposal.

Assets: Resources used within the business for its activities.

Authorised share capital: The maximum amount of share capital that can be issued by a limited company. It is stated in the Memorandum of Association.

Balance (of an account): The overall difference between the total on the debit side and the total on credit side of an account at a point in time.

Bank reconciliation: The process of checking why the cash book bank balance and the bank statement balance are different from each other (as they should be the same in theory).

Bank reconciliation statement: A statement explaining the differences between the cash book bank balance and the balance on the bank statement.

Bank statement: A document issued by the bank of the business showing all bank transactions for a period of time.

Bias: Prejudice in favour of or against one thing, usually in a way that would be considered as unfair.

Book of prime entry: A book, or journal, in which transactions are first recorded before being posted to the double entry accounts.

Book-keeping: The process of recording the financial transactions of a business.

Business document: A document received or issued by a business when a transaction takes place. It contains information relevant to the transaction.

Business entity principle: This principle states that the financial affairs of a business must be maintained separately from those of the owner.

Called-up share capital: The total amount of money that will be due to a limited company from the issue of shares.

Capital expenditure: Business expenditure used to purchase or improve assets that are expected to be used in the business for more than one year. It also includes the cost of getting those assets ready for use. Capital expenditure is not classed as an expense on the income statement of a business.

Capital: Describes how much a business is worth. The capital of a business represents how much the owner(s) of the business have invested. It is calculated as Capital = assets – liabilities. Also known as owner's equity.

Capital receipts: Business income that is not part of the normal operations of the business. Capital receipts are not classed as income on the income statement of the business.

Cash book: A combined cash and bank account which records all transactions involving payments and receipts of money.

Cash discount: A reduction in the amount owing on a credit transaction to encourage prompt payment.

Cheque: A written document authorising payment from the bank account of a business to another person or business.

Cheque counterfoil: Part of the cheque which is kept by the business as a record of the payment made by cheque. It may also be referred to as a 'cheque stub'.

Closing inventory: Value of inventory held by the business at the end of the accounting period.

Collateral: An asset that is pledged as security for the repayment of a debt. In the event that the debt cannot be repaid, the asset will be taken by the lender.

Commission: An error caused by a transaction being entered into the wrong personal account.

Comparability: Financial information is comparable when accounting principles and policies are consistency applied from one accounting period to the next and from one business to another.

Compensating: Two or more errors are made that affect the debit and credit columns of the trial balance by exactly the same amount. The totals of the debit and credit columns of the trial balance are the same but the totals are incorrect.

Competitor: A business that is engaged in commercial competition with other businesses.

Complete reversal: A transaction is entered in the correct accounts and with the correct amount but the entries are on the wrong side of both double entry accounts. The totals of the debit and credit columns of the trial balance are the same but the totals are incorrect.

Consistency principle: This principle states that, when faced with choice between different accounting techniques, an accountant should not change accounting policies without good reason.

Contra entry: A double entry where both the debit and credit entries are in the same account.

Credit control: The monitoring of credit sales and the collection of payments from credit customers.

Credit note: Document issued by a business to a customer when goods are returned to the business because they are unsuitable.

Credit transfer: An automated payment of money into a bank account.

Current assets: Resources of a business that are likely to be converted into cash within one year.

Current liabilities: Liabilities that occur through day-to-day business activities. These debts are likely to be repaid within one year.

Current ratio: A measure of the liquidity of a business which compares current assets to current liabilities.

$$\text{Current ratio} = \frac{\text{current assets}}{\text{current liabilities}}$$

Debenture: A legal document that is given to an individual who has loaned money to a limited company.

Debit note: A document issued by a business to the supplier when the goods received are unsuitable.

Debt factoring: Occurs when a business sells its outstanding customer accounts to a debt factoring company. The factoring company pays the business a set percentage of the value of the debts (80–90%) and then collects the full amount of the debts. Once collected the business will receive the remaining amount less a charge.

Deed of partnership: An agreement that outlines the conditions that partners have consented to. It may also be referred to as a partnership agreement.

Depreciation: An estimation of how the cost of an asset should be allocated over its useful life.

Direct costs: The costs incurred in physically making the products; they are related to the level of output.

Direct debits: A regular automated payment of varying amounts made from a bank account (usually for utility bills).

Discount allowed: A reduction in the invoice total offered by a business to its credit customers to encourage early settlement of invoices.

Discount received: A reduction in the amount a business owes to the credit supplier of the business to encourage early settlement.

Dishonoured cheque: A cheque presented to the bank which the payer has insufficient funds

in their account for the bank to transfer money to make payment.

Double entry book-keeping: A system of recording business transactions by making two entries (one debit entry and one credit entry) for each transaction.

Drawings: Assets (money or other resources) that the owner withdraws from the business for personal use.

Duality principle: This principle states that a business transaction always has two effects on the business and requires two entries, one debit and one credit, to be made in the accounts; also known as double entry.

Economy: The system by which goods and services are produced, sold and purchased in a particular area.

External stakeholder: Any individual or group who has an interest in a business but may not be directly involved with the business. For example, a local resident.

Equity (of a limited company): The value of the shares issued by a limited company.

Financial analyst: An individual whose job is to review the financial performance of a business to assess whether it is a sound investment.

Financial statements: Statements produced for an accounting period summarising business performance. They include an income statement and a statement of financial position.

Float: The amount of petty cash available at the start of each month.

For a limited company:

Return on capital employed (%)

$$= \frac{\text{profit for the year}}{\text{capital employed}} \times 100$$

where capital employed = issued shares + reserves + non-current liabilities

General reserve: A reserve created for general purposes in the future. It forms part of the capital of the company.

General journal: The book of prime entry used to record transactions not found in any other journal, sometimes referred to as the journal.

Going concern principle: This principle states that a business's financial statements should be prepared on the assumption that the business will continue to trade for the foreseeable future.

Goodwill: An intangible non-current asset that represents the value of a business in excess of the assets that physically exist.

Gross margin: The gross profit of a business expressed as a percentage of revenue generated by sales.

Gross margin (%)

$$= \frac{\text{gross profit}}{\text{revenue}} \times 100$$

Gross profit: Sales revenue less cost of sales.

Historic cost principle: This principle states that an asset should be recorded in the financial accounts at the cost for which it was purchased, not its current value.

Historic data: This is financial data or information from the past. In an income statement, this is traditionally the last year.

Imprest system: A system of maintaining a petty cash book by always ensuring the opening balance of the petty cash book is the same amount for each time period.

In arrears: An expense paid in arrears is one which is paid for after having been received, for example electricity is often paid for in arrears – the amount owing is calculated after the electricity has been used.

Income statement: A financial statement showing a business's income and expenses for an accounting period and the resulting profit or loss.

Indirect costs: The costs involved in the operation of a factory that cannot be directly linked to the goods that are being produced.

Intangible asset: An asset of a business that does not have a physical existence. Any valuation is subjective.

Inter-firm comparison: This is where a business compares its financial performance with another business of a similar size in the same business sector.

Internal stakeholder: Any individual or group that is directly involved with the business. For example, employees, managers, owners.

International accounting standards: A set of internationally agreed principles and procedures that inform businesses how to present their accounts.

Interpretation (of financial ratios): Comparing financial results with benchmarks or targets, previous years or similar businesses.

Inventory: Goods held by a business for resale. They may be in the form of finished goods, partly finished goods or raw materials.

Inventory valuation statement: A report including the different valuations for each type of inventory held by a business.

Invoice: A document issued by a business when making a credit sale.

Irrecoverable debt: An amount owed to a business by a credit customer that cannot pay or will not pay the money that is owed. The amount is written off.

Issued share capital: The amount of share capital that has actually been raised by the company by the sale of shares.

Liabilities: Amounts borrowed to fund business activity.

Limited company: A business that has a separate legal identity from its shareholders.

Limited liability: Shareholders of limited companies are not personally liable for the debts of the business.

Liquid (acid test) ratio: A measure of the liquidity of a business which compares current assets excluding closing inventory to current liabilities.

Liquid (acid test) ratio =

$$\frac{\text{current assets} - \text{closing inventory}}{\text{current liabilities}}$$

Liquidity (of a business): A measure of the ability of a business to pay its short-term debts.

Liquidity (of an asset): A measure of how easy it is to convert an asset into cash without it losing its value.

Management accounting: Using financial information to make business decisions concerning costs, revenues and output.

Manufacturing account: An account in which it is calculated how much it has cost a business to manufacture the goods produced in a financial year.

Matching principle: This principle ensures that incomes are matched to expenses in a particular accounting period. Income and expenses need to be entered into a business's financial statements as they are earned or incurred, not when the money is received or paid.

Matching principle: This principle ensures that incomes are matched to expenses in a particular accounting period. Income and expenses need to be entered into a business's financial statements as they are earned or incurred, not when the money is received.

Materiality principle: This principle states that accountants should not spend time trying to accurately record items that are immaterial.

Memorandum accounts: Accounts which are not part of the double entry system.

Money measurement principle: This principle states that only transactions that can be expressed in monetary terms should be recorded in a business's accounts.

Narrative: A description of a transaction entered in the general journal.

Net book value: Original cost of a non-current asset less accumulated depreciation.

Net realisable value (of inventory): The selling price less any costs incurred getting the inventory into saleable condition.

Nominal ledger: Book containing all other accounts not found in sales or purchases ledger.

Non-current asset: An asset bought for use within the business and normally kept for more than one year.

Non-current liabilities: Long-term borrowing that is not likely to be repaid within the next year. These liabilities will appear in a number of consecutive statements of financial position.

Non-profit-making organisation: An organisation formed by groups of individuals to pursue a common not-for-profit goal. They exist with the intention of distributing their revenue to achieve their purpose or mission.

Omission: The entries needed for a transaction are not entered in the accounts. The totals of the debit and credit columns of the trial balance are the same but the totals are incorrect.

Original entry: Entries are made in the correct accounts on the correct sides of each account but the amounts entered are not correct, although they are the same for the debit and credit entry. The totals of the debit and credit columns of the trial balance are the same but the totals are incorrect.

Other payables: See accrued expenses

Other receivables: See prepaid expenses

Overcasting: The amount recorded in the accounts is higher than the correct figure.

Owner's equity: Business resources supplied by the owner of the business. See capital.

Paid-up share capital: The amount of money that has actually been received by a limited company from the issue of shares.

Par value: The issue price of the shares. This is also called the nominal value of the shares.

Partnership: A business that is owned and controlled by a minimum of two owners.

Payee: The person or business receiving payment from the business. The payee may also be called the drawee.

Payer: The person or business making a payment to another. The payer may also be called the drawer.

Paying-in slip: A document used to deposit funds (cheques or notes and coins) into a bank account.

Personal accounts: Accounts of other businesses or people that the business has a financial relationship with.

Petty cash book: A book of prime entry used for small items of payment by cash.

Posting: The process of transferring information from books of prime entry to the correct double entry account.

Prepaid expenses: Expenses that have been paid in advance of the accounting period to which they relate. Also known as Other receivables.

Prepaid incomes: Incomes received in advance of the period in which they were earned by the business.

Prime cost: The total of direct costs of goods produced in terms of the materials, labour and expenses involved in its production.

Principle: The correct amounts are entered for a transaction but they are entered in the wrong type or class of account.

Profit: Total income less total expenses for a period of time.

Profit for the year: Gross profit less expenses.

Profit margin: The profit for the year of a business expressed as a percentage of revenue generated by sales.

Profit margin (%)

$$= \frac{\text{profit for the year}}{\text{revenue}} \times 100$$

Profit maximisation: Aiming to earn as high a level of profit as is possible.

Provision for doubtful debts: An adjustment made to trade receivables based on an estimate of future irrecoverable debts.

Prudence principle: This principle states that revenue and profit should only be recognised when they are achieved.

Purchases: Inventory bought by the business either for immediate payment or on credit.

Purchases journal: The book of prime entry used to record credit purchases.

Purchases ledger: Book recording trade payables. It contains the personal accounts of all the credit suppliers of the business.

Purchases ledger control account: A memorandum account used to check the accuracy of the purchases ledger.

Purchases returns: Inventory previously bought by the business returned to the original supplier due to some problem with the inventory (also known as returns outwards).

Purchases returns journal: The book of prime entry used to record purchases returns.

Qualitative information: Information collected based on an individual's opinions and views.

Quantitative information: Factual information and data that is not based on opinions.

Rate of inventory turnover: A measure of how quickly a business uses or sells its inventory.

Rate of inventory turnover

$$= \frac{\text{cost of sales}}{\text{average inventory}}$$

where average inventory

$$= \frac{(\text{opening inventory} - \text{closing inventory})}{2}$$

Realisation principle: This principle states that revenue should be recognised when the exchange of goods or services takes place.

Receipt: A written document issued by a business when it receives a payment as proof of receiving money.

Recovery of debts written off: When money is received in payment of a debt that had been previously written off.

Reducing balance method: A method of depreciation in which the amount of depreciation charged is greater in the earlier years and reduces with every successive year of the asset's life.

Relevance: A non-numerical characteristic in accounting. Relevance is associated with accounting information that is timely, useful and will make a difference to an interested party when making a decision.

Reliability: Relates to the trustworthiness of a business's financial statements.

Residual profit: The profit for the year for a partnership + interest on drawings – salaries and interest on capital; residual profit is shared between the partners in the agreed profit sharing ratio.

Residual value: The estimated value of a non-current asset at the end of its life.

Retained earnings: This is the profit that is not appropriated (used) to pay shareholder dividends and forms part of the company's share capital and reserves.

Return on capital employed: The profit for the year expressed as a percentage of the capital employed. It informs a business of the profits that have been made based on the resources made available to them.

Revaluation method of depreciation: A method of depreciation in which the amount of depreciation charged each year is the change in the asset's estimated value between the start and the end of the year.

Revenue: Income generated by a business from its normal business activities, usually the sale of goods or services. Revenue may also be referred to as sales, sales revenue or turnover.

Revenue expenditure: Expenditure on running the business. It is clearly linked to a specific time period. Revenue expenditure is classed as an expense on the income statement of a business.

Revenue receipts: Business income that comes from normal business operations. Revenue receipts are classed as income on the income statement of the business.

Royalties: A fee that is paid to the individual who originally invented the product being manufactured.

Sales journal: The book of prime entry used to record credit sales.

Sales: Inventory sold by the business either for immediate payment or on credit.

Sales ledger: Book recording trade receivables. It contains the personal accounts of all the credit customers of the business.

Sales ledger control account: A memorandum account used to check the accuracy of the sales ledger.

Sales returns: Inventory previously sold by the business returned by the customer due to some problem with the inventory (also known as returns inwards)

Sales returns journal: The book of prime entry used to record sales returns.

Share premium: The difference between the par value and the sale price of the share.

Sole trader: A business that is owned and controlled by one individual.

Stakeholder: An individual or group who have an interest in a business and may be directly affected by the activities of the business.

Stale cheque: A cheque that a bank will not process because it is more than six months old.

Standing orders: A regular automated payment of a fixed amount made from a bank account.

Statement of account: A document issued to all customers still owing money to the business. It contains details relating to the transactions taking place between the business and the customer.

Statement of affairs: A list of assets and liabilities at a given date; it is similar to a statement of financial position.

Statement of financial position: A financial statement showing the assets of the business and the financing for these assets, either from owner's equity or liabilities.

Stock exchange: A market where shares are bought and sold.

Stocktake: A physical count and valuation of inventory held by a business.

Straight line method of depreciation: A method of depreciation in which the amount of depreciation charged each year remains constant throughout the asset's life.

Suspense account: A temporary account used when the trial balance totals differ. It is used to ensure that the totals of the trial balance are the same.

Trade discount: A discount given by one business to another business. It is calculated as a percentage reduction in the invoice quantity.

Trade payable: The amount that a business owes to a supplier for goods or services supplied on credit. The supplier may also be known as a trade payable or a creditor.

Trade payables: The sum of the amounts that a business owes to its suppliers for goods or services supplied on credit. All the suppliers of a business may also be referred to collectively as trade payables.

Trade payables turnover: The average number of days that it takes a business to pay its debts to its credit suppliers (trade payables).

Trade payables turnover (in days)

$$= \frac{\text{trade payables}}{\text{credit purchases}} \times 365$$

Trade receivable: The amount that a business is owed by a customer for goods or services supplied on credit. The customer may also be known as a trade receivable or a debtor.

Trade receivables: The sum of the amounts that a business is owed by its suppliers for goods or services supplied on credit. All the customers of a business may also be referred to collectively as trade receivables.

Trade receivables turnover: The average number of days that it takes a business to collect its debts from its credit customers (trade receivables).

Trade receivables turnover (in days)

$$= \frac{\text{trade receivables}}{\text{credit sales}} \times 365$$

Trader: A business organisation that makes profit from the buying and selling of goods. No production takes place.

Transposition: Numbers (or parts of a larger number) are mixed up or reversed, e.g. $142 is written as $241.

Trend analysis: This is where a business compares its ratio results against benchmarks or industry averages and previous years' results

Trial balance: A list of all balances from the double entry accounts.

True and fair view: Describes financial records that are free from misinformation and accurately represent the financial position of a business.

Uncredited deposit: An amount which has been received but the receipt has not yet appeared on the bank statement. The receipt will have been debited to the business cash book when the payment was received.

Undercasting: The amount recorded in the accounts is lower than the correct figure.

Understandability: An accounting policy that states that a business's financial information should be presented in a way that an individual with a reasonable knowledge of business and finance and a willingness to study the information provided should be able to understand.

Unlimited liability: The owner(s) of a business are personally liable for the debts of the business if the business is unable to repay them.

Unpresented cheque: A cheque which has been issued but the payment has not yet appeared on the bank statement. The payment will have been credited to the business cash book when the cheque was issued.

Updated cash book: A cash book brought up to date by the business by the addition of automated transactions and other transactions the business has yet to enter into the cash book.

Working capital: The difference between current assets and current liabilities. It is sometimes referred to as net current assets and is the amount of money available to fund the day-to-day operations of a business.

Written off: Cancelling a debt owed to the business due to the failure to collect the amount owing.

INDEX